Christmas Pieces

*24 Historical Fiction Short Stories
Surrounding Christmas*

Tom Gahan

Christmas Pieces
Copyright ©2024 Tom Gahan

ISBN 978-1506-914-38-1 PBK
ISBN 978-1506-914-39-8 EBK

September 2024

Published and Distributed by
First Edition Design Publishing, Inc.
P.O. Box 17646, Sarasota, FL 34276-3217
www.firsteditiondesignpublishing.com

Christmas Pieces is a work of historical fiction. All incidents and dialogue, and all characters with the exception of some well-known historical figures, are products of the author's imagination and are not to be construed as real. Where real-life historical persons are used, the situations, incidents, and dialogues concerning those persons are entirely fictional and are not intended to depict actual events or to change the entirely fictional nature of the work. In all other respects, any similarity to persons living or dead is entirely coincidental.

For Darla Rae
Who makes every day feel like Christmas.

"The Christmas spirit is the spirit of giving,
the spirit of sharing, the spirit of love."
-- Winston Churchill

Acknowledgements

My personal thanks to all the people who gave suggestions for stories, their help, support, and encouragement along the journey of creating Christmas Pieces. They all performed a role and are listed alphabetically by last name. Also, thank you to the long-gone souls who played a part.

Dr. Ashley Boccio-Hogan, Tammy Cavanaugh, Eileen Curtin, Darla Rae Gahan, Crystal Sjøen-Gahan, Dr. Sarah Geary, Anayeli Gochez, Liz Hanly, Caren Heacock, Mandy Henderson, Darcy Hill, Jen Kane, Christin Kruger, Dr. Katie Owens, Daniella Ronchi, Dave Sapienza, Justin Spates

First Edition Design Publishing

Cover Painting – William A. Gahan

Foreword

It is with great pleasure that I introduce you to *Christmas Pieces*, a heartwarming collection of stories by Tom Gahan, a dear friend I've had the privilege of knowing for over 20 years. Tom is no stranger to storytelling—his previous work, *Harmony Bay*, became a best seller for its vivid characters and emotional depth. In this latest work, Tom takes his gift for narrative to new heights, offering readers 24 unique tales, each set in a different corner of the United States, and ending up just south of the Old City of Jerusalem where all the stories are tied together by the universal spirit of Christmas.

From the snowy streets of New England to the desolate prairie of Oklahoma, and beyond, Tom's stories capture the essence of the season in a way that is both intimate and expansive. Each chapter brings us to a new place, introducing us to characters whose experiences remind us of the hope, love, and generosity that define the holiday season. Whether it's a science fair project in Oklahoma or a sled pulled by incredible dogs in Alaska, Tom's storytelling invites us to experience the magic of Christmas through diverse landscapes and unique traditions.

Tom's attention to detail shines through not only in the stories themselves but also in the thoughtfully curated artwork that evokes a sense of nostalgia and charm. From a Bayou in Louisiana to the bustling streets of New York City, these images transport readers to a bygone era, enhancing the warmth and traditions that radiate from each tale.

But what makes *Christmas Pieces* even more personal are Tom's "Story Notes" found throughout the book. In these sections, Tom reflects on the significance of each story and shares how they connect to his own life experiences. It's in these notes that readers truly see the heart behind the words, as Tom opens up about the memories, emotions, and inspirations that shaped his writing.

Having known Tom for so long, I can say that his love for people and places shines through in every page. His attention to detail, combined with

i

his deep understanding of the human spirit, makes this book a truly special gift for readers. These are stories to be savored, shared, and revisited year after year, much like the holiday itself.

So, as you turn the pages of *Christmas Pieces*, prepare to be transported. Each story will take you on a journey, not just across states and cities, but into the hearts of those who celebrate the beauty of Christmas in their own way. I hope you enjoy this book as much as I have, and that it brings warmth and joy to your holiday season.

Deborah E Gordon-Reagle, Th.D.
Author and Founder of CoramDEOTheology.com

Author's Note

I was taught that no one is going to appreciate your writing unless it educates them or entertains them. *Christmas Pieces – 24 Historical Fiction Short Stories Surrounding Christmas* was a labor of love in which I tried to do both. This book got its start years ago after the successful launch of my historical fiction novel, *Harmony Bay*. On a December day I told my friend Jen Kane I was feeling bored. She said, "You're a writer. Write a story." I asked, "What should I write about?" "It's Christmastime. Write about Christmas," she said.

I've had a long history as a writer. My work was typically commercial pieces for businesses or for newspapers as a columnist, with a few short stories along the way. Until *Harmony Bay*, I never had taken the time to write something at length for my own self-satisfaction. Writing a Christmas story sounded appealing. After watching so many Christmas movies that had an awful script, I wondered if I could write something better. I love the holidays and have many fond memories of them. Although, entwined with great Christmas celebrations, there have been unfortunate years for me as well. *Christmas Pieces* was a way to bring about good thoughts and add some glitter to Christmas for everyone. Let me explain...

When I was seven years-old, at Christmas all my friends got bicycles, ice skates, skateboards, baseball gloves, and such. I got... diagnosed with an incurable disorder and spent Christmas week in the hospital. As a young adult my well pump packed it in two days before Christmas. Try finding a well driller on Christmas Eve! We didn't have water until days after New Years. On Christmas Eve a few years after that, a wicked nor'easter ripped the shingles off our roof. We sat at Christmas Eve dinner with water dripping down through the chandelier and onto the dinner table. Like well drillers, try finding a roofer during Christmas week. Most tragic of all, when I was a young parent my father, who did the cover art painting decades ago as part of a personal Christmas card series for family and close friends, and whom I loved dearly, passed away unexpectedly before dawn on December 22nd. My mother insisted that the funeral would have to be before Christmas so we could all get on with Christmas and our lives. Maybe she was afraid that like the well drillers and roofers, the gravediggers wouldn't be around Christmas week, either. Sadly, four years later, Mom passed away on December 12th. A few other Christmases had strings attached as well. For me, Christmas always seemed to have a tariff. But I never lost my passion for the Christmas season, or my faith in God, which keeps me moving forward. With all those sad Christmases in my rearview mirror, I worked to pump as much joy as I could into the holiday. The idea for *Harmony Bay* came to me as I watched my son at the Christmas pageant rehearsal. Call it Divine intervention… that book did exceptionally well for me on many levels. Which, in turn, pushed me to finish *Christmas Pieces*.

I've been blessed to have visited the locations in the stories, except for a few. Combined with extensive research, my firsthand experiences and travels played a role in writing this Christmas story compilation. Also, parts of my family history were used in several pieces. They, and other anecdotal points of interest, are explained in the Story Notes at the end of those stories.

You may wish to consider *Christmas Pieces* as a guided holiday tour across America in years past. *Christmas Pieces* is a work of historical fiction and deals with several nationalities and their Christmas customs and traditions in those days. To keep things authentic, several stories have words and phrases from immigrant character's native language. Also, there are expressions and slang words that would have been common during the time periods the stories take place. You can use a translation app or go with the flow and let those words be like Christmas ornaments from faraway places. I strayed from some of the rules for writing and used speech patterns and pronunciations that would be typical for the characters saying them. So, the spellings of words, grammatically incorrect phrases, and use of slang is done with purpose and with neither malice nor prejudice.

Some pieces are sheer whimsy, others are to the point, pragmatic historical accounts. Learn and be amused! The reason for 24 stories is there's one Christmas piece for each of the 24 days of Advent leading up to Christmas. My family had a Christmas Eve tradition of reading a short story, poem, or article about Christmas aloud after Christmas Eve dinner and before leaving for midnight church services. It was my mother's family ritual. I often wondered if she did it to keep us busy or keep our mind off of Santa Claus for a few hours before Christmas Day. It was long before the internet and was always a challenge to find a suitable story to read aloud.

It has been my pleasure to write these stories to educate and entertain. I hope you can experience the joys of Christmas during the course of history through them.

If you enjoy the stories in *Christmas Pieces -- 24 Historical Fiction Short Stories Surrounding Christmas,* you may appreciate reading *Harmony Bay – An adventurous slice of waterfront life where mystery surrounds history.* It has a chapter on Christmas as well.

I wish you a Merry Christmas, and good cheer for whatever holiday you may celebrate.

Tom Gahan

Contents

ONE

Manhattan, New York

She pressed her nose up against the glass. Her fingers left other smudges.

"Hey now! I don't mind you looking, but I have to clean that glass," the shopkeeper said. "Take a step back, will you."

The young girl in front of the window stepped back as her eyes filled with tears. A window display held dolls from around the world dressed in their native attire, a train set, and wooden toys of all sorts. Brilliant colors bounced off each other from the slanted late afternoon sun blazing into the window front. An occasional passing wagon added a curtain of shadows.

"Good grief," the shopkeeper said as tears now streamed down the girl's face. She was dirty. More than a street urchin but far below the mostly upper-class customers that usually came to the shop. Her clothes were worn although not tattered. Her thin coat was not enough to fend off the November chill. "I only asked you to take a step back." The girl broke into a full cry, sobbing and heaving as she stepped farther back from the shop window.

"What is wrong?" the young woman from the shop asked. There was no reply from the child. "Hungry?" the woman asked. The shuddering subsided as the girl nodded in response to the question. "Come here to me, Cailín." The shopkeeper hooked her finger in a drawing motion toward her. The girl quieted.

"Looks as though you're having a bit of bad day, eh?" The woman knelt on the sidewalk beside the girl and scooped her in with one arm. "Come in the shop. I have some fabulous cookies. I can't eat them all. Will you help me finish them? It would be a shame to waste them" The girl nodded vigorously, approving the offer.

The girl stepped inside the brightly lit shop and was delighted by the sights, the sounds of chimes, and the meow of a calico cat perched high up on a shelf. "Oh, don't mind her. That's Whiskers. My name is Aileen. What's your name?

"Claire," the girl said.

"Ah! Such a pretty name. That's the name of the county I'm from. Isn't that grand? Spelled a bit different though, I'd say."

"Yes, Ma'am."

"Oh. What do say we just call me Aileen. Is that okay for you?" Aileen said. Claire nodded again. "Hmmm… I think it would be a fine idea for you to have a wash-up before our cookies. Yes?" Claire looked at her hands and placed them behind her back in embarrassment. "Oh, come now. Me hands are gettin' dirty every day. I think if you aren't getting your hands dirty either you're not working hard enough…or you're not having enough fun. C'mon let's wash up. It's right down the hall on the right."

The girl froze. "Come with me. We'll wash our hands together," Aileen said. Aileen realized that other than her name, and yes Ma'am, Claire had not said another word. Rather odd for a child in a toy shop, she thought. She let it go. "I have some lovely hand soap and a lotion for your hands. It will make you feel even prettier than you are." Aileen saw the girl return an approving glance. "Yes, yes, yes!" Aileen said, "And I do believe I have a spare ribbon for that beautiful hair of yours." The little girl smiled.

They washed their hands and applied the lotion. Claire enjoyed the rare luxury of warm water from a tap and marveled at how sparkling clean everything was. Aileen pulled Claire's hair back and tied it with the ribbon in a bow. She lifted Claire up so that she could see her reflection in the mirror. As Aileen held her, Claire reached out for the woman's dark curls and pulled them back, mimicking Aileen's action. Claire could smell Aileen's perfume and the clean smell of her clothes. She wanted to be exactly like her.

"Ah, no. I'm good. The ribbon is much better on you. Let's move on to those cookies."

Aileen opened a brown paper bag that held fresh oatmeal cookies and offered one to Claire. The girl's eyes widened as a smile washed over her face. "Thank you," she said. Her words were almost inaudible. Aileen offered another, then another. Claire ate each one with as much enthusiasm as the first.

"Well, I suppose someone is going to be looking for you any minute," Aileen said. "Where are you from?" Claire's eyes widened then began to tear again. She pointed toward the street.

"Where, child?" Aileen questioned again.

"The butcher shop down there. Hester Street. Maloney's." Aileen didn't notice the girl's eyes welling up.

"Right oh. Out for a walkabout, were you? A little sightseeing? Out to check out the dolls in the case? All good. It ended up being a girl's day." Aileen was pleased that the toy shop was quiet on weekday afternoons. The holiday shopping rush was still a week or two in the distance.

"No, I ran away."

"Why?"

"My Da. I didn't do my chores."

Aileen bristled at the words. "How long have you been out alone?"

"Since sup last night." Tears now streamed down Claire's face. Aileen held her close and wiped her eyes with her apron. She pulled her handkerchief from her skirt pocket and held it to the girl's nose. "Here. Blow." Aileen fought to suppress her anger. She lifted Claire and placed her in a chair. "Stay right here," she said and patted her on the head. Aileen went to the case behind the counter and pulled out a Spanish doll in a lace dress. Good God, this will likely cost me a week's pay, she thought. It's worth it.

"This is for you. She's a lady from Barcelona. It's a little present from me to celebrate being friends. Okay?"

"But…I…I… shouldn't."

"Ah! Yer're fine, Missy. Pretty, isn't she?" Aileen said. The girl grew calm. "Let's call it an early Christmas present."

Aileen knew of Maloney's butcher's shop that was more than several blocks away. She never noticed Claire there. When Aileen's meager budget allowed, she would indulge in some of its offerings. She had also visited there on errands for the toy shop owner and landlord, Mr. Bailey. A benefit of her employment was a fourth-floor walk-up discounted rental flat above the toy shop. She had literally worked her way up from the small room she had behind the shop, which was nothing much more than a storage closet. Her walk-up was one of the first in the neighborhood to have hot running water. Mr. Bailey liked modernization. Aileen appreciated that he did. It was any easy trip home at the end of the day. Mr. Bailey loved the arrangement since Aileen was available at odd hours if one of the wealthier customers came calling after closing time.

Aileen O'Brien arrived in America penniless. She came to work as a domestic. Her life in Ireland had been difficult to say the least. For her family things never really recovered from the days of the great famine decades before, so they pooled their savings and resources for her to immigrate to America for a chance of a better life. On her sixteenth birthday she stepped off the boat from Ellis Island and into the mission of Our Lady of the Rosary on State Street. It was known as "The Home of Irish Immigrant Girls." Those who lived downtown more commonly referred to it as Watson House. Lady of the Rosary Mission welcomed young single women immigrants, sheltered them, and protected them from all the ills of lower Manhattan. Typically, they were girls who came to America to work as servants, as Aileen had. The mission played a role in helping the girls find their relatives, temporary housing, and at times, jobs.

Aileen was at the mission for only several days before being introduced to Mr. Phineas Bailey, a local entrepreneur who also dabbled in real estate. In lower New York City, the term estate held no semblance to crowded tenements that housed thousands. Bailey was happily married and loved his family. Although shrewd and enterprising he was a good and fair man. His family inhabited New York since the days of the American Revolution. They fought as Patriots.

Mr. and Mrs. Bailey called on the mission to find a shopkeeper for the toy store they were creating. For the working class, the luxury of toys was shared by few. Bailey figured if he could offer the most unusual and interesting toys, many parents would make a sacrifice on behalf of their children. There were also a fair amount of well-heeled New Yorkers within a short cab ride of the shop on Mulberry Street.

After exchanging pleasantries with the priest in charge Bailey explained his needs. "The girl has to be polite, honest without question, and good with her sums." Father Riordan nodded in agreement. "And, she has to have a cheerful disposition, be fair of face, and presentable," Bailey said.

"That's quite a list of requirements," the priest replied. "I'd have to give it some thought."

"Perhaps this will help you think more clearly," Bailey said and handed the priest a thick envelope. "Let's say it's a donation toward the outstanding work that you all do for these young women here at the mission."

The pastor's eyes grew. "Ah, yes. I know just the girl. She has only been here a short time, but she meets your description. She's a bit young, though a sweet girl. Will you be providing her housing?" Father Riordan questioned.

Mrs. Bailey invited herself to the conversation. "There's a room behind the shop. It's small, but clean. I'll look after her myself. We're only up the street," she said.

"There will be pay as well and no work on Sundays," Mr. Bailey said.

Father Riordan approved and asked for Miss O'Brien to be sent downstairs. He made the introductions. "Although Miss O'Brien has only been with us for a brief time, I'm certain she will be happy to be moving on. Won't you, Aileen?" The teen nodded in agreement and wondered silently what the future held. Secretly the pastor was glad to be moving out one more girl and, in the process, get a handsome sum for the transaction.

The Bailey's waited as Aileen went to gather her things. She returned with a satchel that held her life's belongings. Mr. Bailey placed the bag in the carriage and helped Mrs. Bailey, then Aileen up to the cab. He took the reins, flicked them, and Aileen headed off to her new life. They headed up Broadway and passed City Hall, turned east on Walker Street taking it five blocks to Mulberry Street. Bailey's horse and carriage clattered up in front of the shop. He announced, "Welcome home." Ten years later Claire Maloney showed up there on a blustery November day.

Aileen pulled on her shawl, helped Claire into her coat, and took her by the hand. She grabbed her umbrella from the stand by the shop door but didn't open it. "Whiskers, watch the place," she said and turned the sign around on the front door that stated -- I will be right back. Thank you for waiting. She turned the key in the lock. They walked up Mulberry to Hester Street where merchants peddled their wares from pushcarts. Aileen counted her blessings as they passed one business after another with signs in the windows declaring Irish Need Not Apply. Signs in other shops were more blunt – No Irish. Aileen walked as fast as she could, but slow enough for Claire to keep up. Aileen arrived at Maloney's a step ahead of Claire. As Aileen pushed the door open Claire hid behind her skirt. A bell jingled to announce their entry.

"Mr. Maloney!" Aileen yelled. "Did you know this girl was out and alone all night? What right, in the name of God, do you have to let this girl be out on the street in the dark and the cold? How could you be so mean to your own flesh and blood? Answer me."

Eugene Maloney stood behind the counter with a cleaver in his hand. He was only a year older than Aileen. "Excuse me, Miss O'Brien?" he said in a churlish voice. His apron was splattered from his work. He wore a brown derby. Maloney leaned forward and brandished the cleaver.

Aileen stepped to the counter and with one swift parry of her umbrella Maloney's butcher's hatchet bounced off the white tile wall and fell to the saw dusted floor. With another swipe she flipped the butcher's hat off his head. "How dare you," she said and leaned over the counter in defiance. Maloney took a cautionary step back. "Don't you dare be threatening me. How could possibly be so cruel? What is wrong with you? Is it drink?" Aileen straightened her back and folded her arms. She let her words sink in.

Maloney was flustered and embarrassed after being bested by a young woman. He hesitated in his reply. "She wasn't being about her chores. Keeping the house clean and all. We argued. She took off and I couldn't find her. I tried. I had to be here first thing." He paused and thought about his next words. "No, it's not about whiskey. Not at all. Well, maybe a bit now and then."

"She's rather young to be a domestic, I'd say," Aileen countered, unfolded her arms and placed them on her hips. "What does Mrs. Maloney have to say about this?"

"She says nothing. She's passed. Her and my other two were lost in that tenement fire two years ago. It's only me and Claire is all that's left. I can't do it all myself with the business and all."

Aileen recalled the fire. She shuddered. "I see. I will pray for their souls. Well then. You best be careful about how you treat others. What you put out as a ripple comes back to you as a tidal wave. If your daughter is all you have left and you turn her away, who will take care of you when you're old and gray? What say you, hmm?"

"It's been impossible to run the shop day and night and raise the girl. I cannot do it by me self. The missus used to take care of the house and help me here on busy days. By the time I get home at night…I'm dog-tired," he said.

Maloney never had it easy his entire life. He immigrated to America with his parents when he was three years old. They lived in the Five Points section of lower Manhattan and by the time he was seven, he was an orphan. He lost both parents to tuberculosis. He had no siblings or any other family. As a boy he lived at the orphanage and apprenticed in the butcher shop for Mr. Kellerher. Unfortunately for Maloney, and even more so for Kellerher, one morning the master butcher slumped over at the cutting table. He was a stone cold gone. With no heirs, it was decided by the community that Maloney should inherit the business and run it as best he could. If he could. He married at eighteen and had three children in rapid succession. Claire was the youngest.

"Right, then. Here's what's going to happen." Aileen said as she once again folded here arms in a defensive posture. "First thing tomorrow morning you will find two neighborhood lads that will want to apprentice in your trade. One should be good with his arithmetic to help with bookkeeping. Understood?" Maloney shook his head in small measures to acknowledge her. Aileen continued, "Starting right now Claire will come to my shop every day after school. There's a small room with a desk behind the shop. If she needs help with her schoolwork she can come to me. I will help her. I will see to it that she gets a good meal every evening. If you must leave for your work before her school day begins, you will bring her to me in the morning as well." Claire peeked from behind Aileen's skirt. Aileen took her by the hand. "You will collect her on the way home in the evening.

"You will do as I say. Most of my toy shop customers are the same women who come to you. They trust me. Rumor has it you've been tipping the scales in your favor. Surely you wouldn't want me giving that rumor some help growing in the neighborhood. Would ya, now?" Aileen winked and continued in a stage whisper. "Oh, and there's a handsome young police sergeant who has taken quite a fancy to me. If you don't do as I say, it will be easy for me to have him, or his detectives, pay you a visit. Eh, Mr. Maloney? Am I clear?"

Maloney shuffled his feet in the saw dust. Inside he welcomed the idea of someone looking after Claire, but he certainly didn't want the coppers around. He would only admit to himself that from time to time he did indeed rest a thumb on the scale when times were tough. "I hear you," he said.

"One more thing," Aileen said. Maloney cringed. "You'll be compensating me with fresh meat and farm goods, eggs, vegetables, and such, when you have them. Be sure not to be giving me anything that's a bit off. I'll be feeding it to your daughter. For starters I'll take a half pound of bacon with me now and a whole chicken. Oh, and toss a brisket in the brine, please. Ten days in the pickle." Maloney followed orders. He wrapped the bacon and chicken in brown paper. Maloney pulled a beef brisket from the cold box and wrote AO in large capital letters on it with a grease pencil and added the date ten days away. It entered the brine barrel with a splash. Aileen learned from the Jewish immigrant women in the area how to corn a beef, turning an otherwise tough cut of meat into delicious tender table fare. The secret to success was the right amount of time for the meat to be in the brine. Some women did the pickling themselves at home. Aileen didn't think it was worth the fuss if she had Mr. Maloney answering to her.

"Mr. Maloney, I know you've been on difficult times, losing your wife and children. It breaks my heart to hear it. Trying to raise a young girl and all is hard. I feel for you. I truly do. I know how difficult things can be living within this city. I grew up on a farm and life was hard in a different way." She paused. "I will see to it that Claire is raised to be a perfect lady. I can promise you that. It will be the best for both of you."

Maloney thought again about the arrangement, searching it for flaws. The only one he could think of was this young woman's domineering nature.

Aileen headed to the door and turned abruptly. "Pick her up on your way home. Don't be too late. And… no drink. Not a drop at all." Maloney winced. "One more thing." She opened the door and the bell chimed. "You will take her to church every Sunday. The both of you will go. Come with me, Claire." Aileen took her hand and left the butcher shop.

They stopped at pushcart vendors for potatoes and a small apple pie. Dinner that evening was a delight for Claire. Aileen took the time to make things as fancy as she could. She hoped she wasn't going to spoil Claire. She reconsidered that there was a lot of damage to be undone. It was bad enough the way she was being raised. It was worse growing up without a mother. Aileen knew that firsthand.

Days spiraled into weeks and crept past Thanksgiving. Every day their routine was the same. Maloney most often dropped Claire off to Aileen well before the school bell. Maloney began to arrive closer to school time and earlier in the evening to pick Claire up. At first Claire didn't do well with her schoolwork, but Aileen could see she was making progress. "Try your best, Dear." Aileen would say. "And I'll do my part. I can see your father is trying to do the same."

A wet wintry mix swirled on Mulberry Street in early December as Maloney arrived at the toy shop. Darkness fell hours ago. His horse and wagon were already put away for the night. He trudged up the steps to the top floor and arrived at Aileen's door wet and exhausted. "Sweet Jesus you look a mess. Like something the cat dragged in…but I don't think there's a single cat in New York that would have anything to do with you."

Claire ran to the door, "Da!" she hugged him not minding his wet mackinaw. "Let's take mercy on him, Claire," Aileen said. "Don't be crushing him to death. Have you eaten, Eugene? I mean Mr. Maloney."

"I can't say that I have," he replied. Odors of simmering pork and onions drifted into the hallway. He pulled off his cap.

"We've already eaten. What do you say, Claire? Should we feed him?" Claire smiled in agreement. "I'd be much obliged," he said.

"Get that wet coat off before you catch a death," Aileen said. She took his coat and hat, draped them on a kitchen chair and pulled it near the stove. "Oven's still good and warm. That'll help. You will sit up there," she said and pointed to the head of the table. Aileen ladled a large portion onto a plate and placed it before him. He picked up his fork and started in.

"Wait!" Aileen said. "Grace first." She and Claire took the two remaining seats, bowed their heads, and prayed.

In the following weeks Miss O'Brien and Mr. Maloney agreed to address each other as Aileen and Eugene unless Claire was present. One morning Maloney arrived at the toy store with Claire and Aileen met him at his delivery wagon with a small box. "What's this?" he said. "Your lunch," she replied. "It's getting closer to Christmas and I'm sure you are scurrying about nonstop with the holiday business and all. You won't have time to get something, right?"

Eugene Maloney was taken aback. Since her first hostile encounter he noticed changes in the woman. She had good reasons to be harsh on him. He wasn't sure if it was politeness for his owns sake or Claire's. Aileen's influence did reset his compass and made him fly true. He hadn't admitted to her that Aileen caring for Claire was a blessing. Not only for himself, but more so for Claire. Her school grades improved, and she was looking tidier. He had more time to focus on the butcher shop and the business was now thriving. He managed to attract several restaurant accounts in addition to his walk in trade and regulars. It dawned on him that the heartache and night horrors of the past couple of years had begun to fade. There was something else he hadn't admitted to Aileen; he was growing fond of her.

"Well, I suppose you're right. With as much food as I'm selling lately I don't get the moment to feed me self."

Christmas was in the air and on display in every shop window. December brought cold, but not bitter temperatures. "Mr. Maloney, I think I will take Claire for a walk this evening after I close the toy store to have a look at shop windows dressed up for Christmas. Care to join us? I know you're tired at the end of the day. I thought it might be pleasant. Maybe even fun. What do you say?" Aileen said. "And you'll join us for dinner afterward, of course," she quickly added.

Eugene Maloney was surprised by the invitation and short notice. "That sounds grand," he said. "I'll have the lads close up and be here straightaway." His pulse quickened. "Won't you need to tend to late customers?" he questioned.

"I'll place a sign in the window about after-hours shopping by appointment only. Aside from that, Whiskers can watch the place."

"I see. Perhaps I should learn to do the same. Well then. I will see you and Claire this evening. By the way, Miss O'Brien, is that a new dress you're sporting?"

"Indeed, Mr. Maloney. Very observant of you," she said. Aileen turned away to hide the blush washing over her face. He noticed, she thought to herself. "Right then; be off with you," she said as she smoothed her dress. I'm sure otherwise there will be a line at your door by the time you arrive. We will see you back here this evening."

Maloney hugged his daughter and climbed up into the buckboard. "Be on your best behavior today," he said to her. "I wouldn't want you to miss out on a fun evening. And to you, Miss O'Brien, until then…" he offered a warm smile, flipped the reins into one hand and tipped his cap, "be well."

Even though Maloney couldn't hear Claire calling out goodbye to her father above the noise of the wagon's iron rimmed wheels on the cobblestones, he turned and blew her a kiss.

That evening the three of them strolled up and down the rows of retail shops decorated for Christmas. Maloney stopped at a pushcart street vendor and bought a bag of roasted chestnuts. "Here have some while they're still warm. They will keep you going until dinner," he said to Claire and Aileen. Maloney noticed the job Aileen had done of grooming Claire for the evening. Her clothes were clean and pressed, her shoes were shined, and she wore a new red ribbon in her hair that was tied back exactly the same way as Aileen's." Impressive, he thought. All of this from the same woman who whacked me with her umbrella not that long ago. They chatted, laughed, and made the best of an otherwise lackluster section of lower Manhattan on a cold winter's evening.

Walking back to Aileen's apartment they sang Christmas songs. "Aren't we the very best carolers?" Aileen asked. Eugene and Claire Maloney answered the question by singing louder. They sang all the way up Aileen's staircase and continued inside her door.

"Hang up yer hats and coats. Dinner will be ready in a jiffy," Aileen said. "I've got a bit of a treat for you 'til then, Mr. Maloney."

Aileen went to the stove and called out, "There's a young man who's a barkeep all the way up on Irving Place in Gramercy Park. It's some place called Healy's Cafe. He tells me some author bloke who came up from Texas to be near his publisher sits in a booth there scribbling a book all day. The scribbler's name is Porter or Sydney or something like that."

"Is Porter or Sydney his last name?" he asked.

"I'd say Porter is the family name. Ever hear of him?" Maloney admitted he had not.

"The bartender visits me at my shop now and then. Every so often he buys a toy for a niece or a nephew. I think he's taken a shine to me. Are you listening, Mr. Maloney? What do you make of that?" Maloney was listening and tried to suppress the jealousy pumping through his veins. Aileen wrapped an apron around her waist and continued. "Anyways, he snuck me a bottle of Bushmills. He tells me there was a big fire at the Bushmills distillery back in '85." Maloney shuddered at the mention of a fire. "All good though. He says what's been coming ever since is pure nectar. It's hardly a lost blend. And, that Porter writer fellow he mentions tipples it all day. Don't know if it helps his writing any."

Aileen produced two short glasses and the unopened bottle of whiskey. "Just a touch," she said as she opened it and splashed a shot of the amber liquid in each glass. "Here's to the season, old Bushmills, and to that Porter chap for finishing his next story... Let's toast them all." Maloney and Aileen raised their glasses in unison. "And, to us. That's covering a lot of bases with one drink," Maloney said. He savored every sip.

Christmas Eve afternoon was a whirlwind for Aileen and Eugene at their work. Last minute shoppers at the toy store anguished over decisions on what to buy. Most often their wants exceeded their earnings. Things were pretty much the same at Maloney's butcher shop. Customers crowded the counter to purchase hams, turkeys, geese, or roasts for their holiday dinner. Orders for the restaurants were delivered in the morning as usual, so he had time to concentrate on his retail customers. Maloney looked at the clock, counting the minutes until closing. Aileen had promised a special Christmas Eve dinner with all the trimmings for him and his daughter. At long last he flipped over the sign in the window from open to closed. He paid his apprentices a fair bonus and wished them and their families well for Christmas and that they should make the best of their day off with them.

Maloney rushed home to wash, shave, and change into his Sunday bests. Claire was already at Aileen's. She promised Maloney that she would have his daughter ready for a wonderful evening and Midnight Mass. He walked the few blocks to Aileen's at a rapid pace, bounded up her four flights, and rapped on the door. Maloney announced his arrival in a loud voice, "It's Christmas Eve. Let the celebration begin!"

Claire opened the door. "Merry Christmas, Father!" she said. "We've been waiting for you." Claire pirouetted to display a new red dress, her hair tightly curled and tied in place with a green ribbon. Maloney was astonished by his daughter's appearance. "Where on earth did that dress come from?" he said. "And you look so lovely. Who fixed your hair?" Claire stopped in mid twirl and pointed toward the kitchen. Aileen emerged looking every bit as elegant and upper class as Claire.

"Good evening, Sir. Merry Christmas," Aileen said as she curtsied. "You're looking a might dapper, Mr. Maloney."

"Aren't we all," he replied. "Where did Claire's new dress come from? Wherever did you find it?" he asked and felt himself begin to choke up.

"Oh, that. Yes, well your daughter must look proper for dinner this evening and Midnight Mass. It's all about the Christmas magic."

"But…" Maloney interrupted. "What did it cost?"

"Never you mind. Doesn't she look lovely? A woman has to know how to turn a hem, trim a sleeve, you know…do magic. Although, the McDonough sisters at the corset shop up the street did lend a hand with a bit of the fine stitching. And they let me use their treadle machine for the long runs."

"And her hair? What did that cost? What do I owe you?" Maloney was bewildered.

"Ah! Only a bit of time with my curling irons was all." Aileen winked and smiled. "We had a girl's time."

"Looks as though you spent a bit of time with that curling iron as well. You look stunning," Maloney said. Aileen's face reddened.

They all sat down at the table, said Grace, and dinned on a sumptuous roast courtesy of Maloney's shop and prepared by Aileen. "My word," said Maloney. "That was delightful. I've never been happier. Thank you."

"Really? I'm pleased. Enjoy being well fed, eh?" Aileen said. All three did the dishes and prepared to make their way to Saint Patrick's Basilica several blocks away.

Aileen knew the Basilica of Saint Patrick, the first cathedral for the Diocese of New York, the second Catholic Church in Manhattan, and only the third Catholic Church in New York State at the time of its completion 90 years earlier served the needs of the Irish Catholic immigrant community. It was designed by Joseph Francois Mangin who was the architect of New York City Hall. Once finished it was the largest Catholic Church in the United States.

By the mid-19th century, the Diocese of New York decided it needed a larger cathedral. "For the glory of Almighty God, for the honor of the Blessed and Immaculate Virgin, for the exaltation of Holy Mother Church, for the dignity of our ancient and glorious Catholic name, to erect a Cathedral in the City of New York that may be worthy of our increasing numbers, intelligence, and wealth as a religious community, and at all events, worthy as a public architectural monument, of the present and prospective crowns of this metropolis of the American continent," said Archbishop Hughes at a ceremony held at the old basilica. Construction began in 1858 for the new Saint Patrick's Cathedral on Fifth Avenue. It took twenty more years to complete.

Aileen had read the archbishop's lengthy explanation. As wordy as his invocation was, she felt it was the best that they decided to build a new St. Patrick's. Catholic immigrants had been arriving in Manhattan in droves for the last 50 years. They needed more church space.

Although, the old Basilica of St. Patrick still held a place in the heart of many New York Irish Americans. In 1913 it would see over 20,000 New Yorkers stream there for the funeral of "Big Tim" Sullivan, a famed Tammany Hall politician.

They walked through the night on Mulberry Street and turned into the graveyard at St. Patrick's and took the path to its front doors. They arrived at the old church early enough to get seats near the front. This delighted Claire since she could take in everything without her view being blocked by too many heads. At the stroke of Christmas morning Claire marveled at the brilliance of the constellation of candles, the full choir, and all the pageantry of the service. She held her father's hand and felt proud to be at his side. She knew he had tried to raise her as best he could. As Claire looked down at her Christmas dress, she realized that she needed Aileen in her life just as much.

Christmas morning saw a veil of snow blanket lower Manhattan. It made the otherwise crowded neighborhoods, and dingy alleys seem clean and sweet. The grandest of holidays didn't change life for many. Stray dogs chased milk wagons down the street and soot churned from tenement chimneys as it had the day before and would do again tomorrow. New Year's Day arrived and still more of the same. Aileen, Maloney, and Claire pressed forward each day as they had done the day before. It seemed it was only the joy of the holidays that added gilding to inner-city life.

Eugene Maloney now found himself comfortable in every way with the brash young women who had embarrassed him with her umbrella. The three continued to attend church together. As the warmth of spring filled Sunday afternoons, they took outings in Maloney's delivery wagon to Central Park to visit the animal menagerie and the Museum of Natural History on Central Park West. Every week Claire counted the days until Sunday. Aileen did, too. Autumn dropped the temperatures and changed the colors of the leaves. It brought the three closer together as they huddled under a quilt on Maloney's buckboard. After visiting the museum their talk turned to Teddy Roosevelt and all his amazing accomplishments including being a founder of the natural history museum. The conversation segued to their citizenship dilemma.

"Years ago, President Roosevelt wrote quite clearly about the responsibilities of citizenship," Aileen interjected. She quoted a passage from Roosevelt's Duties of American Citizenship. 'No man can be a good citizen who is not a good husband and a good father, who is not honest in his dealings with other men and women, faithful to his friends and fearless in the presence of his foes, who has not got a sound heart, a sound mind, and a sound body... In a free republic the ideal citizen must be one willing and able to take arms for the defense of the flag, exactly as the ideal citizen must be the father of many healthy children.' "What do you think about that Mr. Maloney? Let's face it. Neither one of us is ever heading back home." She finished with an impish smile.

Maloney's eyebrows shot up. "He said all that did he? Well. I suppose he's right. Here's what I think. I'm thinking you and I should study and take the citizen's test together. Although according to Roosevelt it seems to be a bit more involved than needing to be fathering a flock of children. Can we be together on this? There's a block captain who covers my shop's street. I've made him a few donations now and then. I'm sure he will help us through the paperwork."

"I accept your challenge, Mr. Maloney. We will. We've been here long enough. It's high time we become part of this fine country's furnishings." Aileen leaned back feeling accomplished. She winked at him.

"Very well," he said. "I agree. The business has become successful over the past year. I think it's the right thing to do and it's time to play more of a part in helping develop the country."

Aileen beamed in the light of the conversation. "Today's the day," she said. "What day is that?" Maloney questioned.

"It's a year ago this very day that Claire came to me," she said.

"A fine day that was," Maloney answered and put his arm around Aileen. Claire was too distracted by the clip clop of the twin horse's hooves and the passing sights of New York to notice. "Let's celebrate with a grand meal," he said. He steered the team through Herald Square, turned on West 36th Street and pulled to the curb in front of Keen's Chophouse. "This will do," he said as he tethered the horses to a post and guided Aileen and Claire into the restaurant. "Keen's is a fine place. They've been going strong since 1885. They've opened the place to women just this year. It was gentlemen only before."

"How do you know that?" Aileen asked. "When you're in the business, word gets around. Both good and bad," Maloney replied.

The three sat at a corner table below the array of churchwarden pipes hanging from the ceiling. Hanging the long-stemmed clay pipes was a tradition in Europe. Clay pipes were too fragile to travel with. In Europe gentlemen would leave their Dutch made churchwarden pipes at inns along their travel routes. Their pipe was entrusted to the innkeeper who would be in charge of its safekeeping until their next visit. Keen's followed the custom, but now the pipes were more for decoration than anything else. Maloney told the waiter, "Nothing but the best for these ladies. Your best steaks with the finest trimmings, please. We're celebrating a special day."

"Will it be whiskey or beer for you today, sir?" the waiter said.

"Sarsaparilla all around," Maloney replied. The waiter's brushy moustache twitched as he rolled his eyes. "Yes, then, the best sarsaparilla it is."

Maloney told tales about the famous patrons of Keen's. "Our president Theodore Roosevelt and Buffalo Bill Cody have dined here," he said. "Other famous sorts and quite a few playwrights, publishers, and newspaper moguls often gather here as well."

"What famous sorts?" Claire asked. "Well, let's see. The list now includes Miss O'Brien and you," he replied. They all laughed.

The afternoon grew late and Claire's eyes grew heavy from the savory meal. Maloney decided it was best to be started home. He paid the bill by candlelight and left a tip sizeable enough to make the waiter's moustache twitch again.

That night as he tucked his daughter into bed, she asked him, "Father, do you love Aileen?"

"It's you I love more than anyone. But I must say, Miss O'Brien does warm my heart."

"It's okay, Father," Claire said. "You can say Aileen." She rolled to the side and fell fast asleep.

Maloney worked hard at the shop and even thought about expanding the business. The Christmas rush began earlier than usual. It was all he and his few employees could do to keep up with the demand. Aileen was equally busy feverishly unpacking deliveries from suppliers, keeping the shelves well stocked, and waiting on customers. Both accepted work as a way of life and that it was a good thing to be healthy and gainfully employed. Others were not as fortunate.

Before dawn on Christmas Eve Maloney pulled his wagon up to the toy shop. He clambered up the four flights to Aileen's with Claire by the hand. He tapped on the door. The door swung open and Aileen said, "My goodness. You're here very early. I haven't put tea up yet. Give me a moment, please." She turned to go, stopped, and once again faced them. "Oh. And a good morning and a very Happy Christmas!" she said and scooted off.

"Wait! Wait! I need you to get yourself together and come down with me to the toy shop," he said.

"But why on earth this early?" Aileen said.

"There's Christmas magic to be done. We need to get started," he said. "Let's get downstairs." Claire shrugged. "Alright, then, give me just one moment, please. I need to fix myself..." Aileen said in frustrated voice.

Maloney cut her short. "There'll be time for that later. And... Christmas only comes once a year!"

As they made their way down the stairs light now began to filter through some of the transoms. The city was about to become alive for another day. The trio arrived in the shop. Aileen folded her arms and gave Maloney a stern look. "Well, Sir. Here we are. It's before sunup on Christmas Eve and I've got dozens of things to do. Would you mind telling me what in the name of St. Patrick this all is about?" Whiskers meowed.

"I'm buying all of them," Maloney said.

"All of what?" Aileen asked.

"The toys, the dolls, the puzzles, the trains. Everything!" Maloney shouted and spread his arms wide.

"Have you gone mad, Mr. Maloney?" Aileen snapped. She took a step back.

"Quite the contrary, Miss O'Brien. Thank you for your concern," Maloney said and grinned in a way that Aileen had never seen before. It was unsettling for her. He was filled with pure joy.

"You poor Dear. You've been working so hard. It's all the stress, isn't it? Can I get you something...shall I call for the doctor?" she hesitated then continued. "Really? All the toys? Everything?"

"Indeed. Hopefully it all fits in the delivery wagon. If not; it's two trips. I'll get a couple of the boys from the shop to lend a hand if we need help, I suppose."

"I take it this isn't some sort of Christmas robbery. Who will be paying for all of it?"

"I will. But no one needs to know. Understand me?"

Aileen's expression grew blank. "Of course, but I do think I need to know. I will have to explain to Mr. Bailey."

"Don't worry about old Phineas Bailey. He will likely read about it in the papers and be thrilled. Plus, you'll be making the biggest Christmas sale, ever. Bailey will be quite pleased," he said in a loud voice.

Claire interrupted. "No fighting. It's Christmas."

The grownups took the advice and calmed their tone and volume. Maloney continued. "You see, business has been better than I ever bargained for, extraordinary actually, much in part thanks to you. And, I've also made a deal with one of the farms over in Brooklyn. They're buying me wagon and horses and picking them up this afternoon. They've paid me in advance and must be over the Brooklyn Bridge and well on their way before darkness. That's why I need to hurry. All of my wholesale accounts have been picking up at the shop and don't really need delivery.

I offer them a small discount for me not having to head out. The lads can continue to make the neighborhood deliveries on foot."

"You have gone mad," Aileen said.

"What about our Sunday wagon rides?" Claire asked.

"I'm thinking of a more proper carriage for our future for all of us, Claire," he said in front of the audience of dolls and stuffed toys. "It all works out."

Aileen was now bewildered. "Whatever will you do with all of these toys?"

"Ah, yes! I should explain that," the butcher said and pulled a large wad of bills from his coat pocket. "Here, count." Aileen's eyes glazed as she outstretched her hands. "We will load everything into the wagon and I'll be taking it straight away to the orphanage. I've already arranged it all with the convent and the nuns were quite grateful on behalf of the children." He hesitated for a moment, looked down at Claire and then to Aileen. "When I lived there as a lad, there was never anything on Christmas morning."

Aileen threw her arms around him. "You are a wonderful man. Merry Christmas." She began to cry and held him for a long time.

"Oh, there's one more bit of Christmas magic," he said and put his hand in the other coat pocket. "I saw this in one of the shop windows last year on that evening just before Christmas. I've had my eye on it ever since. It was that evening when you first had Claire prettied up like a Christmas angel, we went caroling like a family, ate chestnuts, and we raised a toast to us. It was then that I realized how happy you made me. Let's make this Christmas special."

Eugene Maloney withdrew his hand and held out a ring. "I love you, Miss Aileen O'Brien. Will you marry me?"

"Yes, Mr. Maloney, I certainly will. I love you, more. I have never been happier. Merry Christmas!"

Story Notes - Events and people in my life influenced parts of this story. My grandfather William, the son of Irish immigrants, lived with other Irish immigrant families in the crowded Five Points section of lower Manhattan, New York. My father, William, worked as an errand boy and apprentice in a New York butcher shop until the owner died suddenly. This led to him changing his career path and following his dream of being an artist. William A. Gahan was a successful and respected Madison Avenue commercial artist as well as a fine arts painter. The McDonough sisters mentioned were my twin sister, spinster, great aunts who had a corset shop in lower Manhattan. I still have a chair from their shop's fitting room.

TWO

Pittsburgh, Pennsylvania

Hank stepped off the 5:05 a moment after it chugged into Central Station. He had been punching tickets on the Pennsy Pittsburgh line for decades. It was far longer than he cared to remember. Snow flurries swirled around him as he made his way out of the station. Silica dust mixed with the flakes and added more sparkle. Hank pulled his scarf tighter and worked his way through the gaggle of passengers waiting to board the train. "Dang commuters," he said under his breath. He then supposed that not all of them were commuters. After all, it was Christmas Eve and a fair amount of folks were traveling to family or friends for the evening, or longer.

Hank liked working for the railroad. Not a great job, but it was steady work, and it paid most of his and his wife Edith's bills. Hank was on the job long enough to have seniority to pick the "cherry shifts" as he called them. Daylight hours and no more working on weekends and holidays. There were a lot of hard times for sure. They lived frugally up on Mount

Washington. Hank and Edith never owned a house. The down payment money was always a little too far out of reach, often consumed by an unexpected family emergency or paying for the kid's college tuition. They didn't own a car, either. Every day Hank walked to the incline station and walked from there to Central Station to board his shift on the Pennsylvania Railroad. The couple made it through the Great Depression and the tough times during World War II, mostly because they lived within their means and didn't stretch the budget. Hank and Edith attended church on Sundays, spent vacation days going to Pirate's baseball games, and occasionally went to Islay's for a treat on birthdays or anniversaries. They kept it simple. They never complained.

Hank stopped on the street where a young man was selling Christmas trees. "Good evening and Merry Christmas," the seller said and shuffled his feet to stay warm. "I've got a few mighty fine trees left," he said.

"A few is true," replied Hank. "Mighty fine is another matter." He nodded toward the pile of evergreens strewn caddywampus on the sidewalk.

"They will all be gone tonight. Every last one." He pointed at a tree to make his point.

"What will you take for that tree?" Hank asked.

"One dollar and not a penny less. It's a great tree at a great price." He folded his arms across his chest.

Hank laughed and slapped his hands together. "Yes, a great price. It's greater than I will pay. It's worth two-bits. Might be the best offer you get. If you keep looking to overcharge … you might be out here all night. By tomorrow it will not be worth anything. And it's not getting any warmer. Maybe I'll look elsewhere."

"A measly quarter? You've got to be kidding!"

Hank began to walk away. After six paces he turned and said, "Well, Son, I'll give you a half a buck for that tree. Seeing how it's Christmas and all. I don't want you to freeze to death out here. Your lips are turning blue."

The younger man touched a mitted hand to his lips. "Well, all right then. Yes, seeing how it's Christmas and all, I suppose fifty cents will do."

"Very well. Done deal!" Hank handed him five dimes, threw the Christmas tree over his shoulder, and trudged off toward the incline. Hank would have paid a dollar if he had to. He wanted Edith to be happy. It was a nice tree.

"Yinz have a Merry Christmas," he called out to Hank.

Pittsburgh's curious inclines, or vertical railways, were constructed by immigrant labor and served those who worked the Pittsburgh mills and simply didn't have the energy to climb the steep hill to get home at the end of a twelve-hour workday. Hank appreciated it. In particular, on Christmas Eve to take their tree home.

In any other place living high on a hill with a view of the river would be envied real estate. Here at the confluences of the Susquehanna and Monongahela Rivers it was different. Mount Washington was called Coal Hill at one time. The Pittsburgh Post Gazette wrote, "One of the ugliest industrial cities in the world. Honeycombed with mines, fronted by smoke-belching steel mills at its base and virtually isolated with only a few poor roads servicing it, Mount Washington was hardly a prestigious address."

In the interest of improving the appearance of Mount Washington, during the late 1940s the local Chamber of Commerce sponsored a program with school children to plant various colorful plants such as cornflowers, poppies, sunflowers, and "Easter Plants." A local resident wrote to every state and asked for seeds or plants to create a "Garden of the States". Most of the plants died. Those that did grow were able to tolerate the cold winters and acrid coal-soot filled air.

Hank's street was a long string of narrow row house apartments. The area served as home to generations of miners, steel mill workers, and like Hank, railroad employees. All of them were hard working people from strong stock who were the backbone of America.

Hank arrived at their front door as Edith flicked on the light. "Hello, my Dear," she said. "Look at that snazzy tree you've brought me! Put it down and come give me a Christmas hug. I took some time to red up that corner and set the tree stand there. The tree lights needs fixed, too." She put her hands on her hips and sighed.

"What's wrong, Edith?" Hank said as he noticed that his wife looked drawn, and her blue eyes lacked their usual sparkle.

"Well… with the kids moved off Christmas just doesn't feel the same," she said. Their grown son Marshall and daughter Sandra moved out of Pittsburgh years earlier to "find careers in something other than the steel mills," they said. Their college educations offered them many more opportunities. They went their separate ways. One went to Chicago, and the other to St. Paul.

"Oh, gee whiz, heck yeah," the Pittsburgh dad said. "I'm sure they will call on the phone tomorrow morning, they always do. This Sunday after church what do you say you and me take a trip out to Islay's, just for old time's sake? We can have chip chopped ham sandwiches, frizzled and with barbeque sauce, just the way you like it."

"And a Klondike bar?" Edith arched her eyebrows. "Set the tree in the stand, would you."

"Of course, Eddie," Hank said with a nod. "The Klondike and the tree."

"Ralph from number 64 stopped by today. You remember Ralph, yes?" Edith held out a letter to her husband.

"Sure enough, that's my name on the envelope but the street number is wrong," Ralph said.

"Yes, that's why Ralph brought it down. Someone reversed the number; they put 64 instead of 46. Flipped them around. It looks important. The return address says Esq., that's a lawyer."

"Indeed." Ralph's mustache twitched. "I hope this isn't a lawsuit or something bad. Maybe something about an overdue bill? Good grief. Not on Christmas eve."

Edith's eyes widened. "Who would want to sue us? Besides, we are all up to date on our bills. Every last one."

Hank opened the envelope, pulled out a letter, and read it. "Edith, you better sit down," he said in a shaken voice. His hands were trembling, and he motioned his wife toward the couch.

"Oh, dear God! What's wrong? Please, not on Christmas Eve," she said. Her eyes moistened.

Hank joined her on the couch. "It's not what you think. Read for yourself." He handed her the letter.

Edith read aloud. "Please be informed. I am the attorney for your late cousin, Stanley." She interrupted herself. "Yes, I remember Stanley. He was a humble man. He worked for the Pennsylvania Highway Department. He never married. We attended his funeral three years ago."

She continued to read, "I have been charged with dissolving his estate. Stanley's will has gone through the probate court process. All of his outstanding expenses, including his medical expenses, taxes, attorney fees and legal expenses have been deducted from the estate. His will has been deemed valid and is uncontested. He left you as sole beneficiary, having codified his will after the passing of his sibling family members." Edith looked up at Hank. She began to stutter. "Hank… you've inherited $63,111. Good grief!" Edith sprang from her seat and pirouetted in the center of the room. She blew a kiss to the Christmas tree. Hank joined her. They hugged.

"Sixty-three thousand one hundred and eleven dollars." He emphasized each word. "We're rich!"

"We can buy a car," she said.

"We can buy a house," he said and began to sing "I'll be home for Christmas…"

"We can take a vacation," she replied.

"I can retire." They both began to laugh and cry at the same time. "I always liked Stan. He was quite a bit older, but we played together as kids. He never spent a dime, though. I think the Great Depression and two world wars made him think about money and things different than most. I guess between his saving every penny with interest, his pension, and insurance, well… I guess he was rich in a lot of ways. We just didn't think about it."

There was a knock at the door. The couple opened the door and were greeted with shouts of "Merry Christmas! Merry Christmas!" Marshall and Sandra stood in the snow flurries with wide smiles.

"We wanted to surprise you for Christmas!" the daughter said. "Merry Christmas!"

"Yes, we traveled separately by train from Minnesota and Illinois and met at Penn station. We hoped you wouldn't be on the train. That would have spoiled our surprise!" Marshall said.

"Merry Christmas to you!" Edith shouted. "What a wonderful surprise."

"Why are there tears on your face and Dad's?" Sandra asked.

"Come on in and sit on the sofa," Hank said. "I have a surprise, too. There's something I want both of you to read."

"We can trim the tree later on," Edith said with a wink.

THREE

Guymon, Oklahoma

In 1846 Texas wanted to enter the Union as a slave state. Federal law, based on the Missouri Compromise, forbade slavery north of 36°30' parallel north. The Compromise of 1850 settled a boundary dispute between Texas and New Mexico. As part of the compromise Texas agreed to cede its portion of land north of 36°30' north latitude to the federal government. In exchange, the U.S. government assumed the public debt Texas incurred during its war with Mexico for independence.

The sliver of land measured only 170 miles long from west to east and 34 miles from north to south. It was a "neutral slice" without state or territorial ownership from 1850 until 1890. It was officially called the "Public Land Strip" with no form of territorial government and not belonging to any official entity. For decades this piece of land, now known as the Oklahoma Panhandle, was nicknamed "No Man's Land."

It eventually became part of the Oklahoma Territory. Until that time, it was known as a sanctuary for outlaws, a place for land squatters, and often visited by nomadic Native People like the Kiowa and Utes, and additionally, some Plains Apache bands, like the Mescalero Apache, for hunting and raiding expeditions. During the harsh economic times of the Great Depression, relentless drought and suffocating black, swirling, dust storms transformed the region into the Dust Bowl. The Oklahoma Panhandle was not a place for the meek.

The arrival of the Chicago, Rock Island and Pacific Railway in 1901 marked a significant turning point for the center of the new Oklahoma Territory. Just as rivers became the source for early settlements, the railroads did much of the same thing. The rails brought supplies and new people to the territory and shipped out farmed-raised products to across America. A town named Sanford sprouted up along the new rail line. Only a month after the town got its start U.S. Post Office officials renamed the new community Guymon in honor of Edward T. Guymon, who was president of the Townsite Company, which was responsible for establishing the town. Guymon grew quickly and became officially incorporated later that year. Some businesses in the town of Hardesty, 20 miles away, wanted to take advantage of the new railroad and relocated to Guymon.

Oklahoma gained statehood in 1907 and given its central location and rapidly growing infrastructure; Guymon was named the county seat of the newly formed Texas County. It was one of only three counties set up in the Panhandle.

By the early 20th century, the Panhandle experienced tremendous growth in farming. Mostly wheat. Germany was a major source of immigrants who settled in the Panhandle region, particularly Germans from Russia who faced religious discrimination and mandatory military service under the Tsarist regimes. German communities were established in west-central Oklahoma and the Panhandle, forming towns and bringing their strong agricultural traditions. The plains offered wide-open flat land that didn't need to be cleared of trees. Although, tall, thick prairie grass covered the land. A man with a plow, a mule, and hard work could cut the sod and plant crops.

Some say that Russian thistle seeds came to the Americas sewn into the vest pockets of the Russlanddeutschen, immigrants who had left Germany for Russia. Others attest the seeds arrived in America mixed in a shipment of flaxseed imported from what was originally the Russian Empire. It grew easily in the hot, dry climate on the High Plains on the border of Texas and Oklahoma. With its wide-open treeless land, the Plains reminded them of home. The Russlanddeutschen called the thistle, "perekati-pole." Perekati translates from Russian to "rolling" or "tumbling" and "Pole" translates to "field." The hardy, short-stemmed wheat was cold and drought resistant. It thrived in the dry plains, and came to be known as, "Tumble Weed," and became a non-native, aggressive, invasive species. It spread like wildfire. In its early growth stage, it served as livestock feed in place of hay, and during the Depression and the Dust Bowl years, some people ate it to fend off starvation.

German-Lutheran immigrants Karl and Eva Meyer, who came from farming families, arrived on the train in Guymon to settle and begin farming. They were able to get out of Europe before the start of World War I and felt they were lucky with their timing. After arriving in Oklahoma, they realized trouble didn't follow them. It was already waiting there for them before they arrived. During the spring of their first year, they experienced temperatures that spiked the thermometer to over 100 degrees. They were told about tornadoes and didn't look forward to experiencing one. The wind never stopped blowing on the Plains. That wasn't altogether a bad thing. Karl dug a well by hand and built a small windmill to power a pump for the well. Like others, they constructed a sod hut for temporary shelter. They brought little with them from their home country. It was all in their baggage. They sold their property in Germany and saved enough to buy the land, tools, and supplies they would need to get started. Eva brought her prized Weihnachtspyramide (Christmas Pyramid), a decorative, multi-tiered carousel powered by candles representing the Christmas story. Christmas trees were now popular in the old country, but without an evergreen anywhere near Dalhart for their first Christmas in America the young couple improvised with a makeshift tree and relied on an Advent Wreath to keep their Christmas spirits up. Lighting one of the four candles on each Sunday leading up to Christmas Eve gave them comfort during the upcoming days to Christmas.

Clearing the land of its natural grasses and vegetation, along with the elimination of predators to protect livestock, caused other issues. It led to the massive grasshopper swarms that plagued the Oklahoma Panhandle in the early 1900s, particularly between 1860 and 1910. Grasshoppers showed swarming behavior, forming massive migratory clouds devastating crops over vast areas. Swarms descended upon agricultural fields, consuming virtually all vegetation in their path. Grasshopper infestations caused severe crop losses that affected the farmer's livelihoods and caused widespread famine and hunger.

Just prior to 1920 there was favorable weather, the end of the grasshopper plagues, and a high demand for wheat brought about by the war in Europe that caused wheat prices to soar. It was needed to feed the troops when many European farmers shut down during the fighting. Karl and Eva were thrilled. Mechanized farming equipment was starting to become available. Although many farmers didn't have enough credit to take loans from banks for the machinery, private lenders were happy to make a deal at exorbitant interest rates. Farmers put up their property as collateral.

The Roaring Twenties arrived and launched a decade of economic prosperity. It was a period of cultural and social change and a change in societal norms. Jazz and new fashion trends thrived. For some, but not all Americans such as Blacks, Native peoples, immigrants, and ... farmers, the Roaring Twenties ushered in a surge in personal prosperity. It was reflected in their increased ability to afford consumer goods like automobiles and appliances, engage in leisure activities such as going to the movies, and enjoying a more modern lifestyle.

On Christmas Eve in 1920 Guymon saw the arrival of another new resident. Charles Meyer was born to Karl and Eva Meyer in their sod home as the Weihnachtspyramide chimed. Sod houses were a common form of dwelling for the early settlers of the Oklahoma Panhandle and other prairie lands during the early 20th century. With the lack of trees on the prairie for lumber, and the expense of shipping building materials to the Panhandle before the railways were built, poorer farmers built sod huts with what they plowed from the earth. Sod was a practical and free building material that was available in almost unlimited quantities, but extremely labor intensive to obtain. Sod was cut from the top layer of soil in long, rectangular strips usually two to three feet long and four to six inches thick with the prairie grass roots intact. Sod strips would be stacked like bricks to make walls. With good insulating qualities it kept the sod huts relatively cool in summer and warm in winter. Drafts through ill-fitting doors and windows were another story.

A wood frame was sometimes used for supporting a roof that was made with hay, animal hides, or canvas if it was available. Doors and windows were constructed from wood, often scavenged, or animal skins.

Interiors were primitive at best with dark and cramped interiors. Centipedes and other Insects falling from the ceiling and snakes boring through the sod walls were common. Hay thatched roofs were a fire risk. Despite the primitive structure, sod homes often had fireplaces for warmth and cooking. Resourceful homeowners used ingenuity to create a sense of comfort within their limits. When the railroads arrived later in the 20th century lumber became more available and there was a gradual shift away from sod dwellings, or at least major improvements to those that existed.

Karl and Eva did well enough financially with the farm, which gave them enough to build a real house. They selected a Sears and Roebuck home from the catalog, mostly because it would give them everything they needed delivered to Guymon by train. The timing of the new home was perfect since Eva was expecting another child. Their friends from church helped with the construction. Karl, Eva, and Charlie stayed in the sod house while their new home was being built. They couldn't wait for the luxury of a sturdy house with windows, doors, and privacy.

Charlie Meyer grew up on the farm along with his younger siblings, his sister Greta and his brother Albert. They all took part in the farm chores. It was hard work and Charlie wished for more in life. As his father would tell him, "Farming is hard work. You work from before sunup until after the sun goes down. Maybe a little less on Sunday. You work, work, work, until your drawers drop."

Every day at school Charlie started to learn about the things that interested him. Science was his best subject and he excelled in his classes. He loved the laboratory and all the exploration into the unseen world it offered. He thought about what he learned in class and how it applied to life on the farm and in nature. Guymon was still very much a small town and had a small school. But, his teachers, especially Miss Winslow his science teacher, took an interest in him and saw that he had potential. They did what they could. He was certain there was a lot more to know than what his father had been preaching to him for years. He was sure there were things yet to be discovered that would make farmwork, and life, easier.

"Don't be getting your head full of that science nonsense, Charles," his father would say. Karl thought it all was merely a distraction from the more practical business of running a farm. He was a stern and serious man who never knew the pleasure of leisure time. Karl had seen the bumper crop years, drought years, and even years that harvested bumper crops, but the price of wheat dropped so low it wasn't worth anything. Charlie mentioned going to college in the future, but his parents didn't see how that was possible without mortgaging the farm further than the loans they had already taken for farm equipment. Plus, they had two other children to consider. With Charlie being the oldest, his predictable future would be to inherit the farm in the future and work, work, work, until his drawers dropped... permanently. It's what his grandparents, great grandparents, and the generations before them did.

Charlie asked his mother and father for a microscope for Christmas. "We'll see." His mother said. "Maybe for a birthday and Christmas combined." Karl was a little more direct. "How much does one of those gadgets cost?" he said.

Charlie gave a lengthy answer. "I saw one in the Sears and Roebuck catalog. Well, to tell you the truth, there are three. Sort of good, better, and best. The middle-priced one would suit me" Charlie unraveled the specifications in a steady stream. "It has magnification from 100x to 400x, a sturdy brass body, an adjustable mirror to direct light onto the specimen, coarse and fine focus knobs, and an eyepiece with two objective lenses. Yes siree! I could examine any specimen on the farm or in the fields. It would suit me just fine and dandy." He finished with a grin.

Karl responded, "so how much does that thing cost?"

Charlie had made it a point not to mention the price. He thought the features would make the price seem more reasonable.

"Ten dollars," Charle blurted.

"Oh, my word. That's an awful lot of money for us!" Karl insisted. "That stock market crash in '29 affected everyone, even us out here in the middle of nowhere. You've seen the dust blizzards. Everyone's leaving Guymon 'cause of the drought. 15 years ago we were getting $2.20 per bushel for wheat. Now I'm lucky to get 50 cents. Your mother is making clothes for Greta from seed sacks. She's canning tumbleweed for meals. We got nothing coming in and nothing going out."

Eva patted her husband's arm. "Now, now, Karl. Maybe something could be worked out," she said. Charlie recoiled at the rejection. "Charlie," she continued, "How much money do you have?"

"A dollar and eighty cents is all I have," he said sheepishly.

"I see," she said. "What if we came up with half? Could you come up with the other five dollars? You know, meet in the middle..."

Charlie thought about it. "Christmas and my birthday aren't too far off, you know."

"Your father and I are well aware. Maybe for next year? We all need to be patient." Eva glanced at Karl who was glowering.

Charlie felt crushed. Three dollars and 20 cents seemed like an insurmountable goal. He hoped for a Christmas miracle. "I suppose," he said. "You know what Abe Lincoln said, 'Good things come to those who wait.' Let's see what happens."

"That's the spirit, Son," Eva said. "We will pray about it."

Charlie's chin was on his chest as he left the room.

After Charlie was gone Eva turned to Karl. "Karl, you know it's important for our children to have the best education we can give them. Charlie is bright. According to the school, he's brighter than most, if not the very best in some subjects like science and mathematics. Let's not discourage him until he knows his way in life."

On Monday morning Charlie rode their mule named "Dynamite" to school. His sister Greta and his brother Albert would ride in the neighbor's wagon to the lower grade school. Blowing dust made travel unsafe, if not dangerous. During a duster visibility was zero. Guymon had not yet seen its worst days. Charlie took it all in stride. He knew no other world, but he read many books and dreamed about traveling beyond the dusty Plains. He hitched Dynamite and trotted into the school. Miss Winslow greeted him at the door. "Good morning, Charlie. I wanted to remind you about the County Science Fair coming up and ask if you had a plan for entering an exhibit." She smiled softly.

"Good morning, Miss Winslow," he said as he pulled down the kerchief covering his nose and mouth to filter the dust. "To be honest, Ma'am, I hadn't thought about it at all. Work at the farm has been harder than ever.

"Yes, Charlie. I know how tough times are for everyone in Guymon and everywhere else. If it's not the dust, it's the economy. We all have to compromise to get by."

Charlie told the teacher about his microscope compromise offer from his parents, and that he didn't have enough to make it work.

"I see," she said. "Well, golly, there always could be a Christmas miracle! Remember what we learned from what Abraham Lincoln said, 'Good things come to those who wait.' Try to be patient. All the teachers have had their salaries reduced because of the Depression. I know it's difficult when we have our heart set on something. Think about that Science Fair. I will help you in the ways I can. There are some restrictions on faculty being involved. You are my best student. I think you will come up with a wonderful exhibit."

It all was sounding too familiar to Charlie. He shrugged his shoulder and trudged down the hall. His mind wandered from the microscope to the County Science Fair. There wasn't any prize money for the winners. Only your name and picture in the Guymon Daily News. He remembered that Oscar Schultz won last year and had his picture in the paper. Charlie knew he wouldn't have competition from him, Oscar and his family moved to California last year, chased out by the dust and foreclosure on their farm by the lender. Charlie wondered if he did win, would it help him convince his parents to pay for the microscope. Karl would always tell his son, "Don't tell me what you don't know. Tell me what you do know." Charlie thought about what he knew. His life experience was the farm, and that was about it. Every Spring season he watched his father plant seed, only to have his crops ravaged by rabbits, drought, or the winds. And, sometimes there was hail or a tornado.

Charlie made it through the week enduring farmwork, schoolwork, and the endless dust. On Friday two weeks before Christmas Miss Winslow found him in the hallway at the end of the day. "Charlie," she started. "Hold on Miss Winslow. I know what you're going to say about the Fair. I've been thinking and…" "No, this isn't about the Science Fair. Please step into my classroom. I want to have a private discussion with you."

The two entered the room. She closed the door, went to the closet, got her coat, and put it on. "Charlie. I think you have a lot of potential. If you continue to study and keep your grades where they are, you could go far in life," she said. "I've been thinking about your microscope dilemma." The teacher reached into her coat pocket and handed Charlie $3.20. "I want to invest in your future," she said in warm voice. Please accept this as a Christmas gift and go get yourself that microscope."

Charlie was shocked. "I don't know how to thank you, Miss Winslow. It will be a long time before I can repay you."

"It's not a loan, Charlie. There's nothing in return expected. It's a gift and as I said, I want you to have the best of chances in your future. Merry Christmas, and Happy Birthday."

"It's a Christmas miracle," Charlie said.

"Miss Winslow, there's something I've been trying to tell you!" Charlie exclaimed.

"Oh? Do tell. What's on your mind?"

"I've been thinking about that Science Fair project all week. I'm thinking what I know the most about is farming. Well, actually, why it ain't working for folks around here anymore."

"Please tell me more," his teacher said.

"I am going to need some help gathering up the supplies. I can't afford to buy them, but I'm hoping I could borrow them from the school."

"Hmm, I see. You know that if I can, I will. It will depend on what you need to borrow."

Charlie rattled off a list of the supplies he would need to borrow, and what he had available from home. Miss Winslow raised her eyebrows. Charlie finished his list with, "Remember, mum's the word. Don't let the cat out of the bag. I'm fixin' to win!" Miss Winslow nodded that she understood.

Charlie wanted to keep his project plan secret and decided he would build it in the barn and ask his father to deliver it to the Fair with his truck. It was too big to bring on Dynamite. He knew the delivery request could get tricky. If his father said no, Charlie decided he could ask his neighbors to borrow their horse and wagon.

Miss Winslow gathered the materials Charlie needed and asked Mr. Jenkins, the custodian, to deliver them to the Meyer farm.

Charlie worked, worked, worked on his entry. He wanted everything to be perfect. He carefully painted his hypothesis on a board. He tested his experiment again and again. As stern as his father was, he wasn't completely unreasonable when doing the right thing for his children. On Saturday, the day of the Science Fair, he and Charlie carefully slid the exhibit in the back of the pickup and covered it with a tarp. They arrived at the auditorium, each took an end, carried it into the hall, and placed it on a table. Miss Winslow greeted them. She shook hands with Karl and patted Charlie on the shoulder. "Tell me, Charlie," she began, "How did you develop your hypothesis?"

Charlie was quick to answer. "You know that Jim in our class is a descendant of Kiowa ancestry?"

"Yes, I knew that," she said.

"His great grandfather told him stories about the High Plains going back to his childhood. He said the prairie grass was so tall that a man on horseback could grab the grass on either side of his horse without bending over in the saddle and then tie it in a knot higher than the horse's back. Also, long drought periods aren't something new. They've probably been happening here since time began and the native grasses always survived." Charlie then pulled the tarp off the hand-lettered board. It said in black and white, "The Dust is a Result of Over-farming and Overgrazing the Land. It Removes the Roots and Topsoil Allowing the Topsoil to be Blown Away by the Great Plains Winds."

Karl was visibly embarrassed by the statement.

Charlie went on, "That ancient prairie grass had roots up to 20 feet deep. Anybody who's ever plowed sod knows that. Those roots hold the soil in place and the grass shades the ground to keep the moisture from evaporating." He paused. "Wheat and other crops aren't so deep-rooted. And it gets harvested every year leaving the topsoil exposed to the winds. In the case of grazing, it does the same thing."

Charlie was happy to tell his story, and it gave him practice for telling it to the judges. He pulled the cover off his exhibit. Hiis father grimaced but said nothing. Beneath the canvas was an extra-large fish tank. Instead of water it held more than several inches of sand on the bottom, which in turn was covered by a lesser amount of topsoil. Charlie had painstakingly inserted broom straws in on one end of the tank, buried to the bottom with several inches protruding the surface. It resembled a field of grass. The opposite side was barren. A small electric fan was inside at the end of the tank with the bare soil.

On a placard Charlie listed the causes of soil erosion and some possible remedies such as intercropping shallow rooted plants along with deep rooted plants and planting cover crops in the winter to protect the soil.

Charlie was waiting for the judges before starting his exhibition. When they arrived at his table, he told his story once again and then plugged in the fan. It blew off all the topsoil and a fair amount of sand off the unprotected side. The broom straw kept the soil at the other end stable.

One judge, who was a newspaperman, turned to the other Judge and said, "I suppose this really gives us something to think about." He scribbled something on his notepad.

On Monday morning the headline on the Guymon Daily News read, "Student Dusts The Competition Calls Out Farming." There was a front-page photo of Charlie and his exhibit along with an editorial saying that maybe it was high time to reconsider the destructive farming practices that changed the face of the High Plains and its people with dire results.

Spring arrived on the Plains and Charlie continued to toil at school, the farm, and his microscope. On Sunday morning April 14th, 1935, the skies were clear and blue. The day didn't end as well. In the afternoon an endless black cloud lowered on the horizon. It blocked out the sun and turned day into a dark night. A wall of dust hundreds of feet high coursed across the Plains at speeds of more than 50 mph. It was Black Sunday in Guymon and most of the Great Plains. It was the worst dust storm in recorded American history. It coined the term "Dust Bowl."

People huddled indoors trying to seal windows and doors to keep out the suffocating dust. Visibility was near zero. The winds wiped the soil clean carrying millions of tons of it east to s far as the Atlantic coast. Crops, homes, and cars were buried. It was an epic agricultural disaster. It dealt the finishing blow to many people who had already suffered through years of drought and the Great Depression.

It was a dreary year for the Meyer family. Life as they once knew it was disrupted, but they never gave up hope and continued to work, work, work. A hot, dry summer rolled into a rainless autumn. December arrived and two days before Christmas Eva sat at the kitchen table and wrung her hands worrying about what to do for the holidays to cheer the family up. Karl was in the front yard and saw a plume of dust in the distance that announced the approach of a vehicle. It wasn't altogether unusual. But it struck him as odd. Then again, a lot of people got lost because the terrain had changed so much, and street signs were almost nonexistent.

The Studebaker pulled up in front of Karl. "You lost?" Karl asked the man. "I tell you what. If I've found the home of Mr. Charles Meyer, I'm not lost," he said. "That's my son," Karl replied.

"Can I see him?" the visitor inquired. Karl called for Charlie who was in the barn. "Charles, git on out here. It seems you've got company."

Charlie was puzzled as he made his way to the front yard. He wasn't expecting anyone. He wondered if he was in trouble. The newspaper article about his Science Fair project earlier that year caused quite a flap with farmers in Guymon, and beyond.

"Hello Charles," the man said and extended his hand. Charlie shook it. "I'm Mr. Arbuckle from up in Stillwater Oklahoma. I work in the admissions office." Charlie shuddered since he knew college was never going to be a possibility for him. Arbuckle reached into his car and pulled out a stack of papers. "Here you go, young man. We got wind, no pun intended, of that newspaper article about your science project." Charlie was sure he had somehow gotten into hot water.

Arbuckle shoved the papers towards Charlie. "Am I under arrest?" Charlie asked.

"Heavens, no!" Arbuckle said with a laugh. "The school, Oklahoma Agricultural and Mechanical College, is granting you a full scholarship. We got a letter from your teacher, Miss Winslow and took a look at your outstanding grades, and we learned about your strong work ethic, and your intuitiveness of your project. Not to mention the courage it took to say what you said. That Palm Sunday dust blizzard once again proved your point. Times are tight for everyone, but the college wants to invest in your future. Everyone has to compromise. We've graduated a lot of students since we opened in 1890. Many of them became successful businessmen and donated to the scholarship fund. Merry Christmas!"

What's this gonna cost us?" Karl questioned.

"Not a penny," Arbuckle said. "His room, board and books are covered."

"Well, I'll be darned. How's he supposed to get there?" Karl wanted to know.

"We have another student over in Goodwell. His family has agreed to give Charles a ride back and forth to Stillwater at the beginning and end of each semester and for the Christmas break.

Charlie bolted and headed towards the house. "Mama! Mama!' he called out.

Eva met him at the door and Charlie told her the news. "Miss Winslow never let the cat out of the bag!" he said. "It's a Christmas miracle," she said. "I'd like to meet this gentleman and thank him."

Eva approached Mr. Arbuckle and extended her hand. "Mr. Arbuckle, if my husband hasn't already properly thanked you, please allow me to do so. Please come in the house for a coffee. It's not chicory or roasted barley. It's the real McCoy. A friend at church gave it to us as a Christmas gift."

"Please, call me, Stewart," he said. "And it's my pleasure to be the bearer of such good news. Undoubtedly Charlie is delivering the good word." He quoted Romans 14:19-20, "Let us therefore make every effort to do what leads to peace and to lift each other up. Do not destroy the work of God for the sake of food."

Karl turned to his son and hugged him. "I'm dog-gone proud of you my boy," he whispered. Charlie was shocked. His father wasn't one to show outward affection towards him. Karl was disturbed that he would lose Charlie's help around the farm but remembered his wife's wise words during the discussion about the microscope... *"it's important for our children to have the best education we can give them... Let's not discourage him until he knows his way in life."* A college education was something that Karl and Ever Meyer could ever afford. This scholarship was a true blessing.

The following August Charlie went to college. He studied biology, chemistry, and botany. Four years later he graduated with honors. He returned to Guymon and taught his father to plant Eastern red cedars as wind breaks called shelterbelts. Charlie explained, "Eastern red cedars, *Juniperus virginiana*, are native to Oklahoma and are well-adapted to the climate here. These conical shaped trees are fast-growing and disease-resistant, and tolerate drought, heat, cold, and poor soil. They have a dense branching habit that makes them effective at blocking wind and will stop those nuisance tumbleweeds in their tracks. The U.S, Government Works Progress Administration will provide us with hundreds of seedling trees to get started at no charge. They self-seed and propagate quickly."

Father and son planted the bushels of evergreen sprigs on the perimeters of the fields. Within a short time, they were surrounded by scores of Christmas trees that blocked the wind … and saved the farm.

Story Notes - In the Spring of 1938, a climate shift came with some increase in rainfall across the Panhandle Region, although significant drought conditions persisted. By 1941 most areas of the Great Plains, including the Oklahoma Panhandle, were finally receiving near-normal rainfall amounts, marking a significant end to the Dust Bowl era. As technology advanced, large-scale agricultural irrigation from wells in the Ogallala Aquifer across the Great Plains, including the Oklahoma Panhandle, began in the late 1940s and early 1950s.

Oklahoma Agricultural and Mechanical College officially became Oklahoma State University on July 1, 1957.

Agriculture in the Great Plains relies heavily on irrigation from the Ogallala Aquifer. The rate of water pumped for irrigation far exceeds the natural rate of recharge so the aquifer is being depleted faster than it can be replenished. Water levels in the Ogallala Aquifer have been steadily declining for decades in many areas. Continued over-pumping could eventually lead to the depletion of the aquifer.

My childhood next-door neighbor was Mr. Meyer. He was a farmer who had a mule named Dynamite. I have many Eastern red cedars on my property… and one microscope.

FOUR

Philadelphia, Pennsylvania

Since colonial times, the city of Philadelphia has celebrated New Year's Day with Mummers. On New Year's Day in 1901 the tradition of the modern-day Mummer's Parade began. Every New Year's Day Mummers bands, comics, and magicians strut in brightly colored costumes and masks. Mumming is derived from an ancient Greek word, *Momus*, the personification of mockery and satire.

Mumming on New Year's Day became popular in England during colonial times. People dressed in disguises and costumes would visit from house to house, where the occupants would have to guess the identity of the Mummer. "Mommer," meaning miming, masking, and frolicking, can be found in the old English language. It is easy to see the connection of the word to the cultures.

However, it wasn't the colonial British who fanned the flames of this holiday tradition in the colonies, most notably in Philadelphia. Scandinavian immigrants brought mummering to Philadelphia, which had a large Swedish population during Colonia times. They would hold lively celebrations to ring in the New Year, and bid farewell to the devils, demons, and hardships of the past year. This combined with the traditional British play, St. George and the Dragon, which included outlandish costumes and silliness, set the stage for the Mummers Traditions on January first in the City of Brotherly Love.

The first documented somewhat Mummers-like parade first came about in the Colonies during the Revolutionary War. In 1778 the British gave a farewell sendoff to William General Howe, who became the British commander-in-chief in North America in 1775 and led the British to victory in the Battle of Bunker Hill, although at a considerable cost. Howe's goodbye celebration was a wild and exaggerated party that included many particulars similar to a modern-day Mummers Parade.

Mummering carried over to the citizens of the new nation. President, George Washington lived in the President's House at 6th and Market Street. From 1790 to 1800 Philadelphia served as the nation's temporary capitol while Washington DC was being built. George Washington took note of festivities and contributed to the effort to continue the Mummers Day Parade. During the seven years he lived in Philadelphia, he called on the Mummers to celebrate the New Year's Day holiday and involve everyone. Costumed Mummers went door to door to tell jokes, deliver poems, perform skits, and do impersonations of Washington. This was done for General Washington and area residents as well. Visiting Mummers received baked goods and libations for their theatrical contributions.

Runar and Greta Andersson and their children Bjorn and Astrid immigrated from Mora, Sweden to the Colonies prior to the American Revolution. They settled in Philadelphia among other Swedes. Runar was a cabinet and clock case maker.

The classic Swedish curvy longcase clocks started in Mora. Clockmaking began there after a series of drought years farming families turned to cottage industry for income. Each family would be in charge of making a specific part for the clockworks and the cases would be made separately by craftsmen.

Runar Andersson had his own unique style of longcase violin-shaped clock cases with his own signature painted designs that included long-plumage birds. He was a Master Craftsman. His curvaceous Mora clocks were sought after, but his inventory started to exceed the demand. Times had turned bad in Mora after the dry seasons. Ordinary people in Sweden couldn't afford the clocks, except for some aristocrats in Stockholm. During the Mora region's height of clockmaking families made an estimated 1,000 clocks per year during a 50-year span. Eventually the cottage industry shut down when Swedes began importing foreign clocks from Germany and North America. Runar felt his chances for prosperity were better in the New World. He heard that quite a bit of wealth was developing there, particularly in the shipping cities. He considered Boston and New York but settled on Philadelphia because of the large Scandinavian community already there. He knew there would be plenty of hardwood forests nearby that could supply him with the raw materials he needed for his trade. His only worries were the news of unsettled times and high taxation in the British colonies.

Runar and Greta and their children arrived in the spring and settled into a small house with a large outbuilding that would serve as Runar's workshop. Greta and Astrid got to work getting the house in order and setting up the kitchen. Runar and Bjorn unpacked the tools they brought from home: saws, planes, spokeshaves, scrapers, chisels, mallets, hatches, adzes, and measuring tools. Father and son went into the woods and searched for the best hardwood trees that included sugar maple, red oak, black cherry and walnut. Pennsylvania's climate and soil composition create forests that hold some of the world's most prized hardwoods. They felled the trees and whatever wasn't usable for cabinet making was used for firewood. Runar saved every scrap from the wood that was milled for woodworking. They worked hard every day harvesting the lumber, taking it to the sawmill, then to Runar's shop where he worked his magic. Greta and Astrid kept them well fed and brought meals to the workshop so they wouldn't have to stop. Roughhewn planks gave way to smooth planed boards. The boards were cut and fitted together perfectly. Runar was an expert at making beautiful book-matched cabinet doors. He saved this process for select woods in clock cases that would not be painted. He would barter or buy the round glass for the clock face, the eight-day movement, which had to be wound only once a week, the cast iron weights, the pendulum and gong. Parts were becoming difficult to get because of England's tax or embargo on finished metal goods. His customers often included statemen and nobility, so sometimes a blind eye was turned, and papers were shuffled on their behalf when the supplier learned where the clock was going. The buyer could often override the fines. Runar continued his work through the summer.

Runar said to his wife, "Greta, I am becoming concerned. The Revolution has slowed down the demand for our beautiful clocks and cabinets. I'm not sure what to do. We haven't had any new orders in months."

"Have patience," Greta said. "Hopefully, the British will leave soon, and peace will return. Maybe there is something else we can do in the meanwhile."

"I must say," said Runar, "I can sympathize with the Colonist's points. So much taxation and restriction of trade. They are independent and self-sufficient, but still a man has to be able to make a living and support his family."

Astrid joined the conversation. "Papa, Mama, we could make toys for the children of Philadelphia. There is nothing for them during this time. Some are losing their fathers because of the fighting. People may not be buying clocks, but they certainly will want to provide gifts for their children to make them happy. If we make a lot of toys, it could replace some of the lost business that the clocks provided."

"That's a fine idea," her father said.

"It's something we could all work on in-between chores," Greta said as Bjorn entered the workshop and picked up on the discussion.

"I could turn out tops on the treadle lathe," Bjorn said.

" I can paint them in beautiful colors," replied Astrid.

"I can carve dolls and animals," Runar added.

"I can sew costumes for your dolls! It will be fun making children happy," said Greta.

Runar crossed his arms and let out a huff. "But how will we sell them? Maybe if people don't have money for clocks, they won't have money for toys…"

Greta answered him, "We can start by telling our friends at church and ask them to spread the word. A few of the congregation members work for wealthy families in Philadelphia. We will have to have faith. We are doing something good during troubled times. I think we can rely on that to be rewarded. We must keep our spirits up. Let's all get a good sleep tonight and start first thing in the morning."

At first light the family went about gathering the materials needed for toymaking. Runar went through his bins of cutoffs and scrap wood. They worked at a furious pace. One by one a collection of tops, checkerboards, dolls and stilts were lining the shop shelves. During colonial times dolls were generally simple and made from rags, corn husks and or crudely made from wood. Runar said, "I feel that we can improve the quality and look of toys that are available to children today. We can carve more intricate figures, use brighter colors, add more details, and give them smoother finishes. It won't take us very much longer to turn out the finest toys in all of Pennsylvania!"

Astrid thought about what her father said, and repeated aloud, "carve more intricate figures, use brighter colors, add more details, and give them smoother finishes. Mother, Father, Bjorn, I have another idea of something that will be in demand for the New Year and will be attractive to well-off buyers. We know how popular mumming is on New Year's Day. Correct?"

The other nodded in agreement. Astrid went on, "We could create unusual costume masks for the mummers. They would take more work than toys, but they would fetch a higher price because there is no one else selling them. What is out here right now are masks made cheaply with straw and corn husks."

"Brilliant," her father said.

"But we should not stop making toys. Remember our inspiration was to make children happy," Greta answered.

"I agree," said Bjorn.

Astrid answered with a smile and said, "we can make masks that are the characters in the mummers' plays. You know like a hero character, a villain, animals, or maybe even a doctor. We can make some quite comical and in the case of the villain, make them look evil. If we can build a clock, we can make a costume!"

Faced with new tasks, the family worked from dark to dark in the workshop, then by candlelight at the kitchen table until it was time for bed. Greta and Astrid spoke to the women about the toys and the mumming masks and asked them to spread the word. Some women questioned if they were going to stop making the beautiful Molina clocks. Greta assured them that there would be a clock for anyone who wanted to buy one. Runar was growing concerned that their plans for creating items for fun during a time of war may not be well received.

Three days later a man arrived at the Andersson's small factory. "Please allow me to introduce myself," the man said. "I am Mr. Thomas Chenwick. The proprietor of the City Tavern at 138 South 2nd Street on the intersection of Second Street and Walnut Streets. It's one street over from the Pennsylvania State House."

Runar placed his chisel on the workbench and extended his hand. "Yes, I know the place. I'm Runar Andersson, proprietor of the Andersson

Family clock, toy, and mask factory." Runar allowed himself a laugh. Mr. Chenwick laughed as well and said, "You seem to have quite a striving business here."

"Well, time will tell," replied Runar.

"Yes, my wife told me about a visit from Mrs. Andersson and your daughter, and how you are trying to adapt your business in these troubled times. Perhaps I can help you with that. I have a proposal," Mr. Chenwick said. "Please allow me to explain. The members of the newly formed Continental Congress meet at the State House to debate almost every day. It's a little too much arguing, but that's not my business. What is my business is serving them ale, spirits, and a meal at lunch time and in the evening when their day is done, although they do carry their debating on into the evening. I'm sure the rum, whisky and brandy help fuel their arguments."

"I understand," said Runar as he folded his arms, "what did you have in mind?"

Chenwick answered, "Well, Mr. Andersson, those representatives at the State House include some of the most affluent and influential people in the colonies. There's George Washington and Thomas Jefferson from Virginia who are wealthy landowners, Charles Carrollton of Maryland, Benjamin Franklin and Robert Morris both from here in Pennsylvania, and the quite influential John Adams of Massachusetts. They, and other members of the Continental Congress, are in my tavern…sometimes more than once a day."

Runar unfolded his arms and placed his hands on his hips. He was becoming inpatient. "That's jolly good for you, but again I ask you, what do you have in mind? I have a lot of work to finish and not much time to do it."

"Yes, please pardon my unannounced interruption of your day, Mr. Andersson. I only wish to help you, seeing how you are doing good things for the children. So, I propose that you put one of your clocks in the City Tavern on consignment. All those Congress members will pass by it, check the time, and no doubt be struck by the beauty of the design. I will take full responsibility for the clock. And I will gladly refer any inquiries about where it came from directly to you. You have nothing to lose, and I can guarantee without hesitation you will have clock orders by the end of the first week."

Runar rubbed his chin. "That is an interesting proposal, and I accept. I can deliver one the day after tomorrow."

"Very well," said Chenwick. "When you come, please bring your family for a holiday dinner. It's on the house. You deserve it!"

The family was looking forward to celebrating Christmas in their new home. Swedish Christmas starts on December 13th, which is Saint Lucia Day. During the third-century Lucia was a martyr who brought food to persecuted Christians who were in hiding. Traditionally the oldest daughter in the family plays the part of Lucia. In the morning, the girl wears a white robe and a crown of candles and serves her parents buns and coffee or mulled wine. Early on the morning of the 13th Astrid put on the traditional white gown and a crown illuminated with candles. She extinguished the candles and served breakfast to her parents.

Swedes attend church services on Christmas Eve, or Julafton. After Christmas Eve services they go to their homes for a traditional family buffet dinner, a (smorgasbord), that would include ham, pork, or fish, plus an array of sweets.

Following the festive Christmas Eve smorgasbord, someone dresses up as Tomte the Christmas gnome. Swedish folklore says that Tomte is the Christmas gnome who lives in the forest. He was the Swedish pre-Christianity Santa Claus equivalent who hands out gifts. Tomte is associated with the winter solstice and Yule season. The three-foot-tall gnome is said to be a deliverer of good fortune during this time and is the spirit of generosity. Tomte, a small, gnomelike spirit being, is often thought of as mythical presence who lives on a farm and takes care of the homestead or the family while the farmer and his family are sleeping. Tomte can be a gift giver if the farmer treats him and the animals correctly.

Jultomten, or sometimes just called Tomten, is the spirit who brings the Christmas gifts at Julafton, on the evening of December 24. The gifts are called julklappar. Jultomten does not come down the chimney as Santa Clause is said to do. Jultomten delivers Christmas gifts in person. The part of Jultomten is usually played by an older man. He secretly dresses up as Jultomten and arrives at the door with a sack of gifts.

The Tomte is an ancient belief. Some believe that the Tomte was considered a spirit of earlier generations on the homestead, and further beliefs are that they followed the family when they moved. Regardless of its different cultural origins, the modern Jultomte, or Tomte of Jul, is comparable to Santa Claus. The Jultomte of today is a hybridization of the pre-Christian Tomte and the original Dutch Santa Claus.

As Chenwick predicted, within a week of the Andersson's clock being on display, servants of Philadelphia's elite class, and members of Congress, began to show up at Runar's door to place orders for clocks. Word had spread about the clocks, the toys, and mumming masks, being made by the Swedish immigrants. On Christmas Eve Komminister Lundqvist came to the door as well. He was greeted graciously by Runar and Greta. "Good day and Happy Christmas, Pastor Lundqvist. To what do we owe the pleasures of your visit at such a busy time for you?" Greta asked.

"As you know the conflict has begun. I am sad to say that battles have taken place between the British soldiers and the Revolutionists. In addition to many smaller skirmishes, since September the Continental Army has had Boston under siege and, on December 9 there was a battle at Great Bridge Virginia. The Continental Army was victorious, but there were many casualties. And furthermore, as you know, many men from Philadelphia have left their homes to join the effort. This has made children fatherless, and wives left to try to survive without a breadwinner. Ultimately, the children are the most unfortunate victims. God bless the children; they have no voice, and they have no choice."

"I agree, it's terrible and hopefully the matter will be resolved quickly," Greta said.

The frail clergyman continued. "Yesterday a wealthy man from our community came to see me. He is a Patriot who wishes to remain anonymous. He too realizes the plight of the children during these times. He is truly the Jultomte for this Christmas and has given me a donation to cover the cost of 100 toys for children that will be distributed by the church. Before dawn tomorrow the julklappar gifts will be at the front doors of the children's homes. I wish you all a blessed Christmas."

From that day onward the Andersson family was set for life. Their clock business flourished and they continued to make Christmas toys and mumming masks for many years.

Story Notes - Mumming continues in Philadelphia. There is an annual Mummers Parade on New Year's Day on the streets of Philadelphia. The original City Tavern was constructed in 1773. John Adams considered the place the "most genteel tavern in America" It offered a lavish atmosphere for the elite. A fire in 1834 damaged most of the structure, and it was completely demolished in 1854. Years later it was restored to its original format and décor, and featured an authentic menu that would have been used in the time of the American Revolution. Unfortunately, it closed its doors in 2020 from the economic downturn of the COVID pandemic.

FIVE

Oshkosh, Wisconsin

He turned into the driveway and shut off the headlights. The day's work was done. It would exhaust most men, but the sheer joy it brought him was well worth it. He laughed when people told him to get a real job, or that it was only seasonal work. He and his wife moved into the community a year ago. Its uncomplicated Midwest ways made it easier for him than most of the other places they had lived.

He trudged through the ground cover of snow to the front door. "Honey, I'm home," he said as he hung the car keys on the rack. He knew he wouldn't need them for a while.

"Oh, good, Dear. I'm glad. I was hoping you'd be home earlier. You know, a chance to rest a while before tonight's activities," she said as she gave a welcoming hug.

"Well, you know how it is on Christmas Eve. It being the last day and all. The kids are all wound up. I never want to disappoint."

"Come sit. Some of the kids are going to be on TV tonight. I can give you dinner on a tray if you wish."

"Jumping Jiminy Cricket, I almost forgot. Yes, big event and all. A lot of folks told me they'd be tuning in."

"What are they asking for this year? Are girls still asking for Barbie Dolls?" she asked.

He thought about the question for a moment. "Oh, sure, Barbie is still going strong. I think Barbie has a long life ahead of her."

"Really? Good. That's terrific. The boys seem to have so many choices. Not so much for the girls. I could be wrong. What else?" His wife leaned forward for his response.

"Etch a sketch is still popular, but it looks like the Spirograph is giving it a run for the money, for boys and girls. GI Joe is slowing down, I'd say. Rock 'em Sock 'em robots are still popular, too." He chuckled.

She countered, "All of these newfangled toys we have to stay on top of. It was so much easier when it was the usual stuff. You know…bicycles, skates, and baseball mitts."

"Yes, that's all still coming up. And that Sting-Ray wheelie bike. Gee whiz! That's been in demand a lot this year. We'll have to see about that. This year the Hot Wheels Racing sets by Mattel are by far the toy on most lists," he said. She nodded that she understood.

She clapped her hands together, "It's almost time. Go flip on the TV, adjust the bunny ears. I'll get you your slippers. You have a while 'til you have to get dressed."

"Which of the kids are on TV tonight?" he asked. "What channel?"

"Borman, Lovell, and that Anders kid. You remember Billy Anders; he was born in Hong Kong in mid- October, and you had to go out of your way. But they ended up in California. It made things a little easier on the travel," she said and left the living room.

"Yes, yes, yes. I remember it well. Ah yes, those were the days," he said, "before shiny aluminum trees, and pink Christmas ball ornaments." He grimaced at the words aluminum trees.

She called out from the kitchen, "I think it's on NBC. Maybe CBS or ABC, too? I'm not sure. Dial around. This is a big deal. They all may be covering it."

His wife returned to the living room with two steaming dinner plates. "CBS is doing a great job with that Charlie Brown Christmas Show. I'm glad it worked out," she said. "It almost didn't happen. That Charlie Brown tree was just what was needed to get rid of those chrome trees that folks were running out and buying. The plan worked...it gave those folks something to think about. Try fiddling with the horizontal hold. It's been on the fritz lately. Let the tubes warm up for a while."

"NBC comes in the best. Let's try that," he said, turned the dial, and made a final adjustment to the TV antennae. "Forget about those fake trees. We could use some tin foil on the rabbit ears, though. Just like me, this old Motorola doesn't work quite so good as it used to."

"Oh, you're fine. You've got a few centuries left in you. Not so sure about that TV. Turn up the volume, would you?" She paused then blurted out, "Yes, now I remember!" she said in a joyful voice. "The Borman kid was born over in Gary Indiana, and they ended up in Tucson. Jimmy Lovell was born in Cleveland and moved to Milwaukee with his mom. They spent a couple of years in Terre Haut before that. I can hardly keep track of them all."

The couple finished their meals and pushed back their recliner chairs. They remarked on the tension in the commentator's voice. Static filled the airwaves, and a microphone crackled to life. Voices came from the astronauts deep in space, a place where no man had ever been, aboard the Apollo 8 spacecraft. On December 24, 1968, in what was the most watched television broadcast at the time Bill Anders, the pilot of the lunar module said, "We are now approaching lunar sunrise, and for all the people back on Earth, the crew of Apollo 8 has a message that we would like to send to you."

Anders continued by reading from the Book of Genesis, Chapter One, "'In the beginning God created the heaven and the earth.

'And the earth was without form, and void; and darkness was upon the face of the deep.

'And the Spirit of God moved upon the face of the waters. And God said, let there be light: and there was light.

'And God saw the light, that it was good; and God divided the light from the darkness.'"

Astronaut Jim Lovell the Command Module Pilot had come a long way from his boyhood home in Milwaukee, Ohio. Astronaut Lovell continued reading from inside the spacecraft where Anders had left off, "'And God called the light Day, and the darkness he called Night. And the evening and the morning were the first day.

'And God said, let there be a firmament in the midst of the waters, and let it divide the waters from the waters.

'And God made the firmament, and divided the waters which were under the firmament from the waters which were above the firmament: and it was so.

'And God called the firmament Heaven. And the evening and the morning were the second day."

Commander Frank Borman added the last verses, "'And God said, Let the waters under the heaven be gathered together unto one place, and let the dry land appear; and it was so.

'And God called the dry land Earth; and the gathering together of the waters called the Seas; and God saw that it was good.'"

At the conclusion of reading the Bible by the light of the moon he said, "And from the crew of Apollo 8, we close with good night, good luck, a Merry Christmas – and God bless all of you, all of you on the good Earth."

"Hurry, Dear," she said. "It's time for you to get dressed and go. It will be good to know you're not the only one flying around tonight."

He left the room and returned fully prepared for his mission. "Please…" she said, "Do it once for me."

Her husband gave her a warm hug and kissed her forehead. Then he stroked his beard, nodded, winked, stepped to the fireplace, and was gone in a flash.

That Christmas Eve the Apollo 8 spacecraft began ten successful orbits (in 20 hours) around the moon. It marked the first manned flight of the enormous Saturn V rocket that launched Apollo 8 into the heavens. Apollo 8 emerged from the never-before-seen dark side of the moon before heading back to Earth, and a thankful Astronaut Lovell announced to the world, "Houston, please be informed there is a Santa Claus."

Story Notes – It was estimated that hundreds of millions of people worldwide watched the Apollo 8 Christmas Eve broadcast from the moon on TV. American astronauts William Anders, James Lovell, and Frank Borman were the first humans to orbit the Moon.

SIX

Katonah, New York

Marguerite heard a noise in the yard. The sun had not quite risen above the horizon. *Darn it,* she thought. *Something is stirring the sheep.* She thought about whether to wake her husband, Henri. Marguerite knew how grumpy he could be if awoken early. She thought the better option would be to let their dog, Belle, out. After all, that was Belle's job, and what she was bred for.

Coyotes, and occasionally wolves, moved closer to the village during the winter months when food in the wild became scarce. A thick blanket of snow had fallen the day before. It kept prey well hidden within their holes and hideaways. She wondered if it was coyotes after the chickens, or perhaps wolves stalking the sheep. Wolves were common in the area years ago, but now not so much. There had been recent sightings, likely because of the early winter and unusual cold spells.

When the Cross River was dammed up 1897 to create the Cross River Reservoir, many of the animals became displaced. Most moved farther north into the foothills; some moved closer to civilization. In any case, many acres of their former habitat and hunting grounds became flooded. Now even after seventeen years, wild animals prowled the outskirts of the tiny village of Katonah, New York.

Marguerite's grandfather, a French Canadian fur trapper, immigrated to Katonah, which was called Whitlockville during his time. He came to America from Quebec and boarded a barge that sailed down the Hudson River. He brought along a select few prized possessions. Among them was a set of nativity figures that his parents had brought to North America from France. After living in Ossining for a few years, and becoming tired of that growing, bustling town, he moved his family thirteen miles east to Old Katonah and started a farm. After the dam was built and the valley was about to be flooded, his house was raised, placed on logs, and pulled by horse teams to its new location. The new village was called New Katonah, and now was simply referred to as Katonah. Marguerite and her family lived in that farmhouse. It sat near enough to the village to be convenient, yet on the edge of the glorious woodlands, streams, and the reservoir. Henri's parents, Jacques and Marie, were French Canadian and came to America a year before he was born. They visited the young family as time allowed, but always made it a point to be at the farm for Christmas.

She moved silently past her daughter Jeanette's room and whispered for the dog. "Belle, allons. Dépêcher vous!" Like her masters, the Belgian sheep dog was bilingual. She was obedient in both languages. Belle usually stayed in her doghouse near the sheep pen. On the coldest nights, Marguerite extended an invitation to Belle to sleep in the kitchen. The dog never turned down the offer.

Marguerite and her husband used French and English interchangeably, but always tried to speak in English to their daughter, Jeanette, their only child. Although, like the dog, Jeanette understood French perfectly well. Marguerite and Henri were introduced to each other at a church social. A mutual friend thought the couple's shared Acadian heritage would be a good match. It was. They were married in St. Mary's church, which had been disassembled in the old village before the flood and reconstructed in 1899 in New Katonah. Two years later Jeanette was born. They kept up with their French heritage traditions. Particularly around the holidays.

Marguerite opened the kitchen door and the dog knew instinctively what to do. Belle bounded toward the sheep coral and let out as series of sharp commanding barks. Her white fur masked her presence in the snow. When she was satisfied the sheep were safe, the big dog circled the hen house, then crept into the barn checking each horse stall and goat pen. Back outside again she found no one, or nothing except paw prints near the pasture gate. She gave them a cursory sniff, lowered her head, and peered into the pasture and the sun rising behind it. Belle gave the icy air one last whiff and decided that all was well. Her own paws crunched the crusty snow. She trotted back to the kitchen door.

Marguerite opened the door for the dog. Belle licked her hand in thanks. "Ah, all is well, I see. You are back already," Marguerite said as she patted the dog on the head. "Go to your bed. I've started the stove. You will be warm there. Bien?" Belle curled up near the wood stove.

"Jeanette, Jeanette! Time to be up! Time for chores and school," Marguerite called out. She knew it would wake Henri, but it was time for him to tend to his chores as well.

Jeanette arrived in the kitchen and wiped the sleep from her eyes as she leaned against the wall. "Oh, Mama. It is so cold this morning. Il fait froid," she repeated in French and pulled her woolen shawl tighter. Her mother didn't look up as she placed a half-dozen eggs in a pot to boil.

"Yes it is. Good morning, my Dear. Come give Mama a hug," Marguerite said. The two embraced. "It will be warm soon. The sun will be full up in twenty minutes. You can wait until then to feed the chickens." She poured her daughter a cup of tea. "Breakfast will be ready when you are done."

Jeanette skipped to the kitchen door. Once outside she grabbed the tin pail from under the porch and headed to the barn to fill it with grain. The frigid wind tousled her hair and captured her breath. She wished a good morning to their two horses, the goats, and the two pigs huddled in the corner. "Those poor dears," she thought. "One of them will end up on our Christmas table." Jeanette looked away as she filled the pail.

Back in the warm surround of the kitchen Jeanette ate her breakfast of bread and cheese as she prepared for school. Her mother quizzed her again on her studies, but Jeanette knew she was ready for the tests before the Christmas break. She knew the nuns would not tolerate anything less than a perfect score. Jeanette studied hard and worked hard to please her parents. Her schoolteachers were far more demanding. Although, she knew that studying books was far more forgiving than the physical farm work.

"Here, wrap this écharpe around your neck. If you get too warm you can loosen it. I don't want you to have a sore throat for the holidays. I want to hear you sing!" Jeanette tugged at the ends of the scarf to tighten it. "Take these. Put one in each pocket and put your hands in. They will be for your lunch later. For now, they will keep your hands warm," Marguerite said as she slid a still steaming unshelled hardboiled egg in each of her daughter's coat pockets.

As Jeanette walked down the snow covered lane that led from her farmhouse she dreamed about Père Noël and what he might leave in her shoes left by the fireplace. She sang the Hail Mary on her way to school in the way that her mother had taught her, "Je vous salue Marie pleine de grâce..." She would sing that song solo in St. Mary's church on Christmas Eve. She loved it so. She would also sing songs with the choir. Her strong alto voice with its stunning vibrato was in high demand by Sister Margaret the music teacher and choir director. In spite of the cold, the excitement of Christmas filled her thoughts and painted a smile on her face.

Her papa would carry a large cherry Yule log into the house. It was stored in the barn, along with a piece of last year's yule log, and kept aside for the Christmas Eve festivities. The log would be sprinkled with red wine. Jeanette wasn't sure if it was Beaujolais or Bordeaux that papa used. It didn't matter. Either way, it would smell nice as it burned. The charred bit of log from last Christmas would be used to light the new one. It would be left to burn all night along with some lit candles, food, and drinks. This was a custom and done in case Mary, Joseph, and the baby Jesus came to stay the night.

She looked forward to the traditions. A massive Christmas Eve dinner, called Réveillon, would be served after returning home from Christmas Eve Mass. There would be roast goose, perhaps venison if the men had a successful hunt, and ham. Jeanette winced as she thought about the poor pig in the barn. A delicious log-shaped chocolate sponge cake, a bûche de Noël, would be the dessert. In addition to grand-père and grand-mère, perhaps there would be others around the table. They would all sing Christmas hymns, laugh, and eat roasted chestnuts, cheeses, and the madeleines that she would bake under her mother's direction early in the day. And of course, there would be wine.

Jeanette turned on to Valley Road. In the early morning hours, the streets were quiet. Sunlight bounced off the snow and made icicles sparkle like diamond necklaces. It was her favorite part of the walk. It would take her past the front of St. Mary's with its crèche. The hand carved life size statues were the work of a talented woodcarver some years before. The local legend was that the figures were carved from wood gathered from the forest before the flooding began. It was said the wood gave the carved figures mythical, magical powers. Her own nativity at home would feature clay figurines in the French tradition. They were the ones her great grandfather brought to America.

Jeanette always paused for a moment in front of the St. Mary's nativity setting. She would gaze at the carvings of Mary, Joseph, and the infant Jesus. The animal characters completed the scene. There were sheep, a donkey, which she supposed represented the one that carried Mary, and doves. The three magi Melchior, Casper, and Balthasar would be added later in celebration of the Epiphany, the twelfth day of Christmas. *What a perfect place to sing my song,* Jeanette thought. I will offer it as my gift to the baby Jesus. Her words glistened in the crisp air, "Je vous salue Marie pleine de grâce...Le Seigneur est avec vous." She stopped abruptly. There was something not right with the scene. In fact, something was very wrong. She hadn't noticed it earlier, but there was an animal, a large dog perhaps, curled in the hay. Not a carving, but a live animal. She dropped her book bag.

Its sooty fur was matted and its ears were laid back. When the singing stopped the animal lifted its head and jumped up on all four legs. Jeanette was startled by the size of the dog. It was quite a bit larger than Belle. Now staring at her, the animal raised its tail, let out a low, deep grow, and barred its teeth.

"Je vous salue Marie..." Jeanette sang softly. The animal whimpered. "Mon Dieu! You are a wolf," Jeanette said aloud. She and the wolf made direct eye contact, but she was not afraid. "Why are you hiding in the church manger?" She folded her arms in defiance. "Those sheep are not real. You cannot eat them." The wolf growled again, and the smoky gray hackles began to rise on its back. Jeanette became concerned. "Why are you being cross with me? I did not come here to hurt you," she said. "Yes, we are both cold. And perhaps you are hungry?" She slowly reached into her coat pocket and withdrew one of the eggs. "I will be nice to you, and you will be nice to me. Okay?" The wolf cocked his head to one side. "You are too nice to be growling in there with those sheep. Aren't you?" His ears perked up. Jeanette held the egg out with one mitted hand. "Je vous salue Marie pleine de grâce," she sang again. I am going to name you Loup Gris. That is en français for Gray Wolf. Loup, the wolf, sat down. Jeanette tossed the egg toward the beast. He pounced on it and devoured it in two bites, shell and all. Jeanette threw him the second egg followed by the piece of baguette that was wrapped in her bag.

"I must go now. I cannot be late for school. I do not want to upset Sister Theresa. Maybe you can hide behind the crèche and wait for me after school. If you are here, I will sing for you if you wish. Be a good boy."

Sister Theresa was from the Sisters of the Divine Compassion order of nuns. They founded the school at St. Mary's and taught all of the classes. Like Jeanette, her family was originally from France. She still had relatives who lived there. She enjoyed the opportunity to chat in French with Jeanette. It made her feel at home. It was Sister Theresa who encouraged Jeanette to sing at midnight Mass.

In August of that year Germany had declared war on France. By the end of the month the Germans invaded France. With the war going on, Sister Theresa was worried about the safety of her family that was still in France. She prayed for them often. She prayed for everyone.

Jeanette entered the classroom and took her seat. "Good morning, class," Sister Theresa said.

Her students replied in unison, "Good morning, Sister Theresa!"

"I am pleased to tell you that the convent has received word through the Diocese that on December 7th Pope Benedict asked for a cease-fire for Christmas." She paused to let the words sink in. "Please let us pray that the countries listen to our Holy Father and stop the shooting while we celebrate the birth of Christ. Everyone on your knees. And let's pray for end to the war. We will begin with five Hail Mary's and end with five Our Fathers."

No one questioned, no one complained. All of the students knelt beside their desks in the aisle and prayed aloud. Sister Theresa signaled the end with the sign of the cross, "In the name of the Father, and of the Son, and of the Holy Ghost. Amen."

"Class as you know, today is your examination day. For those who do well, there will be a special treat." The children fidgeted in their seats. Some because of the test and what the consequences would be for a poor grade, and others in anticipation of the surprise. "For those who do well, we will read from *The Snow Queen* by Hans Christian Andersen. You may be interested to note that it was published exactly 70 years ago today – December 21st, 1844. Yes, it is fantasy book. But since it shows the battle between good and evil, and how the evil of the devil works in our lives…for those who do not do well you will read from the catechism." Jeanette knew she would be reading the work of Hans Christian Andersen and smiled. "Put your books away and let us give a prayer to Jesus to guide us through this test. "In the name of the Father…"

Jeanette thought about Loup and wondered if she was being dishonest for telling the animal to hide in the manger. She felt it will be for God to decide. After all, St. Francis of Assisi, the patron saint of animals, looked after the wild beasts. Why couldn't she? Jeanette reasoned. What's more, she continued in her thinking, St. Francis created the first Christmas crèche to commemorate the birth of Jesus. Maybe it was fitting for Loup to be there. She hoped he wouldn't be caught...or shot.

At the school day's end she scurried from the room. There was only one more day of school until the Christmas recess. Class was set to resume on January 2nd. Jeanette said goodbye to Sister Theresa and raced out the door. Sister Theresa blamed Jeanette's hasty departure on the holiday excitement. She knew all of the children were a little less controllable at this time of year.

The manger was void of any living creatures when Jeanette arrived. She looked up and down the empty street. "St. Francis, let him be safe," Jeanette prayed aloud. She began to sing, hoping it would draw Loup out if he was near. Gradually increasing her volume, it brought nothing but the start of a tear. She turned the corner and headed down the lane for the long walk to the farm. On each side of the road towering evergreens swayed with the breeze and waved to her with their outstretched arms. She kicked the snow and tried to resist the anger she had for herself for giving her lunch away to an animal that didn't appreciate it enough to stay. "Jeanette, you fool!" She said to her audience of trees. "Oh, well, cest la vie," she shouted to the trees. "I will sing instead and you will all have to clap for me! I will sing you all a choir song that we will perform at Midnight Mass."

The song held a special meaning for Jeanette. Her father schooled her on the history of the song and why it was written. It came as no surprise to her that it was written by a Frenchman who was a poet and a wine commissionaire in a tiny French village. "Wine and poetry are not an unusual combination," her father said. Placide Cappeau de Roquemaure was the poet's name. Jeannette thought it was a bit long. Cappeau penned the song at the request of the parish priest. His lyrics were influenced by the gospel of Luke and his words describing the birth of Christ. "Oddly," her papa said, "the man who wrote the music to go along with those words, Adolphe Charles Adams, was Jewish and did not believe in Jesus Christ. And yes, although it was written by a Frenchman, it quickly became known around the world. It was sung in numerous French Catholic churches on Christmas Eve. The French, and others, loved that song.

"But that was not the whole story," Papa said. "When Cappeau joined the socialist movement and turned away from the church, and they found out that Adolphe Adams was a Jew, the French Catholic church considered "*Cantique de Noel*" not worthy for church services. They said it lacked musical taste and was totally absent of the spirit of religion. Regardless... the people loved it, and sang it, and *Cantique de Noel* has carried on to today."

Jeanette stretched her arms out to mimic the pines, closed her eyes, and tilted her head back. "Placide Cappeau," this is for you, she said. "*O holy night, the stars are brightly shining, It is the night of our dear Savior's birth.*" She sang the hymn loud with perfect tone and measure. The singer moved through the verses and when she arrived at the chorus, she reached deep within herself and delivered it with gusto. "*Fall on your knees, Oh hear the angel voices... Oh night divine...*" The line was punctuated by a piercing whine.

Her eyes popped open as her head snapped forward. Standing in front of her, and now whimpering like a baby, was Loup. "Ah! Loup! You found me. We found each other." Jeanette was not sure what to do next. If she led him home, papa would be furious. "What do you think?" she asked the wolf.

The animal lowered himself to the ground and rested his shaggy face on his front paws. His piercing blue eyes looked up and pleaded with Jeanette. "Well, you ragamuffin, you hardly look like a threat. And, you do look like you have not been eating enough." She threw her scarf back around her neck and put her hands on her hips. "I am heading home. If you decide to follow me, I will know you want to be with me. But, of course, you must behave. I will hide you until we can find a way to explain you to Mama and Papa. We will go through the woods so we will not be seen."

Loup did follow Jeanette. Not only did he follow, but he never left her side. They went through the stands of pines and circled the farm. Arriving at a spot behind the barn Jeanette said, "You will hide here. I will bring you food when I feed the chickens. You have to promise that you will not hurt the farm animals, the chickens, or Belle, my dog. Do you understand me? comprenez vous" Loup sat and lowered his head. "Good. You listen. If you stay a good boy, I will try to make you happy for Christmas."

"Where have you been, Jeanette?" her mother asked. "You should have been home twenty minutes ago. You seem very excited. What is it, my Dear?"

"I stopped by St. Mary's crèche and took a little time to sing to the trees. I need to practice for Christmas Eve."

"Well, you could come home and sing for me."

"It just would not have been the same." Jeanette stifled a giggle.

"And what about your excitement?" her mother queried.

"Oh...well," Jeanette stumbled with her words. "I am excited because I did very well on my examination today, and so, I will be with the students that Sister Theresa will allow to read from Hans Christian Andersen's book, *The Snow Queen*."

"How wonderful! Come give Mama a hug." Jeanette was the first to release their embrace.

"Mama, we are supposed to love everyone, even if we are afraid of them and they hate us, yes?"

"Well, yes, of course. That's true. Sometimes it's difficult, though. Why do you ask?"

Jeanette thought about her reply and changed her response. "Today Sister Theresa told us that Pope Benedict has asked for the shooting to stop for Christmas. You know, the shooting in the war. She had us pray for them. Do you think they can? I mean do you think they can like each other enough to stop fighting for Christmas?"

"Well, yes. I suppose anything is possible. I think it is important for them to try."

"Mama, do you believe in the magic of the nativity figures at St. Mary's?"

Marguerite raised her eyebrows. "I have heard they are special. Why do you ask?"

"I spent time there today. I think Christmas can make miracles happen. Do you?" Jeanette asked.

"Do you mean miracles like the shooting and the war to stop?" Marguerite sat down at the kitchen table. "That's a very good question. I'm sure Christmas holds a magic all of its own."

"Ah, yes, Mama. You are incredibly wise." Jeanette leaned in the doorway and enjoyed the aromas emanating from the stove. "Baking, oui?"

"Yes, of course. It is almost la veille de Noël, silly girl."

"Of course, how foolish of me to say that," Jeanette said in a faint voice and then blurted out her next question. "Are all animals bad?"

Her mother laughed. "Absolutely not. Look at Belle, and our animals in the barn. They are all good animals."

"Oh, yes. Foolish of me again...What about the animals in the woods?"

Her mother pushed her chair back from the table. "That's another matter. There are good and bad."

"Do you think St. Francis loved every animal; you know, God's creatures?"

Marguerite was growing irritated by the questions. "I'm sure he did."

"Well then…we should all learn to be more like St. Francis and enjoy the magic that Christmas brings!" Jeannette grinned, believing she had won the debate.

Marguerite rolled her eyes, shook her head, and thought to herself, *Jeanette has now reached the age of being a silly girl…* Marguerite said aloud, "Yes, that is nice advice from a young girl."

The weather warmed during the night and ushered out the longest night of the year. The first full day of winter started a long series of days when the sunlight would be longer than the day before. Jeannette arose in the darkness and dressed quickly. She entered the pool of yellow light given off by the oil lamp in the kitchen. Her mother was already at work at the stove.

"My goodness, you are up early," Marguerite said.

Jeanette spoke rapidly. "Um, yes. I suppose I am. I want to get my chores done early and be off to school early as well. I can't wait to see the book Sister Theresa has for us. And maybe I will ask Sister Margaret to help me with my voice one last time before we start class. It is our last day before we have our holiday break."

"Excited about Christmas, are you?" her mother countered.

"I am. And, for all the magic that it can bring," Jeanette said as she slung her cape around her shoulders.

Jeanette grabbed a lantern and the feed pail and raced across the muddied barnyard in the false dawn light. She slid the barn door open and pulled it shut behind her. She knew papa and their neighbor had slaughtered the pig the night before. She grimaced at the thought. In the corner of the barn was the result of their work. "It looks like St. Francis let you down," she said. Jeanette grabbed up the loose bits and entrails that had not been cleaned up or saved for sausage. She pulled a long knife from its hay bale sheath and sliced an inch wide swatch from the pig carcass hanging from the rafters. *They'll never miss it,* she thought. Jeanette put everything in the pail and made her way to the door. She extinguished the lantern.

Jeanette raced around the barn and into the woods. She prayed her mother did not look up from her kitchen work and out the window to the yard. She knelt on the wet ground. "Loup. Loup, where are you? Are you here? Loup? Please..." she said as she stood and squinted between the trees. In that moment, a dark figure leapt on her, knocking her to the ground. The pail's contents spilled. She was pinned to the ground and frightened for her life beyond words. In the next heartbeat she realized it was Loup. He was licking her face and wagging his tail.

"You frightened me nearly to death! Behave!" The animal could not contain his excitement. "Lie down!" Jeanette commanded. Loup backed away but chose to sit. "Here this is for you. You spilled most of it on the ground. Perhaps you won't mind." Jeanette gathered what she could and dumped it in the pail. "You have to learn to be calm," she said. "Okay. I will sing for you just a little while you eat." In a voice barely above a whisper she sang the *Ave Maria*. The wolf devoured the pork.

Jeanette returned to the house and entered the kitchen. "You are a mess, Jeanette! What did you do?" her mother said.

"Oh, Mama, I slipped in the mud in the yard. I'm okay. I will get cleaned up for school." Jeanette replied and hoped her mother hadn't watched her outside.

Christmas Eve arrived in Katonah as it had for more than nineteen-hundred years. As always, it arrived on December 24th perfectly as scheduled, a few days past the winter solstice. Jeanette sang with the choir at midnight Mass, and she sang her solo. Marguerite and Henri beamed with pride. "Come now, back to the house. It is time for Réveillon," Henri said. "Let's celebrate the beauty of Christmas and Jeanette's beautiful voice."

Celebrate they did. There was venison, roast goose, pies, cheeses, and of course, ham. Sister Theresa and Sister Margaret were invited to celebrate but had to decline. Henri planned to bring a basket to the convent on Christmas Day. Henri, Marguerite and Jeanette's grandparents, Jacques and Marie, sipped wine and told stories of Christmases in days past. Jeanette noticed that the stories seemed vaguely familiar.

"Papa, do you believe in the magic of Christmas?" Jeanette asked.

"Indeed, I do, my Dear." Henri said and roared with laughter. "Tonight, everything is magic. The food. The wine. Pere Noel. All magic!" All of the adults nodded in agreement.

"Do you think that everything that comes from within a nativity is blessed?" she asked.

"Mon Dieu." Henri's voice softened. "That is a good question, my little one. Certainly Christ, Mary, and Joseph are blessed. Everything else is well...just the animals."

"But, yes," Jeanette countered and chose her words carefully. "God made the animals."

"He made them because they are necessary. That is how we ate tonight," her father said and moved closer to the fireplace.

"What about Belle? We won't eat her."

Henri laughed. "Goodness, no. But Belle does serve a purpose."

"I asked Mama if we should love the ones who don't love us. She said we should," Jeanette said. Henri glanced at his wife.

"Yes, I suppose we should. Forgiveness and unconditional love is what we believe," her father said and took a sip of wine.

"What about animals?"

"Jeanette!" Henri stammered.

"What about those without a home?"

"Jeanette...it is Christmas Eve. Can't we just please sing a song?"

"Papa...if God made the animals and there is an animal that needs love...shouldn't we love him?"

"Jeanette! Is this about the pig?"

"No Papa. But I do imagine some wild animals deserve a chance. They are homeless on Christmas, just like Joseph, Mary, and Jesus in the manger."

"Jeanette, please..."

"And there are those who hate each other and are shooting each other. Shouldn't they love each other?"

"That's different. Besides, that is in Europe, not here."

"We prayed for them, Papa."

"That is good. I guess we can pray for the homeless animals that need love, too?" Henri said as his parents snickered.

"Oh, good," Jeanette said. "You agree." She put her arm around her father. "Then we should open our home for an animal just as we would for Joseph and Mary..."

Henri cut Jeanette's words short. "Jeanette!"

"Papa...I want something for Christmas."

"What, Jeanette? What do you want?" Henri already knew what Pere Noel would leave in Jeanette's shoes; an orange, petite fours, and a brooch that belonged to his grandmother. Marguerite and Henri felt that Jeannette was now old enough to have it.

"I want a pet," Jeanette said and folded her arms in a defensive posture.

"What...what about Belle?" her mother interjected.

"I want to keep Belle and another pet."

"Is this the reason and all about the animal questions?" Henri said. "Did you trap a chipmunk in the barn and want to keep it in a cage?" Again, Jeanette's grandparents chortled.

"Maybe a bird? Un oiseau?" Jacques said as he flapped his arms like wings.

"Grand-père, Grand-mère, do not laugh at me! It is Christmas. There is magic in the air." Jeanette stood and walked to the kitchen door. "I will show you my new friend," she said.

Henri's moustache twitched. "Jeanette, please, not tonight," he said.

Coatless, Jeanette bolted from the house and into the woods. "Loup, come here to me," she called out. The wolf trotted to her and nuzzled her hand. "I have nothing for you right now. If you are very good, I will feed you plenty. It is Christmas." She rubbed the wolf behind his ears and realized it was the first time she touched him. His dark fur was thick and damp. "You must behave your very best."

She returned to the kitchen door with Loup at her side. She opened the door wide enough to stick her head into the kitchen. "Mama, Papa, Grand-père, Grand-mère tonight is a night that is famous for welcoming a stranger into our home. We leave the candles, and the Yule log lit to welcome them. We leave out foods to nourish them. What if Joseph and Mary were questioned about their intentions?" What if that one life was not allowed to be born into the world? We would have never learned the lessons that He, and you, my parents, have taught me – to love unconditionally and to not judge someone on their appearances."

Her parents and grandparents exchange questioning glances. They did not respond to Jeanette.

"I am about to let a stranger into our house. He is a creature who, like all animals, was created by God. You have nothing to fear. He will love you without knowing you, as you have taught me to do. He is cold and hungry. "

The door swung open and Jeanette and Loup entered the kitchen. Jacques was the first to move. "Mon Dieu, a loup!" he screamed and grabbed the fire iron from the fireplace. He brandished it at the animal. Marguerite shoved her mother-in-law behind the safety of the couch. Henri sat speechless.

"Drop that, Grandpapa. There is no need for that. He will not hurt you. He came from the nativity at St. Mary's." Jeanette said as she moved to the center of the room. Loup stayed near the door.

"*Oh, holy night, the stars are brightly shining, It is the night of our dear Savior's birth,*" Jeanette sang. The wolf cowered and moved to her side. He laid on the floor beside her and rested his head between his paws. The adults in the room cowered, too. "It is okay," Jeanette said. "Show him love and respect and he will return it to you. That is part of the magic of Christmas."

Mama was the first. She reached for a slice of ham and held it out. "I will trust you, Jeanette, and him." Loup took it softly from her fingers.

"Well. If she is not afraid…then neither am I," Jacques said. He offered a piece of venison. And again, the wolf calmly ate. Henri was next, and after a long while, Marie, too, offered the stranger food.

They all sang the chorus of *Cantique de Noel.*

Sister Theresa and her student's prayers were answered. On Christmas Eve 1914 the soldiers in the trenches on the French battlefield declared their own unofficial truce. The firing, the smoke, and the fog of war subsided for the night. They came out to celebrate the birthday of the Prince of Peace and exchanged Christmas greetings in their respective languages: Frohe Weihnachten, Merry Christmas and…Joyeux Noël. Together they sang *Silent Night.* Through the magic of Christmas, for a few hours on that oh, holy night, the stars were brightly shining.

In answer to many prayers, that war ended in November 1918. Christmas that year was joyous for all.

Story Notes – Thank you to Jen Kane for her suggestion of the time and location of the story, and the Belgian sheep dog. This was the second of the 24 Christmas pieces I wrote.

SEVEN

Nome, Alaska

"It's beginning to look a lot like Christmas," her mom, Mildred, said.

"I'd have to agree, Mama," Audrey said as she bustled around the general store and straightened the wreath behind the cash register.

"I want you to be careful and be back here for Christmas Eve. I know you've been making extra holidays runs for the extra cash and Christmas tips. After Christmas what do you say we both take a break?"

Indeed, it was unusual for a young woman to be a musher in 1940 in the remote town of Nome in the Alaskan Territory. Audrey's grandfather came to Nome in 1898 for the Gold Rush. She was petite, which was to her advantage. With less of her own bodyweight to carry she could take on more cargo or run with fewer dogs if there wasn't much payload. Men who laughed at Audrey were shocked after they saw her accomplishments. Audrey was daring. And, given that she was willing to deliver packages and mail to remote locations made her services sought after. Today was no different.

Audrey was preparing to make a run by sled to the fur trapping camp up the Snake River. She wasn't worried. She had made the run with its twists and turns many times and knew the route well. Her dogs knew the way, too. They were always anxious to get to the camp for the treats that would be waiting for them.

"I want you back her in time for the Christmas Eve potluck dinner. I don't want to go by myself."

"Stop fretting, Mama. As soon as it's light enough I will head out and get there before sundown. You know Uncle Ned will look after me and the dogs for the night. I'll head back here first thing in the morning. Be back in plenty of time. I'll be home for Christmas."

"I'm sure he will enjoy a visit before Christmas."

Mildred knew that Audrey would be safe once she got to the camp. Running a sled over the frozen Snake River in the Alaskan winter would be a challenge that few were willing to, or could, do. The Snake River, relatively short at about only about 20 miles in length. As it flows to the Norton Sound from the foothills of Kigluaik Mountains its scenic beauty offers sanctuary to abundant wildlife including polar bears, caribou, walruses, and wolves.

Audrey returned to the task of waxing her sled's runners. A kerosene lantern shed a yellow glow in the storage area of the general store. With the sled laid on its side she inspected the runners for dents or scratches from running over rocks. Since the temperature dropped even further than usual and brought snow that was deep, and crisp and even, she felt it was best to use whale oil. Audrey bartered for the oil with the Kauweramiuts, a sub-group of the Inupiaq, the indigenous people of Nome who hunted and fished the region for more than 4,000 years. Bartering was easy because Audrey's mother owned the general store, and everyone was always willing to trade what they had. Whale oil was the most valued at the time for dogsled runners traveling over flatter terrain. It offered a smooth glide, best friction resistance, and worked better when the temperatures went low. Colder temperatures called for harder waxes like whale oil. For warmer weather mushers might choose softer mixes with bear fat or fish oil. Although, sometimes sledders combined bear fat with whale oil for better durability. Audrey didn't have any bear fat on hand and didn't worry about it. A run halfway up the Snake wasn't as far a distance as some of her other runs. Even so, she didn't want her team to have to work so hard. Everyone deserved a break for Christmas. She buffed the finish and applied another coat of oil. Finaly satisfied, she tilted her sled up on one side and lowered it to the upright position.

Twilight wouldn't happen for a couple more hours. Audrey had become used to the long times of darkness during the Alaskan winters. It was a way of life there. Although technically not within the Arctic Circle, Nome has all the characteristics of the arctic. Its subarctic climate has long, extremely cold winters, short cool summers when the sun didn't set until almost midnight, and terrain with permafrost and tundra vegetation. It was a way of life that was different than almost any other.

Audrey's grandfather taught her how to handle a dog sled. At first it was only for fun with a couple of dogs. As she got older her team grew and now she was the proud owner of eight sled dogs that included fearless Alaskan malamutes and Siberian huskies. The huskies were much more playful, but the malamutes were always ready to work and enjoyed pulling the sled.

She checked over her safety and survival gear: a spare musher line – a strong lightweight line to connect her dogs to the sled, anchors and picket lines to secure the dogs during rest stops or overnight, first aid kits for the dogs, a first-aid kit for herself, matches, flint and steel, tinder, and for protection the .30-06 rifle her grandfather gave her on her thirteenth birthday was cleaned and loaded. Her outerwear was all from the Kauweramiuts. She figured if it was good enough to keep them warm and alive after thousands of years of trial and error, who was she to try to reinvent their success.

She added Pemmican to her kit. Pemican, a Native American superfood, was high in calories and was made from dried pounded meat and berries. Her concoction was made from caribou meat and fat. They wouldn't be on the trail long enough to need a meal, but this was enough to hold her over until she got to Uncle Ned's cabin. As an added treat, she brought a half pound of dark chocolate for herself and a large bag of kibble for the dogs.

All the necessities got first priority for space in the sled. Now it was time to add the deliverables to the men at the outpost cabin. A sack of mail, beans, bacon and flour, coffee, sugar, two bottles of whiskey, and two gallons of kerosene for the lanterns. They stopped using whale oil long ago when kerosene became cheaper and burned brighter. An unusual addition to the load were two windows. Her mom was sending them as a Christmas present to Uncle Ned. Although they wouldn't be installed until spring, they would offer the cabin some interior daylight, even if the winter days were short. Audrey wrapped extra canvas around the window frames.

Early in 1940 the U.S. Army recognized the strategic importance of Nome, and the U.S. Army-Air Force started flying in and out of Nome City airfield for reconnaissance and logistics. By April that year construction was begun on Marks Airfield for military use alongside the Nome City Field. Established in the 1920s, Nome City Field first handled small, single-engine planes used for mining exploration and local transportation. Much to the delight of Nome residents, by the 1930s Nome City Field went from a fledgling airstrip to a bustling transportation hub. Although air deliveries were expensive, it offered a much quicker way to receive vital supplies and mail. By late 1940 Marks Airfield was completed and all military operations moved there. With its addition of a longer 3,000-foot runway Nome locals now saw the arrival of light cargo planes and military support aircraft.

Audrey marveled at the planes and wondered what it was like to soar above the clouds like a bird. As she finished lashing the windows and other cargo to the sled, she heard the rumble of aircraft engines starting in the distance. Airmen would often come to the general store for supplies they needed to get the engines started in the sub-zero weather. The engine oil became so thick in the cold that it was almost impossible to turn the engines over by hand. Locals who were used to Arctic aviation and had been flying into Nome over the years knew some of the tricks. Blowtorches became a popular item. The heat could be directly applied to the engine cylinders and oil pans. Her mom charged a king's ransom for them, and the aircrews were happy to pay it. Audrey appreciated meeting the young, and sometimes handsome, army personnel when they came to the store. In particular, a young lieutenant, Bob, who was not much older than herself. He was a sturdy man who was bright, witty, good looking and single.

Audrey heard the sound of aircraft engines starting in the distance, which signaled her that civil twilight would soon arrive. Nome experiences a period of polar night during the winter months. The sun remains below the horizon for 24 hours and typically lasts from approximately November 30th to January 12th. During this time, even though the sun is below the horizon, it illuminates the upper atmosphere and creates a soft, faint light. The only other light comes from the moon, stars, and aurora borealis. Audrey and the pilots would have to navigate in the dimness.

Mildred entered the storage area. "I just wanted to say goodbye. See you tomorrow," she said. "Here's a new pair of goggles for the run."

Audrey flipped her hair back, strapped on the goggles, and perched them on her forehead. "Oh, and, by the way, I invited that nice Lieutenant Bob to the Christmas Eve community dinner. He's a long way from home, he says he's from down in California. And... one more by the way thing ... it seems he's taken a shine to you. He said he would love to come."

"Oh, Mother! Please stop meddling in my life. I'm a grown woman and can choose my own ways."

"Let's face it, Audrey. You're not getting any younger and decent men are a little hard to come by around here."

Mildred continued, "The lieutenant tells me he's in command of a crew that has come up here from Mt. Rainier in Washington to train in extreme arctic conditions and learn about dog-sled travel that they might use in other parts of the world. I'm sure you could teach him a thing or two about sledding."

"Mother!" Audrey grimaced.

"It seems there are efforts underway to form a group called the Alaska Scouts for Arctic warfare who may be useful in European mountain battles. Last year during the Winter War between Finland and the Soviet Union, Finnish Troops made extensive use of skis to get around in winter conditions to their advantage. The Fins are used to snow and are excellent downhill and cross-country skiers. They moved quickly and silently through the forests outflanking and ambushing the Soviets. I'm told their actions stirred an interest with the Americans to create specialized winter warfare units.

"I suppose adding dogsleds would give them further range, although, let's face it, the dogs can be noisy."

Audrey lifted the garage door and called the dogs. As usual Bandi was first. He was the lead dog, the alpha male. Bandi was an overly large huskie with a black mask that gave him his name, which was shortened from Bandit. He nuzzled Audrey. Then came Mina, Bandi's mate, shaking the snow from her coat, followed by the rest of the team. They gathered around Audrey vying for attention. She gave each dog a fish that was devoured without hesitation. When the meal was finished she attached their harnesses and lead lines. The sled was already pointed toward the open door. Audrey connected the lead line to the sled and took her place at the back atop the runners. As always, her mom would shut the door behind her so Audrey wouldn't have to dismount and leave the team. With her parker hood pulled tight the first gulps of arctic air filtered through her scarf and filled her lungs. It would take a few minutes to adjust.

Audrey snapped the reigns and hollered, "Mush! Mush! Line out Line out! Straight on!" Her team started slowly at first as they adjusted to the weight of the sled and followed Bandi's lead. They were yelping as they went and reached full speed quickly. Audrey watched for subtle landmarks that would lead them to the river. The frozen tundra offered no clues. So, she relied on man-made markers. Lights at the end of the Nome City airfield acted as her guide and aimed towards them. She knew there was a clearing to the riverbank just ahead and didn't want to overrun it. "Whoa, whoa!" Audrey called to slow the dogs and gave a light pull on the brake. At the right moment she commanded "Haw! Haw!" and the team pulled left towards the frozen river. Now it was time to make a sharp right turn and head up-river. "Gee, Bandi, Gee!' she yelled to her lead dog, and they turned right. "Good boy, Bandi! Good boy!"

Bandi was loyal to his master and would follow any command she gave but didn't really need them. He had done the run so many times he knew what to expect in advance. Once the sled was aligned with the frozen river the eight dogs pulled hard and increased their speed. "Mush! Mush! Let's fly!" she called out. "Straight on!" Audrey, the dogs, and the cargo-laden sled sliced through the sub-zero air. They still had a long way to go, and Audrey planned to rest the dogs a couple of times along the way.

Audrey thought about Christmas, and about her mother's comments about Lieutenant Bob. She wouldn't admit to her mother, or herself, that she had grown fond of him in a short time. He was responsible, had a steady job, and knew how to take charge of a situation. She saw that he was respectful to his men, and they appreciated him for it. Maybe sledding together wouldn't be such a bad thing. Her thoughts returned to Christmas. It was a bright spot for Audrey in the long arctic night. She made sure there were nice gifts for her mom, uncle Ned, and many of her Kauweramiut friends who had helped her through the years, and some of the customers and the postmaster who gave her steady work. She didn't have many other friends her age. Once they grew up, they left for more hospitable climates. Her thoughts were distracted by a plane overhead. She had no idea where it was headed but she followed the taillights until they faded away. Blinding snow began to blow across the Snake River from right to left. "Easy, easy. Steady, straight on!" she called out to the team. Bandi lowered his head and pulled on. Between the low light and the driving snow visibility could only be wished for. Audrey was determined to get through it. She didn't worry. As they headed up the river the dogs knew the way to pull the sleigh in the deep and drifting snow. She wiped her goggles with the back of her mitten.

She knew they were half way to Uncle Ned's trapping cabin. Trapping was a key part of the local economy around Nome at the time. In the early 20th century, there was a boom in the fur trade in Alaska. 1940 was still within the peak of the boom until it trailed off in the 1950s due to market fluctuations and regulations. Nome had access to endless wilderness. And through a network of sledding the traders could make a good living during the dire winter months when other work was scarce. Furs could be traded for food and supplies. It had been an integral part of Alaskan Native life for generations.

Arctic fox fur, especially silver fox fur, was the most valued. Beaver pelts were warm and durable. Muskrats were trapped for a variety of uses and additional income. Also targeted were wolves, caribou, marmots, and other species depending on the season and the demand.

Ned did the best he could with what nature offered. Every spring he questioned whether he would do it again for another winter. It was harsh conditions and dangerous work. With the addition of the Army base, he figured some things may change for the better in the near future and he could find year-round work closer to town. Some men were still mining for gold. The amount of gold sifted or dredged from the rivers wasn't nearly the same as what was harvested during the earlier rush, but production was still significant. Nome remained the most productive gold district in Alaska throughout the 1940s.

Two days before Christmas Lieutenant Bob walked into the general store. "Good morning, Miss Mildred," he said. Quite a squall that moved through yesterday. Glad we were able to get all the aviators backed to base." Mildred remained silent.

Bob noticed the tense look on Midred's face. "Is there something wrong?" he asked. "Audrey hasn't returned," she said.

During the snow squall the day before a pack of wolves chased a herd of caribou across the Snake River from right to left. Audrey's team sensed the herd's rapid approach and tried to avoid them by swerving to the left. Audrey was caught off-guard and tilted far to the left. "Whoa! Whoa!" she screamed. In the instant the words left her lips a huge caribou broadsided the sled. It rolled over three times. The lead line broke free from the sled and the dogs were scrambling and yelping. Audrey was face down in the snow dazed and confused, with a searing pain in her left leg. She lifted up on one elbow and uttered, "Bandi..."

Bandi came to her side dragging the team along with him. He licked her face and rubbed against her. All the dogs were whining. Audrey had only seen the caribou at the last second when it burst through the wind-driven snow. She had a fairly good idea of why the animal was running in the blinding snow. She winced and undid Bandi's harness. Then Mindi's followed by each dog as she called them by name: Bolt, Stormer, Timber, Tundra, Scout, Shadow. If there were wolves on the hunt the dogs would have a better chance of survival if they were free. The dogs milled around her in a tight circle. In the dim light she could see that some of the cargo was strewn about and given her condition there was no chance of her righting the sleigh by herself. She knew that survival was going to be difficult. The weather and the wolves each played a part, and a passerby would be highly unlikely. She wondered if her leg was broken. She couldn't tell and wasn't about to remove her outer gear to check the damage. 'Come on, Audrey,' she said to herself. 'We can get through this.' She slithered towards the sled and found her day bag with some necessities. Pemican, matches, flint, first aid kit, knife, and the block of chocolate. Wind blew through the wreckage and made a flapping noise. Audrey realized the sound was being made by the canvas she had wrapped around the windows. She lifted the canvas and was astonished to see that the windows were intact. Fighting through her pain and dizziness she pulled the windows free, propped them against the side of the sled, and pushed snow along the base to hold them in place. They would help block the wind and the snow would drift up against them offering even more protection. She found her rifle still lashed in place and the two gallons of kerosene. She couldn't find the kibble and hoped her dogs wouldn't wander off looking for food.

"Oh no!' Bob said. "Oh, yes," Mildred replied. "She's long overdue That's not like her."

"I tell you what," Bob blurted. "Let me get back to the base. The weather is clear. We can send up a scout plane. If Audrey stayed on or near the river they might be able to spot her. And I'll call out the cross-country ski squad. We've trained for this kind of thing. They can be ready to go at a moment's notice. We will find your daughter." Mildred was all too aware of the hazards, the weather, and the wildlife that roamed the territory.

Audrey survived the night by burrowing into the snow and gathering the dogs around her for warmth. The blowing snow had created a blanketing dome over them as it built up around the windows. She prayed, ate some of the chocolate and wondered if anyone had missed her yet. She kept her rifle by her side and knew to stay calm to conserve her strength.

Morning tried to push the sun above the horizon, but the best it could do was deliver the subdued glow of civil twilight. Audrey heard the plane before she saw it. She grabbed her knife and a section of canvas and poured some kerosene on it. Using the knife, she dug down and found some arctic lichens and stuffed them in the canvas. She tore up some of the wrappings on the other packages and thought about adding some of the mail from the sack to the pile. She dropped the idea of burning the letters knowing it would be wrong and there might be important things going to people at the camp. If nothing else, it may be their Christmas cards. With numb hands she struck the flint and steel into the makeshift torch. A flame erupted. She held her breath and prayed the plane might see it.

Lieutenant Bob went to the barracks and instructed his men that they were going on a rescue mission of a civilian. "Be ready to go in 15 minutes. Bring only enough provisions for two days," he said. Six men jumped to attention and began donning their arctic survival gear. It was mostly military issue with some additions they learned from the Kauweramiuts. Besides their usual supplies each man carried extra line, a head lantern, a small pixaxe, and the cross-country skis they would travel with, but also strapped snowshoes on their backs if they were needed. Everyone carried a rifle. "Let's go, men!" the lieutenant commanded. They followed him out the door and put on their skis. They crossed the frozen terrain, found the break in the riverbank and headed north. "Keep an eye out for clues or for anyone who might have seen her pass by." They pressed on up the river side by side with Lieutenant in the lead. After several hours he held up his hand. "Whoa, rest you merry gentlemen, take a break." he said. Although the ski patrol members were hand-picked from the most physically fit and athletic among their peers, the men were relived for the opportunity to rest even for only a moment. "Sir," said one of the men. Do you hear what I hear? Bob pulled back his hood and heard the faint buzz of a plane. "I hear it. That could be Scotty in the patrol plane. Let's keep moving and see if we can spot him." Snake River with its many bends made it difficult to see in a straight line for a long distance. They double poled as they looked up to try and see the plane. Their efforts were rewarded several bends later. One of them pointed skyward with his ski pole and shouted, "There it is! He's circling!" Bob's team pushed harder heading toward the running lights that were turning in a tight pattern.

Scotty keyed his mic and radioed the airfield. "I'm getting glimpses of what looks like a small campfire on the river. Hope Lieutenant Bob and the boys make it up this way soon. I'll circle for as long as I can."

After coursing through three more river bends the rescuers came upon the overturned sled. The dogs popped up from their snow blanket cover and began to howl. Audrey, who had been focusing on the path of the plane and didn't see the men approach grabbed her riffle. She didn't recognize Bob in his hooded parka and goggles.

Scotty saw the men arrive. Wagged his wings and headed back to base.

"Well hold on there a minute Miss Audrey," Bob said. "On behalf of the United States Army, we wish you a Merry Christmas and a Happy New Year! And better than that, we are going to get you home for Christmas Eve. What happened? Are you okay?"

Audrey pushed up on one elbow. "Oh, Lieutenant Bob! Thank you for coming to the rescue. I got run over by a reindeer on my way to Ned's before Christmas Eve. I think my leg is broke."

She explained to Bob how she survived the night with her dog team around her and prayed for a miracle. "Let's get you out of here," he said. Bob and the soldiers used their pickaxes to chip away the ice that was welding the overturned dogsled to the frozen river. Once they freed it Bob order the men to empty the sled, hack down some pine boughs, and lay them in the sled. He scooped up Audrey and let her down slowly in the evergreen lined cargo bay.

"Okay men. Leave your snowshoes here. If you stay on the river, you won't need them. You can pick them up on the way back. Load up with everything that was on the sled and take it all to Mr. Ned's cabin."

"Please find the kibble for the dogs," Audrey insisted.

"What about the mail?" a soldier asked. "I think they can survive without the letters for now."

"Take everything except Miss Audrey's personal belongings, and yes, take the mail." Bob answered. "I know you can handle it.

"What about those windows?" another wanted to know. "Wrap them up in that canvas and tow them behind you," Bob instructed. "I don't want to spoil anyone's Christmas surprise."

I'm getting Audrey down to the Marks Station Hospital." Bob assured Audrey, "Audrey, there's a doctor and a couple of medics there. They will take care of you. Station Hospital is closer than town and by the time we get there the town will be rolled up for the night."

The dog food was found and doled out to each one. Audrey showed Bob how the harnesses were attached to the dogs and the men were able to retie the tug lines back on the tow line and then to the bow by using Audrey's spare musher line.

"Have you ever driven a dog sled before, Lieutenant Bob?" Audrey asked. "Not yet," he replied and chuckled. "Just hang on back there," she said. "I'll tell the team what to do." The dogs were confused by the new arrangement, but Audrey's voice calmed them. "Extra food and Christmas treats for all of you critters when we get home," she told them.

The soldiers now with fully laden packs pointed their skis north on the iced over river. Audrey gave them directions on how to find Ned's cabin. "It will be easy to find them," she said. "It will be the only human habitation you'll pass."

Audrey gave Bob a quick lesson on how to operate the brake and where to hold the handlebar. With Audrey in place and Bob on the riser in the rear she gave the command, "Mush! Line out! Straight on! Let's go home!" From time to time, she slowed the dogs to ease the rough ride and to make it easier for Bob. '*Poor Dear*,' she thought. 'What an introduction to sledding.'

Audrey knew the clearing through the riverbank was just ahead. "Whoa! Whoa dogs!" she shouted. "Bob, tug the brake." They slowed to a walk. "Haw, team!" Audrey said and her dogs dutifully followed her order to turn left into the clearing and away from the river.

The six soldiers found Ned's place. He was surprised to see them. "Where's Audrey?" he asked. They explained what happened and how she was rescued, in good hands, and being sent to the Marks Station Hospital at the airbase.

Ned invited them into his tiny cabin. He helped them unload their packs and sorted through the delivery, marveling at the two framed windows that would add light to the cabin. He was cordial and found everyone a place to sit, warm up and rest. He shared some of his newly delivered whiskey and raised a toast for a good Christmas. They were now rested, but anxious to return to the base and left.

Ned added kerosene to the lantern, lit it, and smiled in the amber light as he began sorting through the mail. Most of it was for the others in the camp, but there was one addressed to him marked confidential. The return address wasn't of anyone familiar to him. Ned raised his eyebrows and slid his thumb under the flap. As he unfolded the message, he could see it was on the letterhead of an attorney's office. His hands began to tremble as he read it and was overcome with a sudden rush of emotion. The cabin door burst open followed by a gust of wind. A large, bearded man stood in the entryway. "Merry Christmas" the visitor shouted then laughed heartily. "Did I scare you, Ned?" he asked. Ned stood up. "No, Pastor Jim, it would take a lot more than your jolly self to worry me. Merry Christmas. What brings you here?"

"I finished making my Christmas visits to the outposts. I was on my way into Nome to give a blessing and a message at the Christmas Eve potluck dinner. I thought I'd stop by to see you for a Christmas visit. How have you been?"

Ned held up the letter. "Bad and good, I got this," Ned said and added the news about Audrey's accident.

"Hmm. Do you want to talk about it?"

"I will after I speak to Mildred and Audrey. You say you're headed down to Nome? Any chance I can hitch a ride on your sled? I want to see Audrey and I have some news for her and her mother. I'll drive and you can take a break, that is, if there's enough room."

"Ned, I'd be happy to get you down there to celebrate Christmas and spend time with family. If there's not enough room, we'll make room."

"All right then, it's getting late. Stay here tonight and we can leave in the morning," Ned said.

The two men fed and settled in Jim's dogs. Ned stoked the fire as they sat in the lantern's light and shared stories, and a round of whiskey.

Lieutenant Bob arrived at the airbase hospital and had the medics get Audrey a stretcher. "Oh, really. I'm fine, I can do this," she said. "I'm sure you can but let's not take any chances," Bob said as he helped them get Audrey on the gurney. He sent a soldier to tell Audrey's mother that Audrey was found and okay but would be at the hospital overnight.

On Christmas Eve morning the weather was clear. Jim only had a few dogs, but they were sturdy enough to pull them. Jim got in the berth, Ned covered him with beaver pelts, and they headed to Nome.

On Christmas Eve fireworks lit the sky at five o'clock and alerted Nome to start the holiday festivities. The people of Nome stood outside the community center under the galaxy of fireworks. They were different ages and from various backgrounds and ethnicities. It didn't matter. They all had the same thing in common, the celebration of Christmas. With the addition of the crews from Marks Airfield, the gathering was bigger than ever. Everyone brought something to share. All the food had been brought to the community center earlier. It was a mix of hearty and traditional fare based on what was available or that had been flown in. The feast included ham, turkey, goose, salmon, mashed potatoes, gravy, roast vegetables, and an assortment of breads, and pies.

As the crowd gazed up at the last burst of fireworks, they didn't notice the arrival of Mildred and Audrey in a Jeep driven by Lieutenant Bob, the six arctic patrol soldiers on cross-country skis, Scotty the pilot, Uncle Ned mushing Audrey's sled and Pastor Jim who was right behind on his own sled. "My goodness," Audrey said. "You're all here!"

Pastor Jim responded, "There's no place like Nome for the holidays."

They followed the crowd as they shuffled into the hall. Pastor Jim made his way to the front of the room and stood on a chair so all could hear. He blessed the food they were about to have and offered a prayer for peace and prosperity. He clapped his hands together and said, "Let's eat!"

Audrey made her way on her crutches to a chair. Her mother made her comfortable. Bob offered to get plates and serve Mildred and Audrey dinner. The ski patrol was already starting their second helpings. Ned pulled a chair between Mildred and Audrey. He cleared his throat and began in a low, measured voice.

"Audrey, as you know, your father and I had another brother, Henry."

"Yes, I knew that," Audrey answered. Mildred nodded in agreement.

Ned continued, "Unfortunately, I'm sad to tell you this on Christmas Eve, but Henry has passed on." Mildred and Audrey looked at each other and bowed their heads. "What you may not know is that although Henry was miserly, he was shrewd and successful. He owned a fishing fleet in Anchorage. And, in spite of the Great Depression he was able to build a lucrative shipping business and bought a lot of properties as well including 600 acres in a place called Lake Tahoe, California. It's snuggled up against Nevada in the Sierra Mountains. He thought it might have a future and the land could be worth something."

Mildred chimed in, "California is where Lieutenant Bob is from!"

Ned pulled the lawyer's letter from his inner coat pocket and slowly unfolded it. "Audrey, see this letter? It was in that sack of mail you were delivering." Audrey flinched as she recalled almost burning the mail. "It seems these folks tracked me down." Ned explained the contents of the letter. "Henry named me the executor of his will and sole inheritor of all his assets. The fishing fleet and shipping business were sold off for a princely sum, and that money is in his estate. It's up to me to decide who gets what. Seeing how as the three of us are family and we've always looked after each other, what I'm going to do is split up everything three ways.

The money and the properties. That piece in California will give us 200 acres apiece side-by-side. Don't worry, Audrey they get plenty of snow in the wintertime, but longer, warmer summers…and a lot more daylight to enjoy it in.

"Mildred, there's more than enough money that will allow you to sell off the general store, if you wish, move to California, build a house on your 200 acres, and retire. Audrey, same for you. You can build yourself a house and start a new life on your own land. As for me… yes, I will move to California. I'm told that growing wine grapes is getting to be a big thing down there. I think I'll take a look into that and give it a go. Oh, I'll build a house, too. It will have a lot of windows." Audrey and Mildred were speechless.

Lieutenant Bob overheard the conversation. "I'm from Sacramento, California. It's only a few hours from Lake Tahoe. I sure wouldn't mind visiting you all once I'm done with the service."

Audrey stood with her crutches and said in a loud voice, "What a Christmas! We are truly lucky. God bless us, everyone!

Story Notes - Thank you to Dr. Katie Owens for the suggestion of the time and place of this story. In part it is inspired by the U.S. Army 10ᵗʰ Mountain Division, which was originally designated as a mountain warfare unit that trained for Alpine combat. Although stationed at Fort Drumm, NY, in its early days the unit did spend time training at Mt. Rainier's 14,411-foot peak in Washington, and later at Camp Hale Colorado, elevation 9,200 feet. My uncle Robert Gahan was a member of the 10ᵗʰ Mountain Division and served heroically during heavy combat in Po Valley, Italy during World War II in 1945. Marks Airforce Base at Nome closed in 1950, and an air base squadron was at Nome Airport until December 1956. On January 3ʳᵈ, 1959, the Alaskan Territory became the 49ᵗʰ State. I was heavily influenced by Jack London's 'Call of the Wild' and 'White Fang' as youngster. On a playful note, I included a few lyrics and phrases from Christmas songs throughout the story. How many did you find?

EIGHT

Everglades, Florida

Nokosi grew up on the banks of Lake Okeechobee, the headwaters of the Everglades. He was a descendant of Tustenukke, one of the survivors of the Christmas Day Battle of Okeechobee. Nokosi was born 63 years after the war. The battle was part of Second Seminole War, which forced the relocation of the Seminole people from Florida to west of the Mississippi as part of the Indian Removal Act of 1830. It was intended to clear eastern lands for white settlement. The Treaty of Payne's Landing, signed in 1832, included provisions for compensation, but many Seminoles found it insufficient and wrong. The Seminoles gave up 28 million acres. They rebelled. On Christmas Day 1837 fighting broke out between 1,000 federal troops led by General Zachary Taylor and less than 500 Seminoles who were led by chiefs Alligator, Billy Bowlegs, Abiaka (Sam Jones), and Coacoochee. 37 lives were lost that day on Northeast shore of Lake Okeechobee, Florida. 26 were U.S. soldiers, mostly Missouri volunteers. The surviving Seminoles escaped into the swamps and used their knowledge of the terrain to evade the army. With its vast wetland wilderness of sawgrass marshes, mangrove swamps, and slow-moving waters, it was easy to hide. Alligators and snakes were treacherous for the unwary, the Seminoles had dealt with those hazards for centuries and knew how to avoid them. The Christmas Day Battle earned General Zacharly Taylor the nickname, "Old Rough and Ready." Even though its strategic impact was exaggerated, public opinion celebrated his victory. In any case, the outcome played a considerable role in forming his image, which launched his political career towards becoming the 12th President of the United States.

Tustenukke, who escaped into the swamps, was Nokosi's grandfather many generations ago. Tustenukke didn't understand the significance of Christmas Day. To him and the others, it was just another day in the early winter when the days were short and the temperatures were cooler. A battle against a white army would have been the same to him on any other day. Tustenukke and the others hiding with him relied on hunting, fishing, and gathering wild foods such as nuts and berries for survival. They lived in chickees. "Chickee" is the Seminole word for an elevated house constructed of palmetto leaves and cypress-log stilts. They were always on the lookout and always on the move if scouts spotted soldiers in the area. They managed to keep to their traditions and perform the green corn dance. Tustenukke and the tribe asked for miracles to end their oppression. They grew as a community. Life carried on. And they continued hoping for a miracle.

Nokosi had heard all the stories about the troubles of the past. The marshlands and the surroundings area were beginning to change. Tensions between the white settlers and the Seminole had calmed down a while ago, and Indian missionaries came to Florida Seminoles living east of Lake Okeechobee.

The Episcopal Church started Glade Cross Mission in the Big Cypress in the 1890's. By 1907, the first the first Indian missionaries came to the Florida Seminoles living near Indiantown 14 miles east of Mayaca Florida on Lake Okeechobee. The missionaries were Creek Baptist Indian missionaries from Oklahoma. The northern group of Seminoles were targeted, as like the missionaries, they spoke the Creek or Muscogee language.

Conversions were slow. Most native people wanted to stay with their beliefs and customs. Or at least only somewhat embrace the new religions presented to them. Nokosi saw both sides. He attended services at the mission on Sundays and took part in tribal events. He was befriended by Josie Billie, who lived by him in Indiantown. Josie Billie was a prominent medicine man and bundle carrier. A bundle carrier was an Elder, a medicine man honored with having the bundle of natural medicines and cures. Josie was baptized in 1920 and Nokosi followed him soon after. Nokosi grew and left his Seminole name behind, which meant "Bear." When he was baptized he took the name, Joseph.

It was a strange time for Joesph, vacillating between the old tribal ways and Christianity. He spoke English, but understood Mikasuki, the language spoken by his parents and elders. He attended school and read everything he could. He was fascinated by life far to the north and the weather that was vastly different from the weather in Florida. He was curious about snow. The more he read, the more he began to understand the messages of the missionaries.

Joseph was also fascinated by the story of the first Christmas when a poor young couple rode on a donkey to a faraway place to have a son who would change the world. The Seminoles didn't celebrate Christmas traditionally. Their customs concentrated on seasonal driven events and ceremonies. With the arrival of the missionaries, they were introduced to Christmas and its meanings. Some adopted the new traditions, some didn't. Joseph also learned that there was another form of Christmas. It involved unusual beliefs, and included a character named Santa Claus, but had long standing traditions among the whites. Joseph tried to cover them all.

Joseph listened to the parables and Bible passages about Christmas, learned the Christmas hymns, and prepared simple gifts for giving to his family and Josie Billie. He was influenced by the father of Jesus, Joseph who was a carpenter. He hand carved small, wooden figures from cypress for all of them. He was excited about the coming of Christmas day. It would mean a large, special meal shared by his family along with aunts, uncles, and cousins. There would be traditional foods, storytelling, dances, and carols adapted from their language, along with gift-giving and presenting his carved figures. He was envious of the people in the far north who would have bright white snow that would decorate the trees during Christmas. He wondered if there could ever be a miracle for snow to fall in Indiantown. He felt it surely would be a sign and often thought about the passage from Matthew 28:3 on the resurrection of Jeus; "His appearance was like lightning, and his clothes white as snow." Joseph felt that was a perfect way to think about snow.

Joseph continued to improve his woodworking skills. He carved birds and alligators from local wood and sold them to visitors. Now that he was finished with school it provided him with a suitable income. Birds and alligators grew into much larger sculpting projects. He was even commissioned to carve a church altar, and later statues of saints for the Catholics. Many people said his hands were gifts from God Himself.

Nokosi Joseph toiled on. His artistry improved and now, being able to command a little more money for his work, he was able to buy better tools. Knives, chisels, gouges, scribes, planes, and saws now rounded out his assortment. He was now duplicating the fine intricacies of man and nature in greater detail.

Christianity and the prosperity began to spread throughout the region. One family of Florida Seminoles living at Indiantown moved to the Dania (now named Hollywood) Reservation and formed the core of a small group of Christian Seminoles. The 497-acre Hollywood Reservation is one of six Seminole Indian reservations governed by the federally recognized Seminole Tribe of Florida. Today, the reservation is the location of several cultural attractions, including the Ah-Tah-Thi-Ki Museum and the Everglades Theater. Missionary activities continued among the Creek-speaking Seminoles around Indiantown. Another Episcopal mission was set up at Everglade, Florida in 1933.

In 1936 a Seminole conference was located at today's Monument Lake Campground. Approximately 275 Seminole Indians attended. Florida's governor and other officials gathered to discuss how the federal government could help the Tribe during the Great Depression. They declined and asked to be left alone.

Joseph saw all the changes; it didn't affect him or his work. The land was beginning to be heavily logged for its durable and rot-resistant cypress wood. It was harvested to be used for everything from ship hulls to bridges and railroad ties. The logging operations made it a little easier for him to obtain the larger slabs he needed for furniture and other pieces. Joseph had learned a long time ago from his father and those before him of the durability of cypress wood. He used cypress along with mahogany to produce carvings that could last for centuries.

A mission was dedicated in 1948 on the isolated Big Cypress Reservation. By 1949, mission work was being accompanied by a Seminole among the non-reservation Indians along the Tamiami Trail. Joseph paid keen attention to the spread of Christianity and the potential for more business. His Christmas carvings became high in demand.

Despite its glut of natural resources many saw the swamps as useless land. Joseph didn't. Hunting and fishing in them provided plentiful food. And as always, a constant supply of materials for the Seminole to build chickees and for himself to work his magic with wood.

While most people considered the area worthless, a former journalist for the Miami Herad newspaper, Marjory Stoneman Douglas published a book titled *Everglades: River of Grass* that pushed for the preservation of the Everglades. In 1934 Congress had been urged to designate the Everglades as a national park. The government had to come up with the land and money needed to create the park. It took another 13 years to acquire. Douglas's book was published in 1947, and the Everglades became a national park the same year. On December 6th, 1947, the United States Government set aside 1.5 million acres of protected land (a mere fraction of its original size) as Everglades National Park. Douglas was credited for giving the name Everglades to the region. Marjory Stoneman Douglas, who lived to be 108 years old, spent most of her life working for Everglades restoration and preservation.

Joseph kept carving. The creation of the park boosted tourism to the area and that was good for business. He kept carving for the churches, too. One autumn he felt the urge to create something special and meaningful in wood. Something life-sized. He selected the best pieces of pond cypress, which is harder and more durable than lighter bald cypress, but can be more challenging to carve, for the overall form, native mahogany for the inlays, and rare Lignum Vitae, known as "ironwood," the densest and hardest wood of all for the small detail pieces that would polish to a brilliant luster. All the wood species he chose were resistant to rot, insects, and saltwater. He wanted his piece to last far into the future.

He was getting on in years and the work was harder for him now. His hands ached as they ran a spoke shave over the raw wood. He started at sunup and worked until dark. The days were beginning to grow shorter and cooler. His goal was to finish for Christmas. Nokosi Bear Joseph pressed on. He worked when it rained. He worked harder when he thought he couldn't do anymore. His muscles felt as stiff as the wood he was carving. He finished the figures in time for Christmas. There was one last task. In a prime plank of mahogany Joseph carved. "A Journey That Changed the World."

Early in the morning on December 24th Joseph loaded the statues onto his trailer and took them to the mission. They were heavy and he struggled as he put them in position in front of the mission beside the door. He wanted everything to be perfect. When he was finished he said, "Thank you, Jesus, for giving me the skills and talents to carve wood that has grown because of your grace that has made so many people happy." He blessed himself and left silently.

That evening he took his family to Christmas Eve Service at the mission. The weather had turned exceptionally cold. It was a cold front from the north that caused freezing temperatures in Indiantown. Everyone wrapped themselves up as best as they could in the unusual weather. He pulled his truck up to the mission as snow began to fall.

"It's a miracle," Joseph shouted and pointed. "Look!" Joseph had carved life-sized figures of Mary on a donkey, clearly expecting a child, and Joseph leading them. Snow covered the figures shrouding them in pure white cloaks. The eyes carved from ironwood shined, the mahogany details glistened, the cypress took on a new life. "My prayers have been answered." Joseph continued to celebrate Christmas for all his years in all the ways, Christian, Seminole, and commercial.

NINE

Williamsburg, Virginia

Clara MacKenzie was overwhelmed. She had only landed in America a few weeks ago, but now she questioned if it was a wise move. When Clara arrived in Richmond Virginia she was put aboard a bateau, a shallow-draft, flat-bottomed boat for hire, for the final 60-mile leg of her journey on the James River to Williamsburg Virginia. It was late May and the weather was already hot. Hotter than Clara would have imagined. It was already much warmer than Glasgow, even on the warmest day she had ever experienced there. She wilted in her heavy woolen clothes. The girl felt badly for the young man poling the bottom mud. It was slow going, but she didn't complain, minded her manners, sat beneath the small canopy, and watched the passing scenery. She had little knowledge about the place she was going. It made her nervous.

At the dock in Williamsburg Clara was met by a dark-skinned man with a straw hat who was driving a wagon. "Miss Clara are you?" he called out.

"Indeed. I am she. Clara MacKenzie of Glasgow Scotland," she said with a thick brogue.

"Glad you made it. Big Esther says to take you directly to her. She wants to show you to your quarters and give you a good feeding and let you rest up before you start your work tomorrow. Y'all look awfully young. How old are you?"

"Big Esther's hospitality will be rather welcomed and much appreciated." Clara paused and removed her bonnet that exposed her radiant red hair. She fanned herself with her hat. "I turned 16 years of age last week," she replied.

"Like I say. You look mighty young. So, I suppose you had your birthday on the ocean."

"Aye, we were at sea when I turned 16. It wasn't so awful. I never have had any celebrations for my birthday. I may be 16 but I can hold my own. I'm sorry. I dinnae catch your name, Sir?"

"Y'all didn't catch it 'cause I never said it. I'm Amos. Originally from South Carolina right near Charleston. Master Campbell purchased me and brought me here to help run his plantation. Y'all can toss your bag in the back and take a seat back there too. I wouldn't be allowed to sit next to y'all, Miss Clara, but I got to drive this here rig."

"Oh. I see. Very well. As you wish." Clara gulped and suddenly felt claustrophobic. "Well, Mr. Campbell didn't purchase me. Let's just say he owns me for a few years to come."

Clara thought about the name Campbell. She knew it came from the Scottish Gaelic roots. *Cam*, which means "crooked" and *beul*, meaning "mouth." *So, there we have it, she thought. I've gone half-way around the world to work for a man whose name means crooked mouth for a period of seven years.*

Amos pondered then spoke. "Master Campbell tells me that ship you arrived on will already be loaded down with tobacco and cotton and be headed back across the water in a couple o' days." In his mind he wished he could be aboard the boat.

"You dinnae say," said Clara. "That much tobacco should fill a fair number of pipes." She looked down at was once her pale white skin that had started turning crimson from exposure. She thought to herself, *I wouldn't mind sailing back with that pile of tobacco and cotton if I don't have to return to my wicked aunt and uncle.*

1850 was a pivotal year in America. Even if Amos and the other slaves ran to freedom, they would have to be returned to their owner if captured

The newly enacted Fugitive Slave Act, which was part of The Compromise of 1850, required the return of escaped slaves to their owners, even in free states. This greatly angered abolitionists.

The Compromise of 1850 was a collection of five separate bills passed by Congress in September 1850. It defused tensions for a moment between slave and free states in the years leading up to the Civil War.

However, The Compromise of 1850 didn't ease the tensions at all that continued to divide the North and South during the next ten years, and it didn't establish a principle that was applicable clearly to territories outside the Mexican Cession. Both Abolitionist and pro-slavery advocates were upset with the Compromise. It was the beginnings of a war that wouldn't start for another 11 years.

Indentured servants, although not considered slaves, were in many cases not much better off. Slavery issues continued to divide the free states and slave states. Pro-slavery and anti-slavery sides clashed politically and socially, and the festering conflict continued to escalate throughout the decade.

Clara was an indentured servant. Her aunt and uncle signed an agreement to give her to Campbell for seven years. After her term of service Clara would be independent and free to do as she wished. Many indentured servants suffered harsh conditions, although they received basic needs like food and shelter. Some servants managed to learn a trade from their work on the estates and plantations and go off on their own after their service. As compared to slavery, indentured servitude was a type of bonded labor, but with an end date that led to their freedom. Poor Europeans often sold their labor to pay off passage to America.

Indentured servitude started to decline in America during the late 17th century after Bacon's Rebellion that took place in 1676. The rebellion by servants in Virginia against the government highlighted the rough conditions the servants faced. Bacon's Rebellion revealed the discontent and poor conditions of indentured servants and led to changes that improved their treatment. Regardless, as an indentured servant, Clara was counted among the working poor.

A shifting agrarian economy saw the rise of larger plantations in the South. It increased the demand for lifelong, cheap labor to increase profits. It made slavery a more appealing option for plantation owners.

Amos delivered Clara to Big Esther's kitchen. "Here's yo' new scullery girl, Clara, Miss Esther," Amos said. Clara could see how Esther got the title of big. She was thick and wide. Esther had a smile that was wide as well. Esther showed Clara to a room off the back of the kitchen. Esther spoke first. "This is y'all's workroom. I expect ya to keep it as clean as it is now. There's a wash basin, cup, plate and spoon for ya on the sideboard. It's there so's you don't have to carry water up to ya room. Sleeping quarters is upstairs above this here space." Esther pointed to a wooden ladder at the far wall. We start before sunup. So's I'm givin' y'all the rest of the day to rest up and get used to things round here. There's an apron for you hanging behind this door."

Clara was told there would be a mansion on the plantation and she assumed she would be living in the manor. In those times the kitchen was a separate building away from the main house. Kitchen fires were common. By keeping the kitchen away from the main house it eliminated the possibility of the main house being consumed in a fire. Early kitchens with open hearths and wood stoves were hot, messy places. They were often smoke filled, had soot, and strong cooking odors. Separating them kept those elements away from the living areas in the main house. Kitchens separate from the main house weren't quite as common in northern colonies, although fire risk could be equally high. Historians speculate that social factors and climate were reasons. Heat generated from cooking would help warm the house in the north. Southern homes were already significantly warmed by the climate.

In more affluent homes, the kitchen was sometimes isolated to maintain a more pleasant environment for entertaining guests. Servants would scurry back and forth between the house and kitchen to serve meals on an outdoor path…in all weather conditions.

It was common for a scullery maid to live within the kitchen building. It would be Clara's job to keep the kitchen and scullery clean, wash dishes, help with food preparation, bring water from the well, feed the chickens and collect their eggs. She also had to care for the small cottage garden behind the kitchen that provided herbs and tender vegetables that would not do well in the open fields.

Esther spelled out all of Clara's chores. "I'm not going to have you do any slaughtering. The men can do that. But, once they bring a slab here, y'all will have to do some butchering. Nobody, including me, likes doin' it. So, Girl, learn to get good at it real quick. The quicker ya'll learn, the quicker it's done. Feed any scraps and bits to the chickens. Don't leave nothing lying about. It'll bring rats, ya know."

Clara shifted from foot to foot. She hadn't spoken since she arrived at the kitchen. She nodded that she understood. "Can you milk a cow, Child?" Esther asked.

"Aye. As a matter of fact, I can," replied Clara. "I was made to do it by my uncle. He did not like to get out of bed early. Always hisky-fied, dinnae you know, that led to a collie shangie by mid morn."

"I may have y'all milk the cows if there ain't a farm hand around. Sometimes they get busy like at harvest time. Milking is somethin' else I'm not fond of," Clara said with a sudden burst of laughter.

"Now and then I might send you to the market. Don't get any fancy ideas. Master Campbell ain't going to let you carry money. The plantation has accounts with most o' the sellers. Y'all tell 'em where the goods are goin', and the overseer or plantation mistress will settle up later. It's a fair ways away. Even farther coming back if you is carrying a load." Esther laughed again.

"I tell you what. You is one scrawny child. I don't know when the last time was you had a good feed. Get washed up and take a seat at the kitchen table. I'll feed you good. Work 'round here sures builds an appetite. I can't have you fainting on me. Oh, and drink up plenty o' water. The weather here will dry you out somethin' fierce, ya know."

Clara liked Big Esther. Although they had nothing in common including race, education, family history, and size, Esther's smile and hearty laugh made her lovable to Clara. And, even though Clara had a long list of chores to handle, she figured she was stuck at the Campbell plantation and would try to make the best of it and make Esther an ally.

Clara poured water from the bucket into the wash basin and washed her face, hands and sweaty neck. She carried her bag up the ladder. She was horrified by the tight quarters. It made her room in Scotland seem luxurious. Clara was growing depressed. She descended the ladder, smoothed her skirt, and went to the kitchen table.

Esther slid a plate of fried chicken, beans, collards, and cornbread dripping with honey, in front of Clara. Clara thought it tasted delicious. She was famished and would have eaten anything. She ate every morsel in silence.

"Tell me about Master Campbell," Clara said. "And his wife."

"Master Campbell is fairer than most, I'd say. He pretty much rewards good behavior and we all's gets new shoes at Christmas. That Missus Campbell is a beautiful woman and she comes from a family with a lot o' money. That Master Campbell is one lucky man. She be around first thing in the morning to give a talk about what we is cooking for the day. Missus Campbell is very kind. If one of the workers gets sick or injured, which happens a lot, she makes sure they's gettin' looked after. Truth be told, Ima almost always the one doin' the lookin' after." Esther laughed. "All in all, Master Campbell's plantation is the best one I've been traded to. I hopes I ain't leavin' here any time soon, 'cause I don't think I'll ever be free."

Hearing Esther's description of Master and Missus Cambell lightened Clara's mood a bit. "Coming here wasn't my plan. Do you think I'll survive?"

"I'll see to it that you do. It was never a plan of anyone here," Esther said and sighed.

Clara wondered about the whole slavery thing. She knew from her schooling that the Slave Trade Act abolished slavery in Britain in 1807. The Act made it illegal to transport enslaved people aboard any British ship. By 1838 The Slavery Abolition Act outlawed owning slaves throughout almost the whole British Empire.

Clara responded to Esther, "Aye. My grandmother was part of the Glasgow Ladies' Emancipation Society. They helped pressure Parliament to end owning people in Scotland, and the rest of the Empire. Hopefully, your time will come soon."

"I hope so," said Esther. "Master Campbell says there's change a comin'. It's only a matter o' time. I ain't gittin' any younger. I hopes it's soon." Esther gazed out the window and tried to imagine what it would be like to be free. "Truth be told, change may be comin' for Master Campbell sooner than he thinks. Amos tells me the fields are getting tapped out. They been farmed for over a hundred years and there ain't much good left in the dirt.

"So… tell me, Child. Tell me yo' whole story about how y'all came to be here in Big Esther's kitchen."

Clara paused for a long time. "I lost me mumm and da not too long ago. Life was good then. I was allowed to attend the parish school and learned to read and write. I loved that."

"Hold on there," Estha interjected. "Y'all kin read and write?"

"Yes I can," replied Clara. "And quite well, I might add."

"I can't do neither. It ain't allowed for us folks, Esther said and heaved her shoulders. "It's illegal."

How dreadful, Clara thought.

"Well, I could read for you. Or to you if you would like," said Clara. "I do have one book. It was a gift from Minister Robertson. I am grateful. Books are expensive and hard to come by."

"Missus Campbell has all o' them bookshelves in the main house. Maybe once you kin get her trust you could read some of those. Any ways, what's the rest o' yo' story."

Clara sighed. "Once I was orphaned it was said either I would be sent off to the horrible workhouse, or possibly taken in by the parish for an apprenticeship, which is only slightly better than the workhouse, to learn a boring trade like sewing or lacemaking. As it all turned out... I ended up with my evil Uncle Archie and Aunt Agnes. After a while they said I was a burden and couldn't afford to keep me. Although, they put me to work as hard as in a workhouse. They were abusive. I was fashous. Uh, trouble. There was always a caw can. That's a pointless argument." Clara leaned back in her chair. "Minister Robertson had a parish member who was a friend of the Campbells. One thing led to another and off I went and here I am. Is that enough of a story for you?"

Esther folded her arms. "Well, I'd say so. At least yo' free, or at least will be. No worry. Big Esther will look after you real good. Ain't nobody gonna touch you as long as I is around."

That night Clara slept soundly and was awakened by Esther's singing. Clara dressed in the darkness and climbed down the ladder. Esther put her to work. Clara was sent to the henhouse to collect eggs, then to the well for fresh water. She scurried about the kitchen cleaning up as Esther cooked. Esther gave Clara biscuits and milk. "Eat this to start y'all's day off right," Esther said. "These taste fresh," Clara remarked. "They is. Only jes' came out o' Big Esther's oven a moment ago."

The sun was now up and dried the morning dew. Mrs. Louisa Campbell stood in the kitchen doorway. "Good morning, Esther. I'm here to meet the new wee waif and discuss today's menu. Don't worry about lunch for Mr. Campbell. He will be in town for the day on business."

Clara was stunned by Louisa's beauty. The well-groomed Louisa Campell stood with perfect posture and extended her hand to Clara. "Good morning, my dear. I was told you arrived in good order after your journey. I am the lady of the house, Louisa Campbell. You can refer to me as Missus Campbell or Ma'am around others, and as Miss Louisa in private. Things are quite different here in the Commonwealth of Virginia than in Scotland. Welcome to your new home."

"Thank you, Missus Campbell. I am honored to me you." Clara reached out her hands and clasped Louisa's hand. Clara curtsied. "I am Clara MacKenzie of Glasgow. I hope I can meet your expectations."

"You seem rather refined," the older woman said. "How on earth did you end up here?

"With all due respect Ma'am, that's a long story for another day," Clara answered.

"I see," Louisa said as she nodded. "Yes, perhaps another time. We've yet to have anyone from Scotland here on the plantation. Although, my husband's heritage is Scottish, and his family are Campbell clan Scots."

"That is nice to know," Clara replied. "Are you Scottish as well."

"Well, a little bit. My family has been in Appalachia for an exceptionally long time. We are what some folks call 'Melungeon.' It comes from the French word 'mélange,' which means 'mixture.' However, yes indeed, part of that mixture is Scottish. My people came from the Stewart Clan.

"Well then, don't let me keep you from your duties. I don't want Esther to be upset with me. Oh, and Esther, please see to it this girl gets plenty to eat. She is far too thin."

"Ma'am, I will, ya know," Esther said and smiled.

"Ma'am, may I ask a question?" Clara asked.

"Yes, what is it?" Louisa answered.

"Will I be permitted to attend church services on Sunday mornings?"

"Indeed, Clara. It's fine. I encourage you to attend. What denomination do you follow?"

"My family was Presbyterian, for a while they struggled with the Church of England. But that calmed down. Is there a Presbyterian church here?"

"There is," Louisa replied. "It's a long walk."

"I don't mind," the girl said.

"Well, in that case, if we have a wagon and driver available, maybe I can help you out. And, perhaps I will attend with you. And I will see to it that you have a clean, suitable church dress." Clara nodded demurely and curtsied again. Oh, and keep that fair skin covered when you are out and about. Otherwise, you will look like a burned biscuit in short order."

Louisa left and Clara and Esther went about their work. At the end of each day Clara was exhausted. Days faded into weeks and weeks dissolved into months. Each one was hotter and more humid than the last. Clara did her best to deal with the hot weather and the work.

Just before sunrise on an August morning Clara awoke to a quiet kitchen. She was used to hearing Esther sing in the mornings. That, and the birds singing, were usually what pulled her from her dreams. She didn't think Esther would be out in the dark, so she decided to investigate. Clara climbed down the ladder, went through the scullery, and into the kitchen. Esther was sprawled on the floor. "Ach! Clara shouted. "Yer pure done in." Clara shook her and got no response. She could see that Esther was breathing in rapid, shallow breaths. Clara shook the woman once more, and again, there was no reaction. Clara bolted from the kitchen and ran at full speed on the servant's path to the main house. Clara arrived at the rear door and barged in, not knowing that Louisia was behind the door. Louisa stood bewildered in the false dawn light. "Dear Girl, what is going on?" Louisa said.

Clara blurted out the details. Louisa wore a concerned look and instructed two of her chambermaids to come with them. They all walked at a rapid pace to the kitchen. Before they entered, she told Clara to fetch a pail of water. "I do declare, this hotter than usual weather is taking its toll on all of us," Louisa said. Louisa and the two servants went to Esther's side, and as Clara had done, they tried to shake her into consciousness. "Esther, Esther, can you hear me?" Louisa shouted as she patted the cook's cheeks. Clara arrived with the bucket. "Bring it here," Louisa said. Mrs. Campbell then dumped the cool water over Esther's head. Esther blinked once, then twice and groaned. "Clara, run and gather up Amos, have him get Moses and Jasper, and a wagon and get them all here posthaste," Louisa ordered.

Tears began to well up in Clara's eyes as she raced to the slave quarters. Her spindly legs shook like jelly as she arrived and called out for Amos. "Amos! Where are you? Come quick! Big Esther has had a spell," she hollered in between gasps. "Amos? Amos! Where are you?" Amos rounded the corner of the slave cabin, Clara explained what had happened, and gave him Louisa's instructions. "Hey now. Catch yo' breath," he said in a calming voice. "I is gonna ride you back up there in the wagon. I don't thinks y'all got enough left to make it back on yo' own." Amos told Moses and Jasper to go to the stable and get the horse and wagon hitched up and bring it to him. "Git it done quick. Run!" he ordered. "Gie it laldy!" Clara shouted to them. They arrived and Amos helped Clara up and then climbed aboard himself. They clattered off to the kitchen. The cloud of dust in their wake was illuminated by the slanted early morning rays.

Clara was the first to jump off. Louisa was already waiting outside the door. "Missus Campbell. I rode up front on the buckboard with Amos. Please, I beg you, do not be upset with him… or me," Clara pleaded.

"It's fine, Child. It's an emergency. You did good," Louisa answered. She then spoke to Amos, "Esther has taken ill and collapsed. I don't know if it is because of this heat or something else. Amos, we need to get Esther out of this hot kitchen and into the shade and breeze. Let's all work together to get her on the back of the wagon." She turned to the chambermaids, "Ladies, set up a bed in the icehouse. It is much cooler there. Get one of the butlers if you need help. Once you are ready, we will take Esther there.

"Clara, can you ride a horse?"

Clara nodded and was quick to answer, "Yes, Ma'am. I was raised on a farm dinna you ken. It's been a long minute since I have been on a horse, but aye, I can!"

"Very well then, go to the stables. Tell them I sent you and they are to follow my orders. Have them saddle my horse, Chloe." Louisa went into the kitchen and returned with two carrots. "Chloe is gentle and will do anything you ask all day long if you give her these when you get there. First ride to Dr. McCarty's and tell him I need him right now, then go to the manse and tell Pastor Phillips the same."

"Will they take care of a slave?" Clara asked.

"Esther has a body and a soul. Both will need tending to. Optimistically, she will recover and be back in the kitchen once she is well enough. I am asking you to tend to her day-to-day needs and watch over her until she is well. She likes you and trusts you. I don't know what I will do for a cook in the meanwhile."

"I can do it," Clara offered. "Yes, I know you can look after her. We will all be around if you need help," Louisa said.

"No, Ma'am, what I mean to say is… I can do the cooking. Esther has been teaching me these last few months. I can do it until she can come back."

"My word," Louisa said, "very well, then. I will get one of the girls from the house to help you with the heavy lifting and the cleaning. Be off with you now. Go fetch Dr. McCarty. Hurry."

Clara did as she was told. The doctor arrived and told Louisa that Esther had a weak pulse and if she was to be back to normal, bed rest would be the best thing. In the following weeks Clara toiled in the kitchen and tended to Esther who was slow to recover. Clara asked permission to read some of Louisa Campbell's books aloud to Esther, saying it would do them both well. Lousia agreed and told Clara that it was fine if she could find the time. Louisa realized that it was the least she could do since Clara was already doing more than her fair share. Clara read Rip Van Winkle by Washington Irving. She enjoyed reading and Esther enjoyed listening. Clara was saving her own prized book to read later.

Clara's weeks were punctuated with Sunday trips to church with Mrs. Campbell. Louisa liked having Clara along and Clara felt the same way about Louisa. Although Louisa's was childless, her mothering instincts took hold. Also in attendance every Sunday was a handsome young man, Alexander Calhoun, whose parents Louisa knew from social circles. Although Alexander was young, barely not much older than Clara, he was bright and well educated. He taught literature, grammar, and rhetoric at the College of William & Mary in Williamsburg.

Clara, and all the workers, were relieved when the cooler autumn weather arrived. She enjoyed the brilliant colors of the foliage and the crispness of the night air. It reminded her of home. The fall harvest brought the work of canning and preserving many foods for the winter. Louisa sent the girls from the house to help Clara with the chores. The days grew shorter. Early on one December morning Louisa arrived at the kitchen door with a large basket. Clara greeted her. "Good morning, Ma'am. What do you have for me? More canning?" Clara asked. "Good morning, Clara. No, not at all. With the weather changing you will need warmer clothes. I picked these things up at the shop in town. And I found this lovely green dress for church and the holidays...along with some proper undergarments." Louisa didn't let on that she had the seamstress make the new clothes specifically for Clara. "Please try them on and let's see if they need any alterations," Louisa said. Clara did and they fit perfectly. "Thank you, Ma'am. I am grateful and very much obliged. I could never repay you." Louisa laughed and waved her hand. "You deserve these," she said. "Let's see if we can find you some nice shoes to go with them. I think you and I are the same size." Clara was overwhelmed and was determined to work even harder to please Mrs. Campbell. "Clara, I will come get you for church on Sunday. Keep breakfast simple that day. Beauregard is going out hunting early Sunday morning, so there's no need to fuss. Same for lunch. However, tomorrow I need you to make a double batch of hush puppies. Use Esther's recipe. The one with extra salt, double pepper, and a double pinch of cayenne. Use bacon grease. I will explain later. By the way, on Sunday l am taking you to lunch after church." Clara's jaw went slack. "There is something I want to discuss with you," Louisa added.

Esther had recovered, although not to the extent that she could keep up the grueling pace of the plantation's kitchen. She did what she could and helped Clara with small tasks. Louisa still sent house staff to help when they needed it. Clara took it all in stride. She was still filled with joy from Louisa's visit that morning. She decided today was the day to read her favorite book to Esther. She knew that Esther may not understand all the peculiarities of a story that takes place in London, but she would explain things if necessary. After the lunch dishes were finished, and before the time to begin preparing dinner, Clara sat with Esther at the kitchen table and opened her book.

"Esther," she said, "I'm going to read to you from my favorite book. It is a novella published in 1843 and given to me as a special gift from Minister Robertson at home. It's a story about the importance of love, kindness, generosity towards others, and the true meaning of Christmas. Its message is about living in the present moment and appreciating the joys of life that are easy to get. I think perhaps you and I can both relate to some of the characters in the story." Clara began to read... *'Marley was dead: to begin with. There is no doubt whatever about that. The register of his burial was signed by the clergyman, the clerk, the undertaker, and the beadle.'*

"Whoa now, y'all hold on," Esther bellowed. Y'all said this was a story 'bout..." Clara held her finger to her lips and stopped Esther in mid-sentence. "Haud yer wheesht! Just wait," Clara said. "It's also about having patience with others and waiting for good things to come. It will come. Just listen." While trying to suppress her accent as best she could so Esther could understand more easily, Clara continued reading, *'Scrooge signed it: and Scrooge's name was good upon 'Change, for anything he chose to put his hand to. But Scrooge had signed it of all the good days in the year, on Christmas Eve.'* Clara looked up to see if Esther was listening and was delighted to see that she was. Clara kept reading.

As the afternoon began to fade Clara reached the last page. 'Scrooge was better than his word. He did it all, and infinitely more; and to Tiny Tim, who did not die, he was a second father. He became as good a friend, as good a master, and as good a man, as the good old city knew, or any other good old city, town, or borough, in the good old world. Some people laughed to see the alteration in him, but he let them laugh, and little heeded them; for he was wise enough to know that nothing ever happened on this globe, for good, at which some people did not have their fill of laughter in the outset; and knowing that such as these would be blind anyway, he thought it quite as well that they should wrinkle up their eyes in grins, as have the malady in less attractive forms. His own heart laughed: and that was quite enough for him.

Clara closed her book. She knew the last passage by heart. She looked into Esther's eyes. In a loud voice Clara MacKenzie recited it slowly in defined measures.

"He had no further intercourse with Spirits, but lived upon the Total Abstinence Principle, ever afterwards; and it was always said of him, that he knew how to keep Christmas well, if any man alive possessed the knowledge. May that be truly said of us, and all of us! And so, as Tiny Tim observed, God bless Us, Every One!"

Clara could see that Esther's eye had moistened. "That was some story!" Esther said.

"Indeed, it is. It is *A Christmas Carol* written by Charles Dickens. It gave him the reputation of a skilled writer and made him financially secure. In a way Dicken's fortune changed after writing about a change of fortunes."

The next morning Louisa arrived earlier than usual to collect Clara for church. Amos was at the reins of the handsome carriage. He helped Louisa down the step. She grabbed a large satchel and a hat box from the back seat and entered the kitchen. "Clara, I'm here!" she called out. Clara bounded down the ladder, moved through the scullery and met Louisa in the kitchen. Clara was wearing her new green dress. "Good morning, Ma'am. How do I look, Missus Cambell?" Clara wanted to know.

"My goodness! Exquisite, I'd say. Good morning to you. Your day is about to get a little brighter." Louisa handed Clara the hat box. "Open it," she said.

Clara's eyes widened as she opened the box that held a charming new hat. "Well, put it on. Let's see how you look," Louisa said. "Wait, there's more." She gave Clara the satchel. "Go ahead and open it, Clara." Clara did and pulled out a pair of new dress shoes and fine gloves. "If you are going to be in my company, I want you to be dressed properly," Louisa said.

Clara was speechless then finally found the words. "Aye, never have I ever had such finery," she said. "How could I ever thank you?"

"Think nothing of it. Let's get all of these things on you and be on our way. Before you put on your new church hat let me run a brush through your hair."

On the way out of church Pastor Phillips greeted them in the narthex. "Looking fine today, Miss MacKenzie." Clara blushed. In line behind them was Alexander Calhoun. He said, "Good morning, ladies. Fine day, isn't it?" Clara was startled and turned abruptly. Her move caused her to drop a glove. She started to bend to pick it up. Alexander stopped her. "Please, allow me," he said. Young Mr. Calhoun genuflected, snatched up the glove and handed it to Clara. "There you are, Lady Clara. All is good." Once again Clara blushed. "Thank you, Sir. Much obliged," Clara remarked. Louisa interrupted, "Clara, please allow me to appropriately introduce you to Alexander Calhoun. He is on the faculty at the College of William & Mary. And, I might add, he received his diploma from the University of Glasgow."

"I'm charmed," he said. "Please call me Alex."

"Glasgow, you dinnae say! That's me hometown! Oh, and please call me Miss Clara or Clara if you prefer. We can dispense with the royal title."

"Yes. University of Glasgow. I began there when I was 15 years old and was back in America within three years with my degree. I enjoyed my time there. Wonderful people. And yes, I teach English at William & Mary down the road. Mr. and Mrs. Campbell got me the position there. What is it you do, Clara? Are you a houseguest on the Campbell plantation?"

Clara felt uncomfortable. She wanted to make a good impression. After hesitating she replied, "Aye. Let's just say I'm in food management and I do stay at the plantation." Her statement caused Louisa to break into a wide smile. Clara continued, "Ah, yes. Wiiliam & Mary. I've been past there a few times. Interesting place."

Alex was quick to respond. "Food management... it sounds like an interesting enterprise. Yes, the College of William & Mary is fascinating. It is known as the Alma Mater of the Nation. The college has many of America's founding fathers as graduates. George Washington received his surveyor's license through William & Mary at the age of 17 and returned later in 1788 as its first American chancellor. The position of chancellor remained vacant for a number of years following the American Revolution. Until then, Bishops of London had played the role. George Washington was the perfect man for the job. Presidents Thomas Jefferson, John Tyler and James Monroe received their undergraduate education there. The institution was founded in 1693 as a college. Although, in 1779, through the influence of graduate Thomas Jefferson, it experienced a reorganization transforming it into the first university in America. As part of this conversion William & Mary also started the very first law school in the country in 1779."

Clara listened intently and was humbled by the young teacher's depth of knowledge. "Beyond interesting, I'd say." she uttered.

Alex continued, "I have a thought. I would like to invite you to the Yule Log ceremony there next week. It's just before final exams. You can have a look at the campus firsthand."

"What is a Yule Log ceremony?" Clara asked.

"Students, faculty and staff gather together at Wren Courtyard with festive wood-burning torches called 'cressets,' then into the Great Hall for the Christmas Yule Log ceremony. It's really quite nice. It includes Christmas readings by the university president and key students. The William & Mary Choir and an a cappella group, The Gentlemen of the College, perform Christmas carols. A large unlit Yule log is passed through the throng of students for each to touch for good luck during their final exams. Then the students walk through the Great Hall and toss a sprig of holly into the fire to figuratively cast aside their woes and worries. Next, we all have refreshments of hot cider and gingerbread cookies. We all continue the singing and make new friends.

"It all sounds lovely," Clara said. "Missus Campbell, may I attend?"

Clara was smitten. She dreamed that one day she might be a student listening to Christmas stories in Wren Hall. Even more so, she imagined reading from Charles Dicken's *Christmas Carol* to them. Her thoughts faded as Louisa answered.

"I declare, that does sound lovely. Yes, Miss MacKenzie, you can go. I will have Amos take you there and wait for you to return. Mr. Calhoun will see you there at the front gate. Now it is time for the two of us to go to our luncheon.

"We are going to Christiana Campbell's Tavern on Waller Street. Yes, we are related. It was originally established in 1784 by my husband's forefathers. It was a favorite place for George Washington to dine back in the day."

They arrived at the tavern and Louisa whispered something in the manager's ear. He nodded and showed them to a secluded candlelit table in the back of a room decorated with mistletoe and holly. Louisa ordered for both of them, they ate, and then she politely dismissed the server.

"Are you enjoying the day, Clara?"

"Aye, surely I am, Ma'am. Couldn't be happier."

"I want to talk to you about something, Clara. Please listen to everything I say before you answer." Clara nodded that she agreed. Lousia gazed into the candlelight. She lowered her voice as she began. "Clara, as you know, Esther has been through a difficult ordeal. She still has not been quite right since that morning you found her unconscious. I've decided to remove her from the staff." Clara began to interrupt. Louisa held up her hand. "Esther has served us well for many years. I had a thought to send her north to freedom." Clara gave a shocked expression. Louisa went on... "Well Clara, I'm going to tell you the best kept secret in the Commonwealth of Virginia. If you repeat this story, we both might be hanged." Now Clara looked horrified.

"I have something called 'The Christmas List'. Every year around this time I pick one or two of the slaves who I think deserves far better and has potential or has been overworked or unfairly treated...and I get them north through Maryland then to Pennsylvania and freedom. We have people waiting for them when they arrive and have them blend into society there.

"Beauregard has never caught on. I tell him either the person has died, not hard to imagine considering what they're up against, or they've run off after the harvest after being worked too hard. By the time he had realized they are gone, it's usually too late for the paddy rollers to catch them. Amos and Esther knew. They always worked with me. They themselves refused to go. Both wanted to stay on the planation and help the others. There are a few ruses we've come up with over the years. Have you visited the slave cemetery up past the slave cabins?"

"I have," said Clara. "I've placed flowers there for them."

"Very sweet of you. However, quite a few of those plots are empty." Louisa said with a smirk. "Sometimes I let Amos know when I'm sending someone north. He digs a grave, fills it back in and places a marker. He tells Beauregard that the person has passed and been buried. My husband never questioned it and tells Amos not to give him the gruesome details and just find another man. Beauregard never made the connection that he had more help than usual die in December. Oh, and that hush puppy recipe you made...that was Esther's doing. As I said, she knew what was going on. Those hush puppies you prepared are going north tonight with one of the runaway boys. They will be scattered along the trail to throw off the hounds if he's followed. The bacon grease attracts the dogs, the extra pepper makes them sneeze and affects their sense of smell, the cayenne covers the scent, and the salt makes them thirsty and will pull towards water. All in all, it quiets the dogs down. Thus the term, 'hush, puppies'."

Clara grabbed her head, "Braw! Pure dead brilliant!"

"So, you may ask why I'm not sending Esther north now," Louisa said. "For one thing I don't know if she could survive the trip. What's more, even with signed papers, she might likely be returned due to that Fugitive Slave Act that Congress put in place this year. Which leads me to my decision. There is an unused cabin on the plantation. I am going to set her up there and have the servants look in on her and bring her meals so she doesn't have to walk too far. She can stay there peacefully for the rest of her days. I've told my husband this is what I'm doing, and he agreed. I must say, I do always get my way." Clara smiled and started to speak... "God bless you, Missus Campbel! Am I the cook now?" Once again Louisa held up her hand. "Patience, Child. It's not yet your turn to speak."

"I am removing you from the kitchen altogether," Louisa said in a calm voice. Tears welled in Clara's eyes. "As a toss of fate you came here through a decision that was not yours, and to the lowliest of jobs here. I've already admonished Beauregard about his actions and told him your debt is now repaid in full. I have a new cook and scullery maid starting tomorrow. I will be improving working and living conditions there." Clara was growing pale and started to tremble. "As for you, young lady, you have done the work here of three people without complaint in the most dire conditions. You don't belong there. Clara MacKenzie, you are educated, well-mannered, well-spoken, and care more about others than you do about yourself. Don't think I haven't noticed. I am moving you to the main house. You will have your own room and access to the tub. You will be treated as part of my family and live with us as family. You may read our books without asking permission. You will have fine clothes. After a year in my company you will be a perfect lady worthy to attend any ball or cotilion anywhere. I hope you will accept my proposal. What say you?"

"Missus Campbell," Clara stammered. "Dear God, I am shocked. Never have I ever come into such good fortune. I can not believe this is happening to me!"

"But wait. There's more to the story," Louisa said. "Next week is the annual Campbell Christmas Gala. It is rather lively. Our ballroom is decorated with many festive wreaths, and mistletoe and holly is hung from the chandeliers. I have a lot of extra candles brought in for the occasion. Beauregard follows the Scottish Christmas customs. Yes, the Yule Log, a bonfire, shortbread, oat cakes, haggis...not that I can say I savor it, and festive pastries and the like. There will be fine music and dancing. You will be our special guest."

Clara recoiled. "I cannot dance. Not a wee bit! I gonnae no dae that!" Clara exclaimed.

"Not to worry. I will teach you every step well in advance. I am inviting that handsome Mr. Alexander Calhoun. He will need a partner to dance with as well."

"Aye. I see," Clara said. "Well enough. In that case, I suppose I will have to learn. I fancy the gadgie."

"One last thing," Louisa interjected. "In September I am enrolling you to attend Wesleyan Female College in Macon Georgia. The Stewart and Campbell families have been benefactors there, and at William & Mary, for decades. I will take care of everything. You will spend the Christmas holidays and summers here with me."

Clara though she might faint. "Missus Campbell, thank you! What can I say? What should I do?"

Louisa took a long pause. "Well, Clara, you have already said thank you. Just say, Merry Christmas. And what you can do is start calling me Mama...if you wish."

Clara jumped up, rounded the table, tightly hugged Louisa, and whispered, "Merry Christmas, Mama."

Story Notes - Thank you to Mrs. Tammy Cavanaugh for the suggestion of the time and place for this short story. I was further influenced during a visit to Colonial Williamsburg in early May when there was an unusual heat spell with temperatures in the high 90s and I saw how it affected reenactors who had not yet unpacked their summer outfits. And in the summer of 2022, my wife Darla Rae and I attended the Scottish festival at Westbury Gardens on Long Island. Again, it was exceptionally hot, and the term "wilt in a kilt," was common. Darla Rae is of Scottish heritage and is a descendent of the Stewart Clan and the Arbuckle Clan that came from near Glasgow. The name Darla Rae loosely translates from Darling Child in Gaelic Scottish.

The name Clara used for the main character was chosen to salute Clara, the lead role in the popular Nutcracker Christmas musical production in which Tchaikovsky composed the music. The story for the Nutcracker ballet is a combination of the works by E. T. A. Hoffmann and Alexandre Dumas père and shaped for the stage by Marius Petipa and Ivan Vsevolozhsky.

E. T. A. Hoffmann wrote the fantasy story called "The Nutcracker and the Mouse King" in 1816. Alexandre Dumas père adapted Hoffmann's story into a more child-friendly version titled "The Story of a Nutcracker" in 1844. Marius Petipa, the choreographer, and Ivan Vsevolozhsky, the director of the Imperial Theatres, collaborated on a further simplified version of the story specifically for the ballet. They drew inspiration from Dumas' adaptation.

TEN

Embreeville, Pennsylvania

Jeremiah and Charles arrived in Philadelphia, Pennsylvania during mid-November of 1763. They were notable British astronomers and surveyors of the day. From the city of Philadelphia, they would embark on a daunting project that would take them five years to complete. It would take place during frigid sub-zero winters over rough, uninhabited terrain.

Charles was an astronomer employed at the Greenwich Observatory where he learned Mayer's Tables of the Moon. The Lunar Tables were created to answer the problem of how to figure out longitude at sea. It was a problem that had upset scientists and navigators from the earliest days of marine navigation. He worked throughout his life to perfect the Lunar Tables as a method of improving navigation at sea and was later rewarded for his successful efforts.

Jeremiah was an English surveyor as well as an astronomer. One of seven children, he was born in County Durham, Northern England in 1733. His father was a coal mine owner.

Young Jeremiah developed an interest in astronomy and mathematics during his education at Barnard Castle. In his early years he made friends with distinguished intellectuals in the area. Of note were William Emerson, a mathematician, and John Bird and Thomas Wright who were astronomers. In 1763 Jeremiah, now 30-years-old and Charles, at 35, signed a contract with the land barons of Pennsylvania and Maryland to help end the 80-year long boundary dispute between them by establishing a border between the two provinces. The surveyors' assignment was primarily to measure latitude.

They pair were well received in the city of brotherly love. And, although the Quakers didn't celebrate Christmas as a holiday, it didn't give the adventuresome team a reason to pause. Although recognized as a Quaker, Jeremiah often broke the rules by wearing a long red coat and occasionally imbibing excessively. Christmas was no exception. They considered their first Christmas in the colonies exceptional.

Jeremiah and Charles were welcomed in the pubs and taverns, including the City Tavern, which is just down the street from old Pennsylvania State House. It was a favorite hang-out for colonial statesmen arguing points of independence for the colonies. The State House is now known as Independence Hall. The City Tavern remained active and open to well into the twenty-first century.

Perhaps it was here among the din of fiddling, holiday laughter, and dancing that they realized that the mapping they were hired to do would cause them to have to cross the icy Delaware River several times a year.

The pair, accompanied by a group of assistants, began their surveying work in Philadelphia near what is now South Street. Although they completed the first part of their assignment there, to establish a southernmost latitude point of the city of Philadelphia, it was soon realized Instead of enduring the freezing winter temperatures and treacherous waters, they decided to set up headquarters on the other side of the river on the banks of Brandywine Creek in Embreeville, Pennsylvania.

Jeremiah and Charles set up a base at the Harlan Farmhouse, which was owned by a Quaker. Harlan's house was originally built in 1724 close to the forks of Brandywine Creek, is thought to be the first house built in Newlin Township. It was originally a stone constructed two story house measuring 25 by 16 feet. It was enlarged in 1758. The addition was also made of stone and measured 25 by 13 feet. Hardly a large house by today's standards, or ample space to accommodate guests and their equipment. After settling in at the new headquarters they set up their precise telescopes and instruments, which had survived the wagon ride from Philadelphia supported by springs with a feather bed beneath them, in Harlan's garden.

Their new observatory location was near marks that had been made by New Jersey surveyors during the 1730s. They placed a large stone as their own mark, Star Gazers' Stone, determining the latitude at Star Gazers' Stone by observing eight stars.

The surveyors returned to Harlan House many times during the four and one-half year-long survey, and often spent their winter holidays there.

On a crisp Christmas eve the two astronomers, joined by Harlan, stood by the stone they had placed. Some of the assistants gathered as well. Someone posited, "Isn't it fascinating that we are looking up at the same very stars that shepherds set their eyes on almost eighteen-hundred years ago that led them to the baby Jesus?" The group nodded in agreement. "A lot has changed since that day, and the world has become a vastly different, and smaller place. Mostly because we can now navigate the oceans and bring the continents closer together. On this day, Bless Jesus! A Good Christmas to all. Let us celebrate!"

"We agree," said someone from among the expedition. "Bring forth the libations!"

"Well now," replied a Quaker who had gathered with the group. "We Quakers believe that Jesus rules every day, and that we should not set one day ahead of any other. Every day is Christmas."

On New Year's Day, January 1, 1767, Charles measured the temperature at the farm and wrote it in his journal... a temperature of minus 22 degrees Fahrenheit. It gave good reason to hoist a toast or two to the New Year and celebrate their accomplishments.

The two surveyor-astronomers had a reputation of being heavy drinkers. Local legend tells a tale about an obscure nearby tributary to the Brandywine, Punch Run Creek, was named to commemorate their drinking escapades.

After the surveying was completed the Harlan Farm was among the last places they visited before returning to Philadelphia and finally home to England.

Today Charles Mason and Jeremiah Dixon's work, which ended an 80-year border feud between Maryland and Pennsylvania, is best remembered by the latitude named after them, the Mason-Dixon Line. It has long been recognized as the border between the North and the South states. Pennsylvania passed a law in 1780 abolishing slavery, making the Mason-Dixon Line the separation between free and slave states. Some historians say it's possible, that although Dixon was associated with the northern side of the boundary, the Dixie nickname for the Southern United States was drawn from his name. Before returning to England in 1768 Mason and Dixon were admitted to the American Society for Promoting Useful Knowledge, in Philadelphia. Mason continued to work to perfect the Mayer's Tables of the Moon for navigation at sea. His work was recognized in 1787. For Mason's work on perfecting the Lunar Tables he was awarded about $800 and not the full prize of about $10,000 to $20,000, in today's dollars, by the Board of Longitude. The Mason crater on the moon is named after Charles Mason. The Harlan farm, the Harlan house, and Stargazers' Stone were listed on the National Register of Historic Places in 1985.

ELEVEN

San Francisco, California

It has been said that the 1950s were pregnant with the sixties. It could further be said the offspring were the Flower Children, the hippies, and were born in San Franciso. The 1950s grew the Beat Generation. Beat generation influencers included writers Jack Kerouac, Author of On the Road, Allen Ginsberg, Poet of Howl, and William S. Burroughs, Author of Naked Lunch, all of whom lived in San Francisco at various times and later influenced musicians and rock bands such as Jefferson Airplane, The Grateful Dead, Jimi Hendrix, and Janis Joplin and Folk Music Artists like Bob Dylan and Joan Baez. Many rock bands, folk song writers, and music performers got their start in San Francisco. They played to sellout crowds in San Francisco at The Fillmore, The Avalon Ballroom, the Winterland Ballroom, and others.

Some say the term Beat Generation is drawn from a sense of weariness, or feeling beat, as a reflection of exhaustion with social values and norms. Others think it came from The Beatitudes; a series of blessings voiced by

Jesus at the beginning of the Sermon on the Mount. The Beatitudes describe the character and rewards of those who follow God's kingdom. Jesus's words were Blessed are the poor in spirit, for theirs is the kingdom of heaven. Blessed are those who mourn, for they shall be comforted. Blessed are the meek, for they shall inherit the earth. Blessed are those who hunger and thirst for righteousness, for they shall be filled. Blessed are the merciful, for they shall obtain mercy. Blessed are the pure in heart, for they shall see God. Blessed are the peacemakers, for they shall be called children of God. Blessed are those who are persecuted for righteousness' sake, for theirs is the kingdom of heaven.

Beatniks were the precursor of the hippie movement. The hippies promoted peace and love, nonviolence, and understanding among people. And like the beatniks, many hippies were involved in social and political activism. Many of the hippie movement philosophies can be seen in the Beatitudes.

Nick stood under his canopy at the open-air street market at Fisherman's Wharf. Business was slow and some people only stopped by to chat. A young woman approached his table. She had two young children with her. "Good morning, I'm Nick," he said. He noticed without surprise that she wore the typical attire of so many young people in San Francisco. Tie-dye shirt, bell bottom jeans, and fringed jacket. Her straight blond hair was parted in the middle and held in place with a beaded headband. Nick also noticed she wasn't wearing a wedding ring. "Try a piece of my sourdough bread," he said as he pushed a plate of sample slices toward her. "G'day. Thank you. Groovy." Holly's the name, Holly Sullivan," she offered.

Nick knew from the moment she spoke that she was an Australian. "Holly holy eyes," he sang.

Yeah, I get that a lot lately. I was born on Christmas Eve. The folks thought it'd be a cute name. I dread it." Holly took a bite of the sourdough bread topped with sesame seeds. "Crikey! This is far out, man."

"I can't believe it," Nick shot back.

"No, it tastes really groovy," Holly responded.

"No, I mean that you were born on Christmas Eve. So was I! I was named after St. Nicholas, you know, Santa Claus."

Holly rolled her eyes. "Peculiar coincidence. How much is a loaf?" Nick told her the price. She rummaged around in her oversized boho tote bag. Nick waited patiently. He didn't have much business, and she was rather attractive and seemed nice. He didn't mind the wait. "Tell you what. Can

I buy half a loaf?" She held out her hand with half the amount. Nick chuckled. "It looks like you've got a couple of mouths to feed. Here's what I think. The whole loaf is on the house, but only if you tell me what brought you to America."

"Fair dinkum. You're a top bloke, Santa Claus. It is so expensive to live here. It's more of a who than a what. It was me mum and dad. They wanted a better life for me than shearing jumbucks all day at their sheep station. They scraped up enough money to send me to college here. "

"Are those your children?"

"Yes. My twins. My jackaroo is John, we call him Jack, my Jillaroo is Jillian. So, don't say it. Yes, Jack and Jill and yes there are plenty of hills in this town to go up and fetch a pail of water."

"Are you alone?"

"Yeah, nah, I'm a widow. Their father's name was, and still is, John. That's how Jack was named. My mother's name is Jill. We were young and got married while I was still in school. As luck would have it, President Lyndon Johnson ended the exemption for married men. John got drafted and sent off to Viet Nam. I didn't realize I was up the duff until after he deployed. He was over there only two months. Never made it home. Never met his ankle biters.

"We came here to participate in the anti-was march to Golden Gate Park in April of '67. Made some friends and stayed."

"I'm so sorry," Nick said. "How in the world are you coping as a single mother? As you said, things are expensive here."

"Just barely would be the quick answer. I work the lunch shift at Vittorio's. Brother Dominic got me the job. He helps a lot of us out. It's a long walk from where me and the twins live near Clipper and Dolores Streets. Sometimes I ride my bike or catch a lift with a friend when I can to save the streetcar fare. We rent a flat upstairs with a separate entrance from Mrs. Cassady. She's on in years and happy for the company and lets me have it for a song. With them in school now, my work schedule fits in. The manager at Vittorio's lets me be off when there is no school. He knows the hard yakka it takes for me trying to raise them. Every day it's a dog's breakfast. In return I work hard for his place. Growing up on the station I learned all about hard work. I'll decide in a few years whether to go back there again.

"Alrighty, I've told you all my dark secrets, now tell me what's your secret for making this bread?"

Nick mused for a moment. "Well, there's no secret. The family legend is that my family came to California for the Gold Rush more than 100 years ago and brought a starter batch of sourdough with them from the restaurant that had in the French Quarter of New Orleans. They never struck it rich from gold and settled down in Frisco. With the little money they had they opened a hardware store, which did well because of the demand for supplies caused by the building boom then. The family almost sold it off during the Great Depression. The place is still around, and it's still named Duvalle's. I know about the struggles of raising a family. My folks had nine kids, not that I have any children of my own.

"My day job is working at the hardware store slinging nuts, bolts, and everything else. My mother manages the place. She took over when my dad passed on. It gets truly boring at times. Coming home and baking several batches of sourdough keeps life interesting. I sell some here at the market at a fair price, which helps pay the bills, and a restaurant or two buys from me. They haggle with me about the price too much, I might add. It's a bummer. I'm limited on space and making the bread is a time-consuming process, so I guess it's really just a hobby business."

"Keeping that family recipe sourdough going through hard times and world wars is crackin' good. Good on ya, mate! If you're of French heritage maybe they should have named you Père Noël. The fog changed to chilly rain.

"Bring the children and yourself under my tent," Nick instructed. "How did you get down here?"

"Streetcar. My joeys enjoy the ride, it always makes for a rippin' good time. Today was a treat. Your bread is a bonus," Holly said. "Come to mommy before you're soaked through." She pulled them close to her. "They have no raincoats. Brother Dominic drops off clothing donations for them. Raincoats weren't available. No worries. They are growing out of gear so quickly they wouldn't last long."

"Your brother Dominic sound like a good guy, though."

Holly laughed. "Oh, he's not my brother. He's a Franciscan Brother. He works among the hippies who are mostly poor, often sick, and sometimes suffer from drug and grog use. Although they bring a lot of misery on themselves because of their own choices, he doesn't judge them. Personally, I don't think it would harm some of them if they went a got an honest job. He tells me they share some of the same principles the Franciscan Friars have; embracing a simple lifestyle, renouncing personal belongings, they strive to be humble and serve others without seeking recognition, actively working for peace, and living together in community with others. Brother Dom is always quick to add that what they don't have in common with him is chastity and believing in the Lord God." It started raining harder.

"Interesting," Nick responded. "Jack, Jill and you don't have rain jackets. There hasn't been much business this morning. My VW is around the corner. I'm going to pull around here, load everything and the three of you in and drive you home."

Holly wondered how he was going to cram everything into a Volkswagen Beetle. She also wondered if he was taking lessons from Brother Dom. "No wucka's," she told him. "I'll watch your stuff 'til you get back." Holly was relieved when Nick pulled up in a VW microbus. "Let's get the kids in first, and you take the front seat while I load up," Nick shouted over the pelting rain. "I'm going to help you. Least I can do. I'm not afraid of getting dirty hands," Holly answered quickly.

They arrived at Holly's address and she invited him in for lunch. "I got to feed the kids, anyway. They're getting cranky, I think we all need a bit of tucker. And I have great bread," she said as she pulled the loaf from her boho bag. "Aside from the bread it'll be cheese and googies."

"Googies?" Nick questioned as he slid from behind the wheel. "You've got me on that one."

"Eggs," she said. "Egg and cheese cut lunch. I know it's not much. The cupboard is a bit empty at the minute." Nick told her not to worry about it, opened the Volkswagen's side door to let Jack and Jill out, and reached in for two more loaves of bread.

He was impressed by how tidy their modest apartment was. She cooked the eggs and added cheese. Nick and Holly had polite conversation at the kitchen table. "Do you have a Sheila in your life? A woman as you would say," she asked. Nick admitted he did not. "Well, Mate, I hope you don't have any thoughts about dating. I don't have time for romance and raising these two is a full-time job. At the end of the day I'm totally knackered. The only outings I have is getting together with some other women, war widows like me, and wives and mothers of servicemen. Many of them are stationed over at the Presidio. Brother Dom brought us together. Sort of a support group, I suppose. On Tuesday evenings we get together and knit. Mrs. Cassady looks after the kids. When you grow up around sheep, wool is everywhere. It takes a bit to get it to yarn, but it's doable. It's a pity the yarn here is so bloody expensive."

Nick took what she said into account. A relationship hadn't entered his mind, although the thought now dwelled on him. He wondered if Holly was challenging him.

"Well, Père Noël, thank you for visiting with us and for the extra bread. Perhaps we will see each other again."

"Thank you for lunch. Greatly appreciate it."

"No worries, Mate."

The following Sunday Holly, Jack, and Jill were back at Nick's market booth. "I couldn't stay away from your sourdough bread," she quipped. "This week I'm paying full price. I don't want you thinking I'm a dipstick."

"Dipstick?" Nick questioned. "A loser," she retorted.

"Hardly. In any case it's nice to see you again. How did the week treat you?"

"Ah, peachy keen! I got a raise at Vittorios, and I finished knitting a jumper for Jillaroo. Wool is perfect here to protect against the dampness. Even does a pretty good job if it's wet. And, how about you?"

Nick admitted that it was the typical routine. Hardware during the day, making sourdough at night. It was getting toward the end of the day and Nick said, "I'm sold out. It's closing time. May I give you and the kids a ride home again?" Holly thought for a long moment before agreeing. "Oh, and one more thing," Nick added. "I'm stopping for ice cream on the way. I'd like to treat you all. Have you tried the ice cream at Swensen's up Hyde Street past Lombard? It's reckoned to be the first all-natural ice cream parlor in the country. They opened about 20 years-ago." Jack and Jill started cheering at the mention of the word ice cream. Holly looked at them and then at Nick. "I don't suppose I can say no. I haven't had an ice cream in quite a long time, neither have they."

Nick's VW microbus climbed the steep street in the Russian Hill section of town and parked around the corner from the ice cream shop. "All ashore," he said. "Crikey! Glad we didn't have to walk up that hill. It's no joke," Holly said. Nick told them to get whatever they wanted. Holly gave him an angry glance. She didn't want her children spoiled. Plus, she knew she couldn't compete with the expense. He ordered vanilla. "Hey big spender, with all these flavors, why are you getting just vanilla?" she asked. "It's my favorite," he replied. "Not too adventurous a bloke, are ya?" she teased. Nick let it roll off.

"Nick, you seem so levelheaded and grounded. I'd like to ask your opinion on an idea I had this week. It came to me after talking to you about how some of us can't afford to buy yarn, or at least not as much of it as we would like."

"Lay it on me, Holly holy."

"As you know I was raised on a sheep ranch. My folks don't have a lot of moolah, but they have a lot of sheep, which means they have a lot of wool. They know about my situation here. However, I think it's a better life here for my little tackers." She flipped her hair back as she leaned forward. "Here's what I'm thinking. If I can convince my folks, which won't be too hard, to send me bulk wool, we can convert it into yarn. I'll see if they can wash the fleece at the station before shipping it here. It's a messy job and I don't think some of the gals would want to do it. We can hand card the fleece. That's the way it was done centuries ago. Hand cards have been made in the United States since the American Revolution. Back in the day, the English blockaded the colonies. So, people here had to manage their own wool and cotton and started making their own cards to get the job done. If we give it a fair go, we could chip together for a drum carder to save time and womanpower. I can look about at the yard sales and flea markets for a used spinning wheel. That could be a challenge because most of them are passed down as family heirlooms. I suppose, if need be, I could find a carpenter who could make us one."

Nick held up his hand. "How are you going to pay for shipping?"

"Hold your horses, Mate. I'm getting to that. I went to the customs bureau over on Battery Street. It's about a half-hour walk from here. And, as I suspected, there's no import duty on raw wool! It gets better. I asked Brother Dominic if he thought I was galah, silly, and my idea was daggy. He asked the same question you did. Which brings up the final piece of my puzzle.

"I started to think, what are we going to do with so much wool? Well, as you have seen, the hippie movement started a demand for handcrafted goods made with natural fibers and dyes. And wealthy non-hippie types are willing to pay a hefty sum for unique clothing. Quite a few of us in the knitting group are dead broke for various reasons. They all have a good heart, though. Here's the plan… make jumpers, sweaters as you say, and sell half of them to the fancy boutiques straight down Stockton Street at Union Square. That will put a bit of quid in our pockets and help with expenses."

Nick put up his hand again. "What about the other half?"

"Glad you asked. When I spoke with Brother Dom he gave me an idea. If we are willing to give some of the finished knit goods to charity. He will speak to the diocese about getting Catholic Charities to help pay some of the shipping costs.

"As luck would have it, the father of one of the Sheila's is General Manager at a shipping company. I'm going to hit them up and see if they will donate shipping services for the charitable cause for whatever the church can't cover."

"I dig it. Far out and totally groovy!" Nick exclaimed.

"Père Noël, I'm glad you approve. I was beginning to wonder if I was bonkers. We all seem to get along, and Jackaroo and Jillaroo appreciate you. I am taking them to the movies tomorrow to see The Love Bug. There's a matinee and it only cost 50 cents. Would you care to tag along?"

Nick was shocked but quickly accepted the invitation for a family day at the movies. The casual socializing went on for weeks and Holly continued to work on importing the fleeces. Her shipment finally arrived and she put the women to work. They all agreed to do it on a volunteer basis until Holly could find shops to buy the sweaters. If there was money left after expenses they would split the proceeds. They all put in their vote for what charity would receive the donated sweaters. Holly taught them how to card the wool. One woman's grandmother had a spinning wheel in her garage that she donated to the cause. Holly soon realized with the volume of work to be done one spinning wheel wasn't going to be enough. Some were better at carding, others at spinning, and some at working with the natural dyes. The group decided to dye the wool themselves in small batches in bathtubs for the time being.

On a Tuesday evening with the group Holly snapped her fingers. "Crikey! Ladies, I have a thought about how we can get two or three pieces done in the same amount of time it usually takes us to do one. And… we don't have to work any harder." The knitting stopped as the group turned to Holly. "Tell us!" they said in unison.

"We all know Brother Dominic. He told me an interesting story about his order and Mission Dolores. You know the basilica. It's eight streetcar stops from here up Church Street. Saint Francis of Assisi set up the Franciscan Order during the early 13th century, and he based it on the principles of poverty, humility, and service to others. Which, I might add, Brother Dom does a bloody good job at. 550 years later the Franciscans are still around and create the Mission San Francisco de Asís, named after Saint Francis of Assisi. Impressive that the flock stuck together all those years, right? To be fair, Ohlone Native Americans did most of the construction work and created the ten-foot-thick adobe brick walls. It's the oldest still intact church nave in California. The mission was later nicknamed Mission Dolores after the nearby creek, Arroyo de Nuestra Señora de los Dolores. And now of course we have Dolores Park as well.

"Anyhow, back to Saint Francis of Assisi. Many ranchers like me are aware that he is the patron saint of animals because of his deep love and respect for all living creatures.

"What many people including me never realized was that Saint Francis, in addition to being a corker of a bloke, creating the Franciscans, and being the champion of everything ranging from wallabies to sheep and beyond, came up with the very first Nativity manger. He created the Nativity to bring the story of Christ's humble birth to life. Saint Francis hoped to advance empathy and understanding for the suffering of the poor and the outcasts by recreating Jesus' birth into poverty.

"Brother Dom said years ago he met the Beat Generation writer Jack Kerouac at the City Lights Bookstore over in the North Beach neighborhood who told him something far out, 'Life is holy and every moment is precious.' Dom said it doesn't get any more real than that. We are now living in the Age of Aquarius and the Peace movement. The hippies aren't all that bad. Counterculture change is encouraging peace, love, and social justice. Out in New York last year the Woodstock Festival pushed things into high gear.

"As we all know too well, it's bloody expensive living here. Raising a family is rough. Rents are high and increasing all the time. Childcare, if you can find it, is pricey, too. There are young mothers who are hard pressed to keep their runts in diapers, let alone anything fancy. I'll chat up Brother Dominic. He works among the poor in the Fillmore District, the Tenderloin neighborhood, and the Mission District. He is friends with the pastors and staff at Saint Boniface Church in the Tenderloin, Sacred Heart Church in the Fillmore District, and of course Mission Dolores in the Misson District."

Holly took a deep breath and held up her hands. "Here's what I propose…" She looked around the room to be certain she had their attention. "Instead of knitting adult size sweaters, we knit up woolies for infants. We can get at least two or three done in the same time and with the same amount of wool as the full sizes. We get lists from the churches of who in their parish had a baby in the past year and whether it's a lad or a lass. We can stick with one pattern to keep things easy. We can save the woad dye for the boys and the madder root toned down to pink for the girls. We can save the logwood, walnut hulls, onion skins, and red cabbage color dyes for the grownup jumpers. If we don't use as much alum for mordanting the little ones it'll give us softer color for them. What we save we can use on the yarn for the adult sizes. We are going to have to kick things up a notch, Christmas is right around the corner.

"Alright, here's the fun part! We deliver these anonymously to their homes on Christmas eve. The only recognition we will ever give the woolies is we'll sew in labels that say, 'You Are Loved'. I say let's give it a burl!"

The room burst into excited chatter. Questions flew back and forth. Someone asked, "With all the hills in San Francisco, and most of us don't have cars, and we have to be home on Christmas Eve…how we will be able to deliver all of these?"

Holly smiled. "I have just the jolly elf to get the job done."

On Wednesday morning the phone at Duvalle's Hardware Store rang. Nick answered the call. "G'day, Nicky," Holly said. "Can you stop by Vittorio's for lunch today? There's something I've got to ask you."

"Can't you just ask me over the phone?" he said.

"No, it's far too personal. Unless of course you don't want to see me?"

"Oh, please don't say that," Nick stammered. I'll be there by one o'clock."

"Thanks heaps, Mate. I'll save you a table."

Nick arrived before one. Holly showed him to a table for two with a card showing it was reserved in the half empty room. "What can I get you? It's on me," Holly said as she removed the reserved card.

"Oh, just a slice of pizza, please."

"Which one?" Holly questioned as she tucked the menu under her arm.

"Surprise me. You always make good choices." Nick responded.

Holly returned with a slice topped with sweet peppers. She slid the plate in front of Nick, unwrapped her apron, and sat across from him. Nick gave a questioning glance. "Oh, no worries, it's not busy and they said they would cover for me for a bit," she said as she leaned back in the chair and smiled demurely. "Nick, how would you like to spend Christmas Eve with me… alone? It didn't take Nick more than a heartbeat to reply, "are you serious?" He took another bite of the peppered pizza.

Holly unraveled her plot. She explained she would invite Nick and Mrs. Cassady for dinner on Christmas Eve and there would be a birthday cake for Nick and herself. Holly would put the kids to bed and Mrs. Casady would stay behind to look after them. Then the two of them would play Santa Claus by rolling around San Francisco in Nick's microbus delivering the new baby sweaters. She figured that since quite a few of the addresses were close together it shouldn't take too long. "We'll just knock on the door and run," she said. Nick nodded slowly the whole time as he looked intently at his remaining half slice.

"I'm proud of you, Holly. You are innovative and resourceful. I took a lot of savvy to put this whole plan together. I dig it. I'm in. Nicholas Duvalle, otherwise known as Père Noël, is at your service." Holly leapt out of her seat, wrapped her arms around him, and hugged him tightly. She whispered in his ear, "you're a good man."

"I have an idea," he said. "I'll tell you about it on Christmas Eve."

The women knitted at a furious pace and were ahead of the deadline. Holly was able to convince several boutiques around Union Square to buy the adult sweaters at fair price. The shops didn't have any trouble selling them during the Christmas rush. The sales gave everyone in the knitting group extra money for Christmas shopping.

Christmas Eve arrived, and Nick could see that Holly, with the help of Mrs. Cassady, had prepared a wonderful holiday dinner. "It's a shame you had to spend your birthday in the kitchen," Nick said. "And it's a shame you have to spend Christmas Eve and your birthday with me," Holly replied in a cheerful voice, and added a laugh. "Merry Christmas and Happy Birthday, Père Noël!"

Nick opened a bag and pulled out two loaves of sourdough bread. He placed them on the table and told Holly, "One of my favorite quotes is by Dostoevsky who said, 'There is not a thing that is more positive than bread'. Bread is a staple food for many cultures. It characterizes the basic human need for sustenance and survival. For many of those cultures breaking bread together is a regular ritual that symbolizes a shared experience and unity."

Holly thought about what Nick had said. "Speaking of a shared experience, that day at the restaurant you said you had an idea, and I had to wait until Christmas Eve to hear it. It's Christmas Eve. Tell me." She put her hands on her hips.

"Patience," Nick said. "It's like waiting for Santa Claus to come. You have to have patience. I'm not going to tell you. A little later. I'll show you."

Holly shrugged. "Fair enough. No worries. Let's eat."

After dinner Nick helped with the dishes. Holly tucked Jack and Jill in bed and read them a story. As she closed the book she told them magic happens for children on Christmas morning and kissed each one good night. Holly closed the door behind her and pulled Mrs. Cassady aside. "Are you sure you don't mind staying with the kids? I would understand if you changed your mind."

"My dear, Holly," Mrs. Casady answered in a faint voice. "Given why I've been asked to do this, I am thrilled and honored to do my part to put some joy in the homes of many families on Christmas. God bless you and Nick for your good works."

Nick and Holly went downstairs to his van. Nick had picked up the knitwear earlier in the day. He slid open the side door and Holly was delighted to see the women wrapped all the little sweaters individually. Some had pink bows, the others had blue. "This should make it easy to figure out who gets what," she said. "Hey, it smells fantastic in here. What is it?"

Nick flipped back a blanket that was covering dozens of loaves of sourdough bread wrapped in Saran Wrap. "This was my idea. I got the idea from the pizza you gave me that day. Roasted red and green peppers, the colors of Christmas, cover each one. I traded sourdough with the veggie man at the market for the peppers. We'll leave a loaf or two at each door drop off."

"What a great idea. Good on ya. You're a legend! Gold star for you! You better save one for us. I can't wait to try it. Let's be on our way, Santa," Holly said as she waved the list of addresses for the deliveries.

Nick and Holly continued their Christmas Eve and birthday tradition for years. Even though the Viet Nam War ended, the women continued to meet and knit every Tuesday.

Nick's mother retired from Duvalle's Hardware Store and Nick took it over. He and Holly worked together at the hardware store and baked sourdough bread together as Mr. and Mrs. Nicholas Duvalle. She continued to call him Père Noël. Sourdough bread smothered in roasted red and green peppers was on their Christmas Eve dinner table for ever after.

Story Notes - I had the opportunity to visit northern California and San Francisco a couple of times in the early 1980s. It was a beautiful city, and I had a chance to drive down the famous Lombard Street, known as the crookedest "Street in the World." with its eight hairpin turns. I absolutely fell in love with sourdough bread in San Francisco. My wife belongs to a knitting group that meets every Tuesday, which inspired this story. She knits sweaters for newborns in our family and close circle of friends.

$\mathcal{A}$ncram, $\mathcal{N}$ew $\mathcal{Y}$ork

In its day the village of Ancram, originally known as part of Gallatin until 1814, sat alone unnoticed by a growing new nation. Nestled in the hills between Albany, New York and Massachusetts' Berkshire Mountains, Ancram and the surrounding area were blessed with rich deposits of iron ore. The entire Hudson Highlands region from Danbury Connecticut west to the Hudson River and south to New Jersey were greatly mineralized. Enterprising settlers dug the iron ore from local mines and fed it to several forges and a blast furnace in Ancram. Columbia County's rich woodlands provided ample firewood and charcoal to fuel the ironworks that employed almost 100 men there.

Finished iron products such as tools, wagon rims, pots, kettles, and hardware were in high demand to meet the needs of Colonists. Although there were foundries in Pennsylvania and other surrounding colonies most iron products were imported from Britain. Colonists were prohibited from producing iron products. Resourceful Americans began to produce enough iron that they became serious competition for Mother England. In spite of the ban on finished iron items, crafters and blacksmiths began slipping horseshoes, tools, and other iron goods into the colonial commerce stream. Colonial governors turned a blind eye to local iron works churning out competing products in their colony. They could realize a handsome profit for themselves by allowing it to happen. So much so, in 1750 the British Parliament created the Iron Act. It restricted colonial ironworks to producing only bar stock and pig iron. Although, by 1775 it was estimated that the colonies were producing one-seventh of the world's iron ore.

Ancram got its name from the Livingston family homestead in Anchoram, Scotland. Lord of the Manor, Robert Livingston, was the son of a Scotch clergyman. He was born in Anchoram, Scotland in 1654. Many Scots and Scots Irish settled in the area around Ancram and worked the mines and iron mills.

Robert Livingston's grandson Philip Livingston founded the first iron works on the banks of the Roeliff Jansen Kill, New York in 1743. It was the only one of its kind In the Colony of New York. It would play a much greater role in years to come. Ancram was a busy place. Prior to the events of 1776 Ancram grew wheat, and later…Patriots.

At fifteen-years old Owen Pearce was not old enough to work in the mines or blacksmith shop. At least, not old enough for mine work by his mother's account. He was a bookish youth who had his eye on attending Yale University in Connecticut the following year. Owen was wiry and mature enough to earn an occasional bit of money running errands. His father, Simon, did not work in the mines or the mills, either. He was a farrier who nailed shoes on horses, cared for the hooves, and acted as a veterinarian to the degree that he could. He often sent Owen to the smith's shop with an outline drawing or an old horseshoe to match up. At times there were special instructions to form a shoe for a specific purpose such as studded shoes for traction on ice or shoes made to prevent snowballing, the buildup of ice and snow in a horse's hoof.

Winter arrived early in Ancram. Iron snowshoes for horses were rapidly growing in demand. Owen made frequent trips to the blacksmith shop of Archibald "Baldie" MacTavish. MacTavish was a fierce barrel-chested man with forearms as big as his thighs that were developed from years of hammering hot iron on the anvil. His red beard and flowing locks mimicked the roaring flames of the forge. His hair was tied back and pinned in place with an iron nail and leather thong. He feared nothing. His bellow could be heard above the constant clanging of the hammers.

His parents arrived in the colony decades earlier from Scotland. Baldie was born in the colony of New York. He practiced the Scottish traditions but considered himself a staunch Patriot. He believed in the cause.

Owen arrived at the blacksmith shop dusted with snow. He was a quiet and reserved boy who stood in awe of Baldie MacTavish. Owen saw him as a superhero. That was not much of a stretch of Owen's, or anyone else's, imagination. MacTavish always bested the other men at the games of skill and strength during the summer gatherings. Baldie MacTavish won by a wide margin. The blacksmith was burned and injured on a regular basis from working with white hot iron. Baldie always shook it off and pressed on.

"I've been watching those horses trying to make it up the hills on the ice. Nasty business," MacTavish said.

"Yes, sir," Owen said. "Even the big draft animals are struggling on the ice. A horse fell yesterday. Father saved her, though."

"Good thing." MacTavish replied. "Your father is a good man and a true Patriot who believes in the cause. There's a lot of heavy moving to be done in the upcoming weeks. We will be needing those horses. Captain Thomas Machin came to see me yesterday. He's Washington's man for the area below Poughkeepsie. He has recovered from his battle wounds and is set to create a new, stronger chain across the Hudson to keep the British from sailing on New York City. The works down at Chester won't be able to produce all of the new larger links. We have high quality ore here at Ancram. Machin came to me because he knows this shop is run by a steadfast Patriot. A Patriot who knows how to forge the best case-hardened steel in the colonies. He's asked me to make clevises and pins to join the chain sections. He wants something stronger than the chains they had that broke last year." MacTavish stepped back from the fire and pumped the bellows furiously. Sparks flew up the chimney. He used a long wooden handled hand shank ladle to carry molten iron from the fire and cautioned Owen to move back. Owen marveled at the cannon balls lying in the dirt that Baldie had already produced. Baldie moved toward the spherical molds. Owen pointed at the round shot and said, "Aren't you worried about a British patrol finding these?" Baldie poured the iron and acrid fumes filled the shop.

Baldie paused and thought about the boy's question. "Yer not a wee clipe, are ya? You know what I'm sayin', a tattle tale?"

"Of course not, Sir."

"Right-oh, then there's no need for worrying. What do you say we finish up the devil's work for the day? What sort of shoes is your father needing?"

Owen opened his tattered haversack and pulled out a horseshoe. "Here's the size father wants. And these are from mother." Owen handed Baldie four biscuits wrapped in muslin and two freshly made candles. Baldie was a bachelor who lived alone beside his shop. Owen's mother, Priscilla, often sent along a gift of home goods and food for the young man. Baldie was pleased to see that the horseshoe had not damaged the other contents. "Father said to please add studs and harden them. They will be seeing a lot of wear. He said to add the shoes to his tab."

"Ah, good lad! I can always count on you and the Pearce family to keep me busy. How many sets?" the blacksmith asked.

"Father said two sets of four for the time being. If the weather stays icy, he may ask for more."

"Alright, if these will be on the horses moving our provisions to the troops, there'll be no charge." MacTavish folded his arms. "Aye. Yes, the weather is making things difficult. Captain Machin tells me General George Washington and his troops are already camped in for the winter down near Philadelphia. A place named Valley Forge. Snow is already so thick, even the ox teams can't get through to deliver supplies."

"Yes, and it's not yet Christmas. Father said that is a bad sign for the rest of the winter."

"Sure enough, I'll be warm working over the furnace," Baldie replied and roared with laughter. "I can have these shoes finished by tomorrow."

Owen asked questions in rapid succession. "If the snow is deep and thick here, how will we celebrate Christmas? How will we visit? How will you visit us?"

"Whoa, whoa, whoa, laddie. You know I don't celebrate Christmas."

"Yes, but last Christmas Mother invited you and you came for dinner."

"I'm never one to turn down a good meal for any reason," Baldie said and added a smug grin.

"Why don't you celebrate Christmas?" Owen asked in a hurt voice.

The big man grew quiet and sat on a corner stool. He sighed and rubbed his forehead with the back of his hand. "Well, you see. It's sort of a family tradition to not celebrate Christmas as a holiday. The Protestant Scots don't follow the Catholic custom of celebrating Christmas. My parents, and the Scottish Presbyterians, said it was too papist. Scots do celebrate Hogmanay, though, on New Year's Eve and into New Year's Day."

Owen was wide eyed. He wasn't sure what papist meant, and surely didn't know what Hogmanay was. He was in total disbelief that anyone who claimed to be a good Christian did not celebrate the birth of Jesus Christ.

"But why?" Owen demanded to know.

"Christmas, and Catholic Christmas feasts and celebrations, were banned in Scotland as part of the Protestant Reformation," Baldie answered. "It's still banned to this day."

Owen shuddered. He knew that many of the people in the area were of Scottish heritage. Could this mean that Christmas would be outlawed in the colonies as well? He wondered if part of the reason for the Revolution was to save Christmas for those who wanted Christmas as a holiday. Those of British ancestry hosted Christmas dances in the evenings and served elaborate food and drink. Owen knew the German families made even more of a fuss for Christmas. Owen knew that Christmas had to be saved for the good of all. Because the Scots forbade Christmas, it shouldn't be so for everyone and affect those who wanted to celebrate. He wondered if the Scots were just opposed to having fun.

Owen was overwhelmed. Reports continually flowed into Ancram about militiamen and Continental Army regulars from the Ancram being lost at the Battles of Saratoga during September and October. Now to think that Christmas may be at risk was terrifying.

Owen thought carefully about his response to Baldie. Owen was taught to respect his elders and did not want to bring the wrath of his parents or pastor down on himself. He paced for a moment, knowing his response would be disrespectful to the man.

Owen cleared his throat and began. "Mr. MacTavish, you do know that I have every respect for you, Sir. Father and my family respect you for your trade, for your patriotism, and all that you lend to the cause of separating the colonies from the King." Owen felt he was doing well and sounded like one of the selectmen visiting the town square for a public notice. He grasped the lapels of his coat. "We are now here in the Americas. Yes, General Washington may be sitting in Valley Forge awaiting spring. But, at Saratoga, Colonel Daniel Morgan and his men picked off most of the British field officers and Major Benedict Arnold rallied our troops to victory. British General Burgoyne surrendered his army to the Patriots in October. What is left of them is on the run. In a short time, this land will become ours alone and governed by the rules and laws we choose to live by. They will be rules written by wise men with everyone's best interest at heart."

MacTavish's swallowed hard and his jaw dropped. He never imagined that Owen could deliver so much conviction with such eloquence. He rose from his perch and stood by his anvil.

"Furthermore, Mr. MacTavish, I respect your traditions and customs, and you and yours will be welcome to not observe Christmas if you so choose. For the rest of us…the right to celebrate our religion, or Christmas, in the way we choose, will not be taken away."

Baldie did not feel disrespected given that Owen made it clear his own Scottish traditions would be respected as well. The small-town blacksmith could see that this young man would do well at the university, and perhaps later as a barrister or statesman after the revolution. He measured his words too before responding. Baldie stammered and tried to voice his reply.

"Laddie, let me tell you about Hogmanay. It's all I've ever known," he stroked his beard as he spoke. Beards were a peculiarity at the time. Protestant Puritan values made men shave their face clean before God as a sign of respect. Owen wasn't sure if Baldie was breaking the rule for his own defiant sake or ignoring it. "Hogmanay is about visiting your friends and relatives for the New Year," Baldie said.

"Oh, so that is why you visited us for Christmas last year?" Owen asked.

"In a way, yes," Baldie said. "Like I told you, Lad, I wouldn't turn down your mother's cooking. And it was to be polite and accept the invitation. You know…to respect your family traditions."

"But we had singing and games and fine food. Isn't that more than visiting?" Owen asked.

"Well, I suppose you're right. I must admit it was rather enjoyable," MacTavish said as he untied the strings of his leather apron. He was wise enough to know that for Simon and Priscilla's family of six children it was a struggle to put out such a fine meal and include visitors, and provide even small gifts, as well. He also knew it would be hard for the couple to have their oldest son leave for school in Connecticut the following year. There would be one less man around the house to help with the chores.

"Will you join my family again this year to celebrate Christmas, Mr. MacTavish?"

"Aye, Lad. Indeed, I will. It's a fine tradition and here in the colonies it has a bright future of being celebrated by men who govern themselves and respect the customs of others."

In the days following Christmas 1777, in addition to making horseshoes and hardware, Baldie MacTavish worked day and night to carry out the request of Captain Machin. Although the bulk of the work to construct the massive chain was done by the Sterling Iron Works in Chester, New York, the Ancram blacksmith forged key connecting links for the great chain. By April 1778 it would stretch 1500 feet from what is now called Constitution Island in the Hudson River to West Point, New York. The chain was never challenged by the Royal Navy.

MacTavish also continued to produce cannonballs and other round shot in his foundry. Patriots hid them deep in the surrounding woods before being scurried off to Washington's army. At the Battle of Monmouth Courthouse in June, MacTavish's hand-poured rounds were fired by Washington's artillery under the command of Major General Nathaniel Greene. From high ground above a marshy field the well placed shots of Greene's four cannons held the British in their position. This exhausted the lobsterback's will and allowed Washington to attack the enemy's rear guard on both flanks, fighting them to a stalemate. These actions caused British commander General Clinton to withdraw under the cover of darkness and head to New York. The Battle of Monmouth Courthouse was a turning point for Washington, his troops, and the American Revolution. Ancram iron had served the Patriots well.

Owen attended Yale later that summer. Yale University was the alma mater of American spy Nathan Hale and Major Benjamin Tallmadge, Washington's appointed head of military intelligence, and the leader of the Culper Spy Ring. Was Owen Pearce recruited at Yale to participate in intelligence gathering operations as Hale and Tallmadge had? Owen Pearce was like many young men of the time who played roles in the quest for liberty whose stories remain untold. Owen did return home to Ancram to continue the family Christmas traditions.

Baldie MacTavish the Scottish-American, learned about the joy and warmth that celebrating Christmas brings. He started his own Christmas customs and celebrated the feast of peace and light...every year thereafter.

THIRTEEN

Denver, Colorado

"Well, with Doctor Jones gone, and only the midwife Lilian here to tend to the women folk, we need to find a new doctor for the men," the older man said.

"I suppose you're correct, Lester. Our town has been growing right quick. It's hard to keep up," the Sheriff said. "A while back I put word out to a doctor friend up in St. Louis to see if he's interested in starting a practice here. I've since learned that he moved his family to Kansas a few years ago."

"Is he interested?" the gray-haired man asked. "What do we know about him?

"His name is Vic. Dr. Victor LoPriesti. He was a Union Army surgeon during the war," Sheriff Barker said. "I'd say he's qualified to handle most any situation. Unfortunately, he's getting on in years and fixin' to retire. So, he wrote back and said he had the perfect doctor for the job who was willing to start a medical practice in Colorado."

"Do we know the name of the new doc?"

"Sure do. The name is Vic LoPriesti."

"I thought that was the doctor's name?" Les stroked his whiskers.

"You're right. I guess his oldest son became a doctor. Or, maybe a nephew."

"LoPriesti? Ain't that Italian?" Les asked.

"I suppose, I suppose it is," said the Sheriff. "Didn't think much about it. We need help here on the outskirts. We can give Dr. LoPriesti Doc Jones' old place. It's been sitting vacant. We did promise housing to a doctor willing to relocate. I hope he doesn't mind that there's no indoor plumbing."

"It never bothered old Dr. Jones. And… it didn't make him any less than a good doc."

"Like being Italian doesn't make a man any less of a doctor?" Barker asked.

Les thought about it. Accepting change was hard. He grew up poor, the son of Irish immigrants. Although, he figured having come to Denver from Illinois in 1858 during the Pike's Peak gold rush was hard, too.

"I reckon you're right. Let's see how he does," Les replied. He stood and straightened his back.

Sheriff Barker replied, "I got a telegram. I'm told Dr. LoPriesti is already on the way. Should be here within the next week or so."

"Coming by train, Sheriff?" Les wanted to know.

"Didn't say and I don't know."

Henry Barker was pure cowboy. He wore chaps on a regular basis, even while at his desk in the office. His black gambler hat and drooping handlebar moustache were his trademarks.

Three days later a tall rider, sitting straight-backed in the saddle arrived in front of the sheriff's office. Aside from the horse and rider, there were two heavily ladened mules in tow. Barker and Les sat on a bench under the porch in front of the sheriff's office and watched as the rider hesitated.

They weren't sure who it was. A miner? New ranch hand? A tinker? Or perhaps only a traveler passing through. There were many who passed through their town on the distant outskirts of Denver for a variety of reasons.

Les shouted out, "Is you lost?"

The new arrival wore a duster with its collar pulled all the way up to a cattleman crease cowboy hat. A bandana covered more in between. All were covered with layers of trail dirt. Swinging a leg over the saddle and dismounting the horse the rider replied in a high voice.

"If I've found Sheriff Barker's place, I'm not lost." Pulling down the bandana and collar, the visitor removed their hat to unleash a long tumble of flaxen hair. "I'm Doctor LoPriesti. Your new physician. This is my horse Audax, and my trusted mules. I simply call them Mule One and Mule Two. Have I found Sheriff Barker? You fit the description."

Les and Barker simultaneously dropped their jaws.

Les spoke first. "We was supposed to get a doc with the name Vic LoPriesti. You're a woman!"

"Correct on both accounts. I am Doctor Victoria LoPriesti, my father is Doctor Victor LoPriesti. I was named after him. And yes indeed, I am a woman. It's a pleasure to make your acquaintance."

Les was in a state of shock then recovered quickly.

"Is you Italian?" Les stammered. He put the emphasis on the I, pronouncing the ethnicity eye-talian.

"I am of Italian heritage on my father's side," the doctor answered. "I didn't know it made a difference. What is your surname, Sir?"

"It's O'Reilly. Lester O'Reilly. Folks call me Les."

"Very well, Mr. O'Reilly. My mother is of Irish decent," she said pulling the dusty scarf from around her neck. "Is that okay with you?"

"Oh. Well then. I reckon it is." Les paused. "We already have Lilian who's a midwife and takes care of the women folk. We need a doc for the men. Just what kind of doctor are you? Are you any good at it? You're awful young."

Victoria replied, "Like my father I am a medical doctor and general surgeon. I graduated at the top of my class in medical school. I was educated in Edinburgh, Scotland.

"I was further inspired by Elizabeth Blackwell who became the first woman physician in the United States. She earned her medical degree in 1849. Dr. Blackwell began seeking a medical career after a terribly ill friend of hers insisted she would have received better care from a woman doctor.

"I come from a long line of doctors who have been practicing medicine in the United States dating back to the mid-18th century. They were all American patriots and over the decades served as doctors in the American Revolutionary War, the War of 1812, and my father was an Army doctor for the North in the Civil War. In spite of raising five children, my mother is a professor of the English language and speaks several languages. As such, I speak five languages...fluently.

"I may be young, however, in a very short time I gained a lot of experience in rural doctoring. By age 11 I was at my father's side observing his every technique and treatment. By the time I was 14 years old I was assisting in some of his surgeries. Since then, I've treated snake bites, horse bites, broken arms, legs and heads and everything in between. I've treated women and men. Don't fear, Mr. O'Reilly. I've seen it all. The fact is, flesh and blood, skin and bones, and pain are all pretty much the same no matter who is suffering. It is my job to make them well, no matter who they are." She drew a circle in the dirt with the toe of her boot. "And, oh, I can ride a horse quite well. Anyway, I thought the Sheriff Barker would be doing the questioning."

"Well…one more question," Les blurted. "Where's your husband?"

"I'm not married, I'm widowed." the doctor answered. "My husband passed soon after our marriage. It was a tragic farming accident. He was harrowing a field, when the horses started unexpectedly, throwing him under the harrow. By the time he was found he couldn't be saved."

"My condolences, rest his soul," Les said and removed his hat. Sheriff Barker followed suit.

Barker had been taking in the whole exchange between the doctor and Les. He didn't rush to any judgements and wanted to hear what the young doctor had to say. He spoke for the first time.

"My sincere condolences, as well," he said. "Let me be the first to welcome you to our small piece of the Wild West. We started out as a gold-mining town. When no more gold was being found, we became a supply depot for other mines in the mountains. When the first railroad arrived here in 1870, we started growing in size like grass on the prairie. Seems the population doubles every few years."

Barker paused to let his words sink in. "A lot of them are from New York, Ohio, Illinois, and Missouri. Hundreds of the new people come here with tuberculosis in hopes of finding a miracle cure from the dry climate and clean, thin air. I don't know that it helps. I don't know if anything helps. Here on the outskirts we don't see as much of it as they do down in town. To be clear, it's an issue.

"As you mentioned, you ride well. That will come in handy in these parts."

Victoria appreciated Barker's low-key, open-minded manor. "I see," said the doctor. "I will do what I can. Let's all try to stay positive."

Barker said, "Well, so much for what's been going on. As the agreement said, we will provide housing to the doctor who answered our call. Let's get you settled in. We have Dr. Jones' former residence for you. Not to worry. There's a barn for Audax, One, and Two.

"That's quite a bit of baggage you're traveling with. As long as you've got the appropriate apparel for the changes in weather, no one worries too much about fashion outfits here."

Victoria laughed. "Oh, it's not clothes. Those are my medical supplies and equipment. I keep things fairly simple when it comes to my wardrobe. Doctor's clothes, work clothes, Sunday clothes. I'm told that in this part of the country, if you don't like the weather, wait twenty minutes. On some days I may need them all!"

Barker stepped closer to the horse. He pointed to the Winchester lever-action in the saddle scarab. "Do you know how to use that thing?" he asked.

"I can shoot better than I ride. A woman traveling alone can't be too careful. On the trail coming here I tried to fall in with traveling family groups. Safety in numbers, right?" Doctor Victoria unbuttoned her duster and held it open to reveal a holstered Colt revolver. "I'm darn good with this, too."

Les, who had remained quiet for the last few minutes, rejoined the discussion. "Well, what all else are you good at?"

"Well. Let's see. I'm good at doctoring, but I've already told you that. I'm proficient with a fly-casting rod. My father taught me how to fish. I understand the fishing in these mountain streams is quite good. I'm looking forward to an opportunity once I have some spare time."

Les was astonished. "How is it that you're still not married yet?" Barker gave him a demeaning glance. The doctor didn't answer.

Les stammered into his next question, "Audax is an odd name for a horse. I don't think I've heard that one before."

Victoria laughed. "Probably not. It's Latin. It can mean daring or bold in two different ways. Either spirited and courageous, or foolhardy, rash and presumptuous."

"That sort of sounds like you!" Les uttered. Barker knocked Les' hat off with the back of his hand. Lester slowly bent over at the waist to retrieve his hat.

"Lester, show some respect!" the sheriff ordered.

Les replied in a weak voice. "Understood, Sheriff. Understood. Sorry, Doc."

"Well now. Let's change the subject," Victoria said. "Yes, I can, and do ride, which will get me out to my patients. Nonetheless, I want to set up a clinic here in the village, closer to the bulk of the population. That will be easier for people to come to see me."

Lester's pride was a bit damaged after Victoria's blunt rebuttals to his questions and Barker's reprimand. He returned the conversation to make amends. "I know of just the place. The Post Office had to move to a bigger location. They outgrew the old place. There's plenty of space for whatever you want to do. Not to mention, it's got heat and water. Plus, everyone knows where it is. I'll tell them the new tenant, Dr. Victoria, is here to serve them. I'll even see if I can't bargain down the rent."

"Excellent! I appreciate that," the doctor exclaimed. "I can't wait to get started. I will invite Lilian to have space there as well and be available if a birthing mother or their new baby needs medical attention.

"There's one more thing, Mr. O'Reilly. In addition to being a widowed woman, not remarried, a doctor, sharpshooter, horsewoman, angler, and Italian... I am a Catholic. Is that alright with you? I would like to attend church on Sunday. Can you please direct me there?"

Barker answered her question. "In downtown Denver there's that St. Mary's Parish Church on Logan Street. It's fairly hard to miss. Father Joseph Machebeuf, a French Roman Catholic missionary, started the place. He did a lot of good things and increased the number of Catholics in the area and grew his parish. I guess he made a good impression. So, in '68 they made Father Machebeuf the bishop of Colorado.

"St. Mary's is a bit of a hike from here. There is a Catholic missionary who comes here on Sunday mornings and Holy Days to hold services. He tends to the Spanish speaking folks, who are mostly miners who came up from Mexico to work the mines and stayed on, and some of the tribal people who have been baptized.

"Denver land originally belonged to the Arapaho tribe, as stated in the 1851 Treaty of Fort Laramie. Then the Colorado Gold Rush of 1858 undid the treaty when white settlers moved onto Cheyenne and Arapaho land that was supposed to be protected. Next there was that Sand Creek Massacre in '64. Just awful. It's mostly Utes left here now. Sometimes there's unrest, sometimes there's not. I try to get along with everybody, keep the peace, and uphold law and order...

"Anyway, his name is Father Suarez. You'll like him. They hold Mass under a tent when the weather is fair and use the barn out back when it's not."

"That's fine," the doctor said. "The Mass is in Latin and, I speak Spanish and Latin."

Les cleared his throat, "Of course you do," he uttered.

"Sometimes we have to ask God to step in when medicine cannot," Victoria added.

"Maybe you can give Father Suarez some space in your office as well," Les said as he chuckled.

"It's been a long, dusty trip. I would like to get to my residence, unpack, and draw a bath."

The two men looked at each other and exchanged horrified expressions.

"Of course," said Barker with a stutter. "One problem. We didn't expect a new doctor so quick, so Dr. Jones' place is under repair and renovations are being added. It could take a while."

Dr. Victoria looked confused. Les gulped.

The sheriff continued, "I tell you what. We are going to set you up at my sister's place. Emily is about your age and a single woman like yourself. Y'all will get along famously. She has a seamstress shop around the corner. That could come in handy if you need something done up. Les, please take our new doctor and her caravan around back to that barn. You can leave any gear that's not too important there for the time being. If you have anything valuable, I'll have a deputy lock it up in one of the holding cells.

"Emily has all of the conveniences like indoor plumbing, a bathtub, and a spare room."

Doctor Victoria was puzzled by the sudden change of events. "Oh, honestly I don't mind living in the Jones house while it's being fixed up," she said.

"I wouldn't hear of it," the sheriff continued. "It's not a problem rooming at Emily's. She will enjoy your company. Les, take charge here and I will go let Emily know you're coming.

"Emily's house is just up the street past where the old post office was. Les can show you the way.

"Summers here get hot and dry, but when winter rolls in it gets plenty cold and snowy. It will be Christmas before you know it. We want to be sure you're comfortable and have plenty of firewood. The roof is leaking, some critters have gotten into the house, and, uh, the plumbing needs work. He took a long pause and drew in a deep breath. It's a big mess and needs a lot of work. We will get it all fixed up nice for you. We want you to be comfortable. We appreciate you coming here and your patience." He tipped his hat and trotted off in the dust to his sister's house.

Emily greeted Dr. Victoria at the door. "Well, Doctor. It's an honor and pleasure to have you here." Emily tried not to look too surprised by

Victoria's grimy clothes and dirt-streaked face. "You must be exhausted. That's a long way to come alone by horse."

"It was more of an adventure... and, a challenge," the doctor said. She dumped her bag of belongings on the porch of Emily's tidy bungalow. I wasn't alone. I traveled with three good friends."

"I'm delighted to hear that you have the pioneer spirit. You'll fit right in here. Let's get you settled, and I will draw a bath for you. Don't worry too much about what to wear," Emily said.

"I've been told that," the doctor interjected.

Emily continued, "You and I are exactly the same size. I am happy to share what I have here. There's fresh biscuits and honey in the kitchen. I will put up tea. I imagine you're hungry."

Doctor Victoria LoPriesti was overwhelmed by the hospitality and the caring nature of the people she met in her new town. Victoria welcomed it. She was filthy, exhausted, and starving.

"How shall I address you, Doctor?" Emily wanted to know.

"Please call me Victoria. The town folk can call me Dr. Vic. How much will the rent be?"

Emily answered, "Doctor Jones had a custom of bartering his services for what people had. Frankly, most here don't have much money, and I think he made out better in the long run. He never wanted for anything. I made that man more than one suit of clothes in his lifetime.

She hesitated then continued, "If you find a barter arrangement suitable, there will be no rent here. If you don't find it agreeable, there will be no rent anyway as you will stay as my guest. I am overjoyed that we have a new doctor, and a woman doctor at that." Emily waited for a response.

"Bartering for my services is just fine with me. I'm glad to have that arrangement. I didn't travel with much money. I wasn't sure about highwaymen on my journey. Folks looked after me and I looked after myself. Emily, you're my first patient in my new practice."

Dr. Vic had agreed to meet Lester at the old post office first thing in the morning. Just after sunrise Emily prepared a sumptuous bacon and egg breakfast for both of them. "You'll have a busy day, Victoria. I want you to start the day off right. The thin air here increases your need for food and dries you out, even in winter, so drink plenty of water. You should be well prepared before you meet up with Les and the landlord of post office building, that cantankerous old coot, Phineas T. Blake. He's my landlord at my shop as well. He can be difficult."

During the bacon eggs, coffee, and fresh biscuits Emily gave Victoria the lay of the land.

"Back in '61 Denver was an extension of Arapahoe County, Kansas. However, (Emily emphasized the word however) because a county here didn't get organized there was no official government. It was truly the Wild West. Around here it was as lawless as it can get. Vigilantism and vendettas were rampant.

"So, Colorado becomes territory, courts were set up, judges got appointed, and laws and rules were put in place. They didn't always work. Mob justice was common. That's when my brother Henry got appointed Sheriff. It was dangerous at first. He got things settled down after a while. Emily took a sip of coffee.

"The same year we became a territory, and now under the jurisdiction of the federal government, the Civil War broke out. I heard that your father was doctoring the Union troops?"

"Yes, and he still looks after some of the wounded War Veterans in his area," Victoria replied. "I hope to follow in his footsteps and do the same for the war-wounded soldiers around here."

"Noble indeed," said Emily. "Around that time most of the men here had come here from up north for the gold rush and stayed on. Denver's first mayor, John Moore, was a Southerner. Moore was driven out of town along with all the other sympathizers of the Confederacy.

"Territorial Governor Gilpin got the Colorado volunteer militia together. They shipped south to fight the Battle of Glorieta Pass on the Santa Fe Trail. Some folks have called it the Battle of Gettysburg of the West. The Texan Confederates had a plan to head up into New Mexico Territory and seize Fort Union, then invade the Colorado territory with its rich mines that could bolster their war efforts. And then eventually head to the West Coast and control all of the Southwest."

Victoria was astonished by Emily's knowledge of history, "Please continue," Victoria said as she pushed back her empty plate.

"There's more to the story," Emily answered. Although the Union troops won the battle and eventually the war, it could have gone a different way if the Confederates had broken through and gained control of the Colorado Territory and beyond.

"Yes, even though we won, the results were hard for the people of the Colorado Territory. The war campaign tied up all the resources and there was nothing left for mining, farming, or building new roads and railroads. Denver went stale.

"Right around this time the mines started playing out. The mines are what fueled Denver, which was a big supply town. Then all of a sudden, nobody needed any supplies. It had been a place where miners and other folks would come and buy things. That dried up. A lot of people left. Those who stayed behind couldn't find meaningful work. There was a lot of drinking, fighting and gambling away what little they had in hopes for a lucky day.

"During the war years other things didn't go too well for the townspeople. In April of '63 a tremendous fire started in the center of town. Winds fanned the flames and burned down most of the wooden buildings in just one night. The buildings themselves weren't worth much. Some not much more than shacks. It what was in those buildings that mattered much more. They held all of the stores and goods of new businesses. Since then, they passed a law that all new buildings had to be made out of stone or brick. Denver began to look like a more solid town as things got rebuilt.

"As if things weren't bad enough, in the year following the fire the spring snowmelt and torrential rainstorms caused Cherry Creek to overflow its banks. The floods reached into low-lying areas like down in Auraria. City Hall, the Methodist Church, warehouses, businesses, and homes were destroyed. So, what the fires didn't manage to destroy...the flooding did. Some people died, a lot more were left homeless, and a lot of livestock drowned. Contamination in the water was causing sickness on a wide scale.

"They started right quick on rebuilding. You'd think folks would have been smart enough to learn a lesson. Same exact thing happened again last year. Same thing has probably been happening for centuries. With no one living here, who would even know? Before the Pike's Peak gold boom of 1858, there wasn't a soul around, except for tribal people who could move in a hurry.

Emily stopped and folded her hands. "Are you feeling alright, Victoria?"

Victoria replied, "Yes. That was quite a history lesson. At first, I was wondering if I had come to the wrong place. It has had so much bad luck. Though, the more I think about it, the Good Lord has placed me exactly where I need to be."

Emily spoke again, "During the summer of 1865 there were supply train attacks by outlaws, market manipulators drove prices up, a plague of grasshoppers swarmed through completely eating all of the crops and anything else that grew, real estate prices bottomed out. Most wise people moved on. Our population declined greatly. Original town folks like the gold miners and the town's founders were most of those who left. What Denver was left with was quite a few scallywags and scoundrels. Once again, saloon brawls and lawlessness were common.

"When the first railroad came into town about seven years ago the population and businesses started to regrow quickly.

"So now, even after such a stormy path, we've been growing in leaps and bounds. We've had an influx of folks with consumption. They come here hoping to find a quick fix from our fair weather. The only thing they quickly find is that it wasn't the cure they were looking for."

"Yes, your brother mentioned that," Victoria said. "I'll tell you what I told him. Let's try to stay positive. I will do my part the best I can."

"Problem is," Emily said. "We haven't had enough doctors or hospitals. Which brings us to you. That's why we're blessed to have you here, Victoria."

"Thank you, Emily," Victoria said with a warm smile. "I can't argue that dry climate, sunshine and clean air aren't beneficial. Those things, along with exercise and a good diet do seem to make a difference. Overcrowding in the cities has fed the contagious nature of the disease. The TB disease is carried in the air from coughing and sneezing. Therefore, it is more contagious for people in crowded and unsanitary conditions. We should avoid bunching them together along with the healthy like cattle."

"It's been hard for townspeople to keep up," Emily said. "My brother is overloaded with keeping the peace. He works long days that often run into the night. Even with the deputies, there's a lot to handle."

"Tell me, Emily" what is your brother Henry's history?" Victoria sat with her back to the kitchen window. Bright sunshine beamed in illuminating her fair hair that created a halo effect.

"Very much like you, he's tough, but intelligent and kind. When our daddy died several years ago, and our mama many more before that, Henry took over the ranch. We still own it. Henry often goes up there in the morning to check on things. Since becoming Sheriff he's hired men for the daily chores and day-to-day running of the place. Sometimes he will stay up there for a day or two. One of the deputies will fetch him up if he's needed. Otherwise, he has a room above the Sheriff's office. Our family wanted him to attend Law School, and he wanted to go. He very likely would have become a good and successful solicitor. He never married. At least not yet, anyway. Says he hasn't met the right woman. Probably so."

"Interesting," Victoria said. "Speaking of ranch hands, Audax needs shoes. Do they have a farrier at your ranch?"

"Well, not at the ranch," Emily answered. "Although, there is a farrier who makes the rounds. He shoes everyone's horses here. His name is Tom Jennings. He usually can be found at the blacksmith shop or around the general store. I will track him down and chat him up directly. He's a nice man. I think he's taken a shine to me. He sure is handsome. I'm sure I can convince him to get the job done straight away." Emily blushed. "I can't believe I told you that!"

"Oh, don't be embarrassed. From what you've told me it seems like good men are hard to come by in this town," Victoria said. "Maybe it's time for you to be putting yourself out there. Marriage is a wonderful thing. You're adorable, you'll be fine. Just find the right man for the right reasons. I appreciate the help getting to know the people here and who I can depend on."

Emily said, "It's the end of the harvest season here and there's an ice cream social on the lawn of the Methodist Church on Sunday afternoon to celebrate. You should come and meet people. I'm sure there are many folks who would like to meet the new doctor in town. It will be fun. It's all free. Local business chipped in to cover the expenses."

Victoria rolled her eyes and uttered, "Methodist church?"

"Oh, please, Victoria," Emily said. "They don't bite. Please come with me and enjoy yourself."

"I'm sorry, Emily. That came out the wrong way. Of course I will join you, and of course I would like to meet people."

What caused Victoria's response was a thought that passed her mind...*the Methodists had a church, and the Catholics had to meet in a barn and didn't have the luxury of an ice cream social.* She figured, oh *well, I shouldn't judge. After all, Jesus was born in a stable and that started Christianity.*

"No apology needed, "Emily said. "Clearly you are attractive, well-kept except for the filthy riding gear, and obviously you are well-educated and well-spoken. Maybe it's time for you to be keeping an eye out for an eligible bachelor.

"Our hot weather will be ending soon, quickly followed by snow here in these higher elevations. You should think about getting a slider that could be pulled by your horse or mules. Now is the time to look around. Once the demand for sleighs goes up, the prices go up. Also, at some point you will want Mr. Jennings to put studded ice shoes on Audax. These hills can be treacherous."

"Thank you for the advice, Miss Barker. I will keep that in mind. A doctor does need to be able to travel."

It was time to go to the old post office. Victoria thanked Emily for her hospitality and warm welcome. She met Lester waiting at the door. A few moments later a completely bald-headed man with oversized muttonchops joined them.

Les said, "Dr. Victoria, please allow me to introduce the esteemed landlord of many structures in our fine little town, Mr. Phineas T. Blake." He suppressed a laugh as he said it.

"A pleasure to meet you Mr. Blake. How much will the rent be?" Victoria asked.

Blake stated a price that made Victoria gasp and Lester lean back on his heels.

"My dear Mr. Blake, You are entitled to ask for it, nevertheless, I cannot afford to pay you your price. I am only just starting my medical practice here. I charge a fair fee for those who have the money to pay. Otherwise, I always try to work something out. Perhaps you and I can work something out."

"What are you paying in rent at Miss Barker's house?" Blake asked. At that moment the sheriff joined the group. He tipped his hat towards the doctor.

"Fair question, Mr. Blake," Victoria said. "In fact, Emily is not even charging me a dime. We worked something out. Blake smirked.

"Mr. Blake, how did you get so many properties?" Victoria wanted to know.

"That's a fair question, Doctor," he answered. "In '65 when the real estate market bottomed out I was able to pick up many of them for a song. With the growing population, nobody had money to buy but they were easy to rent."

"Right now you have the surplus of one dusty old Post Office that nobody seems to want," Henry said. "You and your wife have six children. I'd say there's a good chance our doctor would be willing to barter her services for rent. Would you be willing, Doctor Vic?"

Victoria answered without hesitation, "Of course."

Blake was flustered by her sudden answer. "I suppose we could work a deal. At least for the time being."

"Alright, let's shake on it. I will provide my physician services to you, Mrs. Blake, and your children in exchange for use of this building." She extended her hand.

Blake shrugged and extended a sweaty hand. "Okay. Deal," he said. "You can move in today."

Later that day Henry, Lester and Emily, along with a couple of deputies moved Victoria's medical supplies into the post office. Bundles that One and Two carried included medicinal goods of the day that were relatively crude compared to modern medicine. Some items were hand-crafted and made from common materials. Late nineteenth-century doctors and nurses were able to provide care for their patients despite what they had to work with. Many advances in medicine occurred during this time.

Unloaded from the packs were: cloth bandages, gauze, forceps, thermometers made with mercury, syringes and hypodermic needles, scalpels and probes, sutures made from silk and catgut, ointments, plasters, stethoscopes, and ether and chloroform for anesthesia, plus bottles of aspirin, morphine, and codeine for pain. Dr. Victoria wasn't sure of what would be available in the far outskirts of Denver, so she carried what she could, and figured she could order what she needed as time went on. Deliveries by train was an option for the future.

Emily took Victoria to the General Store and the saloon where Victoria bartered for supplies she hadn't brought, such as bedding, honey, vinegar, and whiskey.

Sunday arrived cool and crisp. After Victoria attended Mass at Fr. Suarez's makeshift church she and Emily walked through the autumn air to the Methodist church for the ice cream social.

On the lawn of the church Emily said, "Victoria, please meet Mr. Tom Jennings who is our town farrier."

Jennings greeted the ladies. "Howdy, Doc LoPriesti. Good afternoon. Nice to meet you." He thrust his hand forward toward Victoria.

She noticed he had large powerful hands and forearms, the result of the physical struggles of horseshoeing. Emily had told her that there was a story about Jennings knocking out a horse that tried to kick him. It only took one punch.

"My that's quite a grip you have!" she said. "And, I must say, you pronounced my name perfectly. Please call me Dr. Vic. I'm told you stopped by and shoed my Audax yesterday, what do I owe you?"

"Aw shucks, Doc LoPriesti, it's on me. I'm just so glad we have a local doctor again. Me and some of the other fellas are always getting banged up. Sometimes it's not too serious…and sometimes it is. You don't owe me anything."

"I'm much obliged, Mr. Jennings. I will keep that in mind."

"You don't have to call me so formal-like. You can call me Tom, or what the locals call me, 'Horseshoe.'"

Emily was growing jealous. She hoped that Tom Jennings wasn't becoming keen on Victoria now. Jennings was an affable man and a colorful character. He was quick to tell a joke or a funny story. At that moment Henry Barker rode up. He had on his signature hat. Instead of his cowboy clothes, he wore his Sunday bests. Victoria displayed a warm smile at the sight of him. Sheriff Barker dismounted and mingled about the gathering shaking hands with the men and tipping his hat to the ladies. He made his way to Emily, Jennings, and Victoria.

"Hello Henry, out politicking, are you?" Emily asked.

"I reckon so," said Henry. "Elections are in a few weeks. I don't want to take anything for granted." He turned toward Victoria. "It's a pleasure to see you here, Doctor." He bowed slightly and removed his hat. "Are you out drumming up business?"

Victoria chose not to answer, however Emily did. "Nothing of the sort, Henry. From what I've seen the last few days Victoria's services are already in demand. I asked her here today strictly for social reasons. I thought a sarsaparilla and ice cream would be a nice treat."

Days turned into weeks and Victoria was busy with fixing broken bones, performing surgeries, and treating illnesses. On occasion she played the role of dentist if a tooth had to be pulled. The first snow of the season fell and was followed by a second and a third. It painted the Ponderosa Pines white. Victoria loved how elegant they looked in their snowy veils.

Tom Horseshoe Jennings arrived one morning at the doctor's office with a severe limp. "What happened?" the doctor asked.

"Dang horse stepped on my foot. Wasn't his fault though. I wasn't paying attention. Dr. Vic, I'm a darn fool."

"Don't be so hard on yourself. Let's get that boot off and see what we need to do." He grimaced as she slowly pulled the boot off. After carefully examining her newest patient she offered her opinion. "I can't tell how bad the damage is. I don't think there are any major breaks. Hmm, I imagine there are fractures, though. There's nothing we can do for fractures. Your skin is not broken. I believe your boot protected you a bit. That's good because we won't have to deal with an infection. Alright, here's the treatment. Keep it raised up as high as you can. Keep ice on it for intervals.

I will wrap it. These things will keep the swelling down. I will give you a set of crutches to use. And stay off that foot for a while."

"What do I owe you, Dr. Vic?"

"What comes around goes around. This is on me. No charge. Tom, I have a question for you... How's the horse?" She laughed as she asked the question.

"I reckon he's fine. I did manage to get all of his shoes on even with a battered foot."

"Mr. Jennings, I'm going to send Lilian to round up Sheriff Barker. I will ask him to let you stay at his ranch until you're recovered. He's got plenty of space and no stairs. I'll ask him to have his ranch hands keep an eye on you because the pain medication I'm giving you will make you dizzy. They can make sure you are following my directions and are not up and around. We'll get someone with a wagon and let you stretch out in the back. I don't want you on a horse. Please, don't be stubborn about this. I will come see you in a few days to check on you."

Lilian found the sheriff at his office. He came straight away, and his lanky frame filled Victoria's outer office doorway. "I hear you're holding Horseshoe Tom as a hostage," he said with a grin.

"No," Dr. Vic replied. "You're going to hold him hostage. Or prisoner I should say." She explained her plan to Sheriff Barker and asked him if he could get Lester to come by with a wagon and take the injured horseshoer up to the ranch.

"Well, I can do that," he said. "With one stipulation..." She waited for him to continue and sat down.

"Actually, there's two stipulations. First off, please call me Henry. We don't have to be so formal in casual company."

"What's the second issue, Henry?" she said with a concerned look.

He was slow to reply. "This Sunday afternoon at the St. Mary's Church in downtown Denver they're holding a Christmas music recital. I'd like to invite you to attend it with me. I can take you to Mass, we can go have a lunch, and then stay for the music. We can be back here by sundown."

Victoria was stunned. Not only was she surprised by the invitation, but even more so that Henry was willing to attend Catholic Mass. She stammered ever so slightly in her reply. "Well, Henry, yes, I accept. However, I have a stipulation. Actually, two...and a question."

She stood up and placed her hands on her hips. Henry was now the one who had to wait for the delivery of conditions. "Firstly, being gone all day I have to be sure that my patients are looked after."

"We can ask Lilian or Emily to keep an eye on things until you're back. It's only just one day," he replied. "What's the other, Doctor?"

"In casual company please call me Victoria. Lilian has her family to look after on a Sunday. So, I will ask Emily to be on standby. She has learned a lot from me in a truly short time."

"That's easy enough, Victoria. Thank you for accepting my invitation. Let me get ahold of Les and have him bring a wagon around and collect this sad sack and deliver him to the ranch. I will collect you at Emily's first thing Sunday morning. I will get a good wagon from the livery so you don't have to ride horseback into town. If there's snow I will rent a sleigh."

"What was the question?" he asked. Victoria removed her hands from her hips and clasped them in front of her. "Are you ever called Hank?" she wanted to know.

"Nope, never," Henry replied and added, "Is it ever Vickie?"

Victoria mimicked him... "Nope, never."

He nodded and strode out of the office feeling triumphant. Jennings hobbled behind him on crutches.

Sunday morning dawned bright, clear, and unusually warm. Henry Barker arrived at Emily's with a horse and buggy to pick up Victoria. After a spirited although uneventful ride through the Colorado countryside they arrived at St. Mary's. As promised, they attended Mass followed by lunch at a tavern up the street.

That day St. Mary's Christmas concert included songs of the season including *O Come, All Ye Faithful, Hark! The Herald Angels Sing, Silent Night, Joy to the World, O Holy Night, We Three Kings, The First Noel, Away in a Manger,* and concluded with the final chorus in *Händel's Messiah, the Hallelujah Chorus,* a triumphant and joyous celebration of the coming of Jesus Christ. All in attendance, including Henry, rose to their feet during the *Hallelujah Chorus* in *Händel's Messiah* as a sign of respect and reverence for the music and its message.

Standing during the Hallelujah Chorus is a tradition said to have started when Great Britain's King George II attended a performance of Messiah in 1743. King George stood up because he was so moved by the power of the music and its words. The audience followed suit. It is a tradition that continues to today. It is a common practice at performances of Messiah all over the world.

Henry was moved by the music as well. It dwelled on him that he was so used to dealing with unsavory people -- criminals, lawlessness and unrest

-- that he found comfort in the inner peace the music gave him. Henry deposited a donation in the poor box as they left the church.

As they arrived at their buggy Henry said, "You know, I'm thinking... I'm thinking we could build Fr. Suarez a chapel so y'all don't have to be outdoors or in a barn for Services. I can write a letter to Bishop Machebeuf and make sure it's okay. I'm sure he'll be fine with it. Afterall, he built up the congregation here in a big way. I'm sure Fr. Suarez will appreciate it, too. How would you like that, Victoria?"

"Well Henry, would you be building the chapel to please the good Fr. Suarez... or me?"

"I figured we'd be building it for the Almighty, and everyone else can enjoy the benefits."

"I see," she said. "I think it's a wonderful and beautiful idea. And, this has been a wonderful and beautiful day!" They pulled up in front of Emily's house as the sun kissed the peaks of the Rockies good night. Emily thanked Henry for the outing and bid him a good night. "I'll see you tomorrow," she said. Henry replied. "I'm looking forward to it."

Henry wrote to Bishop Machebeuf and received a timely reply and full endorsement for the chapel project. Once word got out to Fr. Suarez's small congregation things started to happen quickly. His churchgoers included men of every trade: carpenters, wood carvers, stonemasons, a glazier, roofers, landscapers and solid workmen who could do the heavy lifting. A sawmill donated lumber. That spring as the chapel was nearing completion Fr. Suarez got a message from the railroad station that there was a large crate for him with instructions to send a wagon and a couple of sturdy men.

A day later a flatbed wagon clattered into the building site. It carried the large shipping crate marked, 'For the Catholic Chapel of Fr. Suarez, Colorado.' The puzzled priest stood alongside the wagon. He hadn't ordered anything and wasn't expecting anything. He asked the workmen to get pry bars and open the crate. They went to work. Within a few minutes the top and sides were opened revealing a bronze church bell.

"Dear Lord!" the priest exclaimed. "This is a gift from heaven! Psalm 100 in the Bible encourages worshippers to 'make a joyful noise.' A bell speaks clearly no matter what language you speak. This bell will ring the news that our church is open to all who wish to be in the presence of the Lord, no matter their race, color, or creed."

Henry stood by watching. He approached Fr. Suarez and said, "The bell is indeed a gift. It came from a worldly place a little closer than heaven, though. It is a gift from Dr. LoPriesti."

"God Bless, Victoria!" Fr. Suarez shouted as he threw his hands in the air.

"Well, okay, but not quite," Henry said while suppressing a smile. "Victoria's father, Dr. Victor LoPriesti, received word from his daughter about the chapel being built and all the materials were being donated. Dr. LoPriesti had this bell sent from a foundry in St. Louis. When Dr. LoPriesti was young he saved the life of the foundry owner's son and wouldn't accept any payment for his services. The bellmaker told the doctor, 'Someday, some way, I will repay you.' So… here it is."

"I am overwhelmed with happiness. Gracias. Mucho gracias. I will write to Victoria's father today that the chapel has received the bell, and it will offer a joyful noise for all to hear and call people to worship. I will say a Mass of thanksgiving and a Mass in his honor."

Within a few weeks a chapel now stood where there was once only a tent on barren ground. In the months that followed Victoria continued to heal the sick and injured. Henry kept the peace. Lillian delivered babies, and Tom Jennings developed a flourishing business in the growing town. Emily had quickly become an indispensable nurse and assistant to Victoria.

On Christmas Eve that year Sheriff Henry Barker stood in front of the chapel beside Victoria and said, "Dr. Victoria Marie LoPriesti, will you marry me?" Without hesitation she said, "yes."

Four months later the chapel bell rang loud on their wedding day. Victoria wore a wedding dress made by Emily, Fr. Suarez performed the ceremony, Audax pulled the wedding carriage. The newlyweds decided to rebuild the old Dr. Jones house for their own home as it was closer to town and was big enough for a family.

Later that year on Christmas Day Tom 'Horseshoe' Jennings asked for Emily's hand in marriage. Emily said, "It took you long enough to ask. Yes! Of course, yes!" Tom and Emily were wed within a month. Victoria was her Maid of Honor.

Every Sunday the chapel bell rang. And it rang again four other times in future years for the Baptisms of Victoria and Henry's babies. Two boys and two girls. Emily helped Victoria through the delivery of her babies. And it rang four more times for the Baptisms of Emily and Tom's newborn babies. Three boys, one girl. Victoria was beside Emily helping deliver the new lives into the world.

The Barker and Jennings families added even more life to the bustling town. Every holiday was spent together by the two families. Christmas celebrations were always noisy and joyful. Lilian and Les were made honorary grandparents and joined in all the family gatherings.

With their children grown, and they themselves getting on in years with successful careers behind them, Henry and Victoria decided to move to the growing city of Denver. By 1900 Denver was home to almost 134,000 and was ranked as the 25th largest city in the US. It was the largest city west of the Mississippi River. Henry had always wanted to be an attorney. He read every book about law that he could find. He retired from the business of keeping the peace and began life as a Justice of the Peace, then elected to be judge. He was invited to be an adjunct law professor at the recently opened Sturm College of Law at the University of Denver. Victoria decided to teach medicine.

They turned their ranch and home over to their children and moved to a large house in the Capitol Hill district in Denver. Henry and Victoria Barker wanted a larger house to accommodate their children visiting with their spouses, and perhaps eventually grandchildren. It was bitter-sweet for Victoria to leave her thriving practice and move away. Emily had become proficient enough, and educated enough by Victoria, to take over at the clinic. Victoria promised to come by on a regular basis to check on things or to give Emily a break if needed.

Once in their new home Victoria learned about a Colorado woman, Frances Wisebart Jacobs, who was known as "Mother of Charities."

In 1843 Frances Wisebart was born in Harrodsburg, Kentucky to Jewish Bavarian immigrants who raised Frances in Cincinnati, Ohio. Frances married the business partner of her brother Jacob, Abraham Jacobs. She went to Colorado with Abraham Jacobs. Jacob Wisebart and Abraham Jacobs started businesses in Denver. There, Frances Jacobs became a motivating force for Denver's charitable organizations and activities, with national exposure. She founded many philanthropic organizations. Frances Jacobs was the mother of three and in 1880 played an influential role in setting up Denver's first free kindergarten for children of poor parents.

Victoria wondered, *"how does she find the time?"*

Victoria heard that Frances Jacobs recognized the need for a tuberculosis hospital due to Denver's large population of patients with the disease. Frances Jacobs teamed up with William Sterne Friedman, a young rabbi. Together they collected enough donations to buy land and build a hospital building on East Colfax Avenue. On October 9, 1892, the hospital's cornerstone was laid. It was an event drew that tremendous crowds. The next day the *Rocky Mountain News* reported, "The exercises yesterday were attended by several thousand people of all denominations, and the cable and electric car lines were taxed to full capacity, while the route to the site was lined with carriages."

Unfortunately, the hospital did not open. It sat vacant for six years.

In 1890 the Sherman Silver Purchase Act required the U.S. Treasury to buy 4.5 million ounces (281,250 pounds) of silver bullion each month. Ultimately, it resulted in shrinking gold reserves, which led to economic panic. A national depression occurred after the Silver Crisis caused a run on currency. Banks closed and businesses and manufacturers were unable to open because there was no cash to make payrolls or purchase materials. After the failure of two of the largest employers in the country in 1893, The Philadelphia and Reading Railroad and the National Cordage Company, the stock market plummeted as businesses that had borrowed heavily to invest in railroads went bankrupt.

After sitting finished, but unable to open for years, Rabbi Friedman approached B'nai B'rith, a national Jewish organization. He convinced the organization to raise the necessary operating funds on a yearly basis.

On its completion the hospital was going to be named the "Frances Wisebart Hospital" after its founder, except she died of pneumonia before the hospital could open. In 1899 the hospital opened two weeks before Christmas, with a new name –The National Jewish Hospital for Treatment of Consumptives. Consumption was an early name for tuberculosis. B'nai B'rith supported the Denver hospital until the early 1950s.

Victoria and Henry were at the groundbreaking festivities in '92 and she followed the progress of the hospital. Victoria had heard the words spoken at the ceremony, "… Pain knows no creed, so is this building the prototype of the grand idea of Judaism, which casts aside no stranger no matter of what race or blood. We consecrate this structure to humanity, to our suffering fellowman, regardless of creed." Along with many others, she was saddened by its delayed opening.

Judge and Doctor Barker attended the opening ceremonies in December 1899. "Henry," she said, "Although we are not Jewish, do you think they would allow me to be on their staff?" Henry answered instantly, "In spite of the name, National Jewish says they will treat anyone, including those who cannot pay regardless of race or creed. I would think they would welcome you based on your skills alone, and not on religion.

They would be foolish not to have you." Victoria thought about his words. After a moment she said, "TB is not my specialty, but there may be patients with other medical needs that I could treat. It could free up the other doctors to do what they do best. The motto for National Jewish is, 'None may enter who can pay -- none can pay who enter.' I can appreciate that. Henry, we are financially comfortable now. Life has been good for us. I wouldn't ask for a salary." Henry said, "You have my blessing. I'm sure they will work something out." He winked.

"Do you remember what Fr. Suarez said many years ago when the church bell arrived?" she asked. Henry patted his moustache with his index finger and mused, "Uh, not exactly. Remind me," he said.

"Well, Henry, Fr Suarez's words were, 'A bell speaks clearly no matter what language you speak. This bell will ring the news that our church is open to all who wish to be in the presence of the Lord, no matter their race, color, or creed.' This hospital is very much the same philosophy."

Henry said, "You've always treated people no matter their race, color, or creed, or their ability to pay. I think the Lord heard your bell and put you in the right place."

Victoria took a long pause. "I'm not asking for pay; however, I am going to ask the hospital board for something in return… a Nativity manger out in front of the hospital. After all, Jesus was born in a lowly manger, a place for animals, not a King, and certainly not for the Son of God. He was born into to a poor, humble Jewish family who probably couldn't have paid for accommodations even if there were any available. The birth of Jesus Christ is a lesson in humility. This hospital is a lesson in humility. I think it would be a welcoming sign for the Christian patients and their families as they arrive at The National Jewish Hospital. It may give them a sense of hope…and peace."

"I'm proud of you, Victoria. You set a fine example of being humble. I will help you get your wish. Merry Christmas."

"Thank you, Your Honor. A very Merry Christmas to you, too!"

The New Year welcomed the start of a new century, and a new hospital with a new doctor on its staff. The following Christmas a new Nativity manger was on display, through a donation made by Henry.

By the following year the new century ushered in many new findings in the field of medicine. In 1901 many new medical discoveries were made including:

Karl Landsteiner discovers the existence of different human blood types. This discovery made it possible to safely perform blood transfusions, which had previously been a risky procedure.

Alois Alzheimer identifies the first case of what becomes known as Alzheimer's disease. This discovery led to the study of this devastating disease.

Frederick Hopkins suggests the existence of vitamins and proposes that a lack of vitamins causes scurvy and rickets. This discovery led to the development of vitamin supplements, which have helped to prevent these diseases.

Ivan Pavlov develops the theory of the "conditional reflex". This theory has been used to understand and treat a variety of conditions, including anxiety disorders and phobias.

Georg Kelling of Dresden performs the first laparoscopic surgery. This minimally invasive procedure is now used to perform a variety of surgeries.

William Crawford Gorgas, a United States Army physician, controls the spread of yellow fever in Cuba through a mosquito eradication program. This major public health achievement helped make construction of the Panama Canal possible.

An improved sphygmomanometer, used for measuring blood pressure, is invented and popularized by Harvey Cushing. This made it possible to more accurately diagnose and treat high blood pressure.

These are only a few of the numerous medical advances that happened in 1901. These advances helped improve the lives of millions and laid the foundation for future medical discoveries. Christmas became a much more joyful time for people who endured the illnesses addressed by these developments.

Doctor Victoria was delighted to hear about all of them.

When National Jewish Hospital opened it had a capacity of 60 patients and an eventual goal of treating 150 patients a year.

The rate of Tuberculosis in Denver started declining in the early 1900s due to the developments of science and medicine that included new treatments such as antibiotics. By the 1950s, TB was no longer a major public health problem in Denver.

Story Notes - Although Victoria, Henry, Emily and Tom, Lester, Lilian and Fr. Suarez are all fictious composite characters based on how people lived back in the day, everyone else had a true history.

Colorado's state capitol building has sixteen stained-glass windows in the dome. Each one celebrates a pioneer who played an important impact on Colorado's development. There is only one woman depicted, Frances Wisebart Jacobs. Of all the organizations she help start the most well-known among them were the United Way and the Denver's Jewish Hospital Association.

The time and place of this story, Denver, Colorado circa 1876, was inspired by Dr. Ashley Boccio-Hogan, a mother of four and a gifted Long Island, NY doctor and surgeon. Dr. Ashley Boccio-Hogan followed in the footsteps of her father, Dr. Richard Boccio. After retiring from private practice, Dr. Richard Boccio went on to serve American Veterans at the Veterans Administration Hospital. Dr. Ashley followed his footsteps there as well.

I lost both of my maternal great grandparents to tuberculosis in the late nineteenth century, which resulted in my grandmother, Mary Dooley, being orphaned at age seven. Mary Dooley loved Christmas. My paternal great grandfather was a nineteenth century farrier in Ireland. Family legend says that John Gahan, a powerful barrel-chested man, knocked out a horse that tried to kick him. It only took one punch.

FOURTEEN

Brooklyn, New York

With the crash of the New York stock market in 1929 the Roaring Twenties came to a screeching halt. It was an epic economic downturn of the American economy. By 1930 with the Great Depression well into its second year, many in New York, and even more across the country, were struggling to feed their families and keep a roof over their head…Although times were tough, for some, Christmas in New York City in 1930 was a time to celebrate.

Jacob Debus was born in 1889 and quickly grew into adulthood. He went to school, became a draftsman, and went to work at the Ridgewood Iron Works on DeKalb Street in Brooklyn. At age 24 he married Mary "Mamie" Dooley, a girl from his Bushwick Brooklyn neighborhood who was introduced by a mutual friend. His career as a draftsman blossomed. Jake was a genial young man. Tall and slim with brown hair and blue eyes he was well-liked by his coworkers and the workmen that he interacted with in the building trades. He continued to learn, quickly moved up the ranks by becoming an architect, and was effective in his craft.

Mary "Mamie" Isabella Dooley, the child of Irish immigrant parents, Joe Dooley and Sarah (nee Kane) Dooley, was orphaned by age seven or eight. She was never sure of her age. Her birth year could have been anywhere from 1891 to 1894. When she married Jacob Debus her age on the marriage certificate was listed as 21, although she may have been as young as nineteen. After living as an orphan at a convent for a few years with her brother Jimmy, she was taken in by her aunt and uncle, Bella and Otto Johanns.

Bella was a member of Mamie's maternal grandparent's family who immigrated to America from Ireland in 1861. Her grandfather Edward was from the Kane clan and was a skilled machinist, her grandmother was from the Burkes family. They were strong people who survived Ireland's Great Famine. Together they had nine children.

Aunt Bella was only 17 years older than Mamie. She married Otto only a year before Mamie came to live with them. Bella's Irish-born mother instilled all the Irish customs and traditions on her family. Bella knew them well and passed them on to Mamie.

Mamie was happy to move to the Johanns stunning home at 529 Gates Avenue, Bushwick Brooklyn, NY. It was a two-bedroom apartment equal in size to two apartments combined, with high ceilings, two fireplaces, hardwood floors, a study, dining room, and a living room. Bella, who had eight brothers and sisters, was used to sharing space.

Bushwick Brooklyn has an interesting history. The Canarsie Indians sold the land in 1638. Settled by the Dutch, Peter Stuyvesant, governor of New Amsterdam, chartered the land in 1660 and gave the name "Boswyck," meaning refuge or town in the woods, to the area in 1664. Although the English toppled the Dutch administration of the colony and renamed New Netherlands to New York, the Dutch settlers developed Bushwick along with most of Brooklyn. In the Dutch language Brooklyn was originally called "Breuckelen," which translates to, "Broken Land."

Among the earliest settlers along with the Dutch were French, Scandinavian and English from Plymouth Colony. They all farmed the land for the next 200 years growing tobacco and food for their own consumption and for the bustling New York markets. There were community owned woodlands used for animal grazing and cutting firewood.

The Dutch dominated the culture, and it was the common language until the 19th century. School children were taught classes in Dutch and English from 1758 until 1800 when English became the exclusive language. Bushwick stayed rural and agricultural until the early 1850s. The quiet Town of Bushwick merged with the City of Brooklyn in 1855. Land was plentiful and homes were built to accommodate a populace that grew rapidly from the influx of new immigrants. Industry began to boom in Brooklyn and a workforce was needed for businesses that included shipping, ship building, ironworks, the manufacture of clothing and pottery, along with printing. Scores of businesses thrived along the Brooklyn waterfront.

During the mid-19th century more than a million immigrants from Germany and Austria settled in northern Brooklyn. The Germans and Austrians created breweries, beer halls and restaurants to boost beer sales, and they organized singing societies and hosted singing festivals. They built many Catholic and Lutheran churches. By 1880 almost a dozen breweries existed in the Bushwick and Williamsburg sections of Brooklyn, by 1904 there were 44.

Brooklyn's rapid development had already begun before the start of the 20th century. Most noteworthy was the completion of the Brooklyn Bridge in 1883, which for the first time connected Brooklyn, and all of rural Long Island, to the island of Manhattan. Later electrified streetcars carried people from Bushwick to Manhattan via the Brooklyn Bridge. In 1905 the Williamsburg Bridge started carrying trolleys to lower New York City connecting riders to subways. On October 27, 1904, the New York Transit Authority began subway service from City Hall to 145th Street. The line ran a total of 9.1 miles from City Hall in lower Manhattan to 145th Street and Broadway in Harlem. It featured 28 stops, including stops at Times Square and Grand Central Terminal. By 1908 the subways were complete, making connections from a booming Brooklyn to Manhattan and all of New York.

The Bushwick section became the second largest American community in Brooklyn for a while. In addition to the growth of long-time Brooklyn families, development continued from the inflow of immigrants from Germany, Austria, Ireland, Italy, Russia, Poland, and Jews from Europe and elsewhere. Many two to six family homes were built throughout the area. Mansions built between 1880 and 1913 for brewers and doctors lined Bushwick Avenue. Well-known architects designed the Bushwick homes following desirable Neo Greco, Italianate, Revival, Romanesque, and

Queen Anne architectural styles. Meanwhile, the Irving Avenue area was developed between 1900 and 1913. In 1913 Bushwick High School opened its doors at 400 Irving Avenue and had as students, financier, entrepreneur and art collector Joseph Hirshorn and Irving Thalberg, an American film producer during the evolving years of early motion pictures. Hollywood called Thalberg "The Boy Wonder" based on his youth, ability to choose scripts and actors, produce an effective staff, and make moneymaking box office hit movies.

During the period between WWI and WWII was the time of Bushwick's greatest prosperity. Streets and sidewalks were spotless. Homes were meticulously kept. It became a renowned entertainment district and hosted the Bushwick Theater at 1396 Broadway between Palmetto and Woodbine Streets. Following The Palace in New York City it was the second most important vaudeville venue. It was less than a mile and half from Bella and Otto Johann's home where Mamie Dooley grew up. Her brother, Jimmy Dooley, found work on the vaudeville stage as a performer during the days of the Great Depression. Those were the glory days of Bushwick and other parts of Brooklyn that sadly fell into decline decades later.

Jake's career flourished. The building boom and the need to feed a houseful of kids drove his success. By 1930 Jake and Mamie had six children, one boy and six girls including Dolores who was born that year. Their house was always bustling and full of music. Jake had added a Victrola record player to their parlor along with a 1912 Bush and Lane player piano that was operated by foot pump pedals. Family attendance at Saturday night sing-alongs was mandatory. Christmas was always a grand time in the Debus household.

Jake loved to cook and would often make "Frikadellen" for the family. Not to be confused with American hamburgers, Frikadellen are a traditional German dish. An American hamburger usually only has ground beef and not much else, aside from a slice of cheese to make it a cheeseburger. A Frikadellen recipe calls for: ground beef and pork, bread, sautéed onions, herbs and spices, and an egg to bind the ingredients together. Jake also loved music, and he loved to dance. He would come home on a Friday evening after work and say to Mamie, "Let's go out dancing tonight!" Mamie would roll her eyes and say to Jake, "Jake, I'm exhausted. I've been taking care of our family all week... but okay." She would grab her hat and away they would go. He and Mamie would take trips out on Sunrise Highway into Nassau County, Long Island, to dance halls that were popular at the time.

During the 1920's they would take their children into Manhattan during the holidays to marvel at the Macy's Thanksgiving Day Parade, which was first held in 1920. By the mid-1930's the family holiday tradition also included seeing the lighting of the enormous Christmas tree at Rockefeller Center in New York City. Christmas displays in department store windows, such as Macy's, Best & Company, and Saks Fifth Avenue, were elaborate Christmas exhibits. Each store's displays regularly featured animated figures, music, and lights. Jake, Mamie and the children visited all of them. Mamie started another family Christmas custom. After Christmas Eve dinner, and long before Midnight Mass, everyone in the family would be gathered in the parlor with stockings hung on the mantle. Each child had to read a poem or short story about Christmas. When they were finished, Jake would read Matthew 1: 18-25 and Luke 2: 1-20. Then, they would all gather around the player piano and sing Christmas carols until it was time to leave for church.

It was the parents' custom to set up their own Christmas tree in the parlor on Christmas Eve after Midnight Mass and the children were asleep. It was to follow the legend of St. Nicholas who brings a decorated tree along with filling the stockings with gifts on the night before Christmas. As the children got older, the tree decorating got later and later. In earlier years their tree was illuminated by candles. "These symbolize Jesus Christ, as the Light of the World," Mamie would say. The candles were held to the branches with small clip-on candle holders. The older children, Edwin and Marie, had to take turns standing guard with a bucket of water in the event of a fire. By the 1930s electric Christmas lights became readily available.

Jake had been enjoying his work as site architect on the Hotel Piere at 2 East 61st Street at the intersection of Fifth Avenue, New York City with a magnificent view of Central Park. Construction had begun in the late 1920s. It was designed by the New York firm of Schultze and Weaver as a 41-story skyscraper with neo-Georgian accents that rises in a blond-brick column from a limestone-fronted Louis XVI base. It boasted 714 rooms, a 3-story copper-plated mansard roof, checkered marble floors, a fantastic ballroom with a grand staircase, and a Rotunda featuring hand-painted murals by Edward Melcarth, an American artist. The cost to construct The Pierre in the late 1920s was $15 million, more than approximately $200 million in today's money.

In late December 1929 Jake was summoned to the offices of the hotel's owners. They didn't say why. He decided to get a shoeshine to look his best. He sat and wondered as his shoes were being polished. He felt he had been doing a good job. There were no labor issues on the job, he had the flow of materials coming in on time, and there were no mistakes in the construction, he made sure to interpret the blueprints for the ironworkers so they clearly understood what needed to be done. He mused... actually... *I think we're ahead of schedule.* Again, he wondered what the owners wanted to see him about. He tipped the shoeshine boy double and wished him a Merry Christmas.

"Please sit down, Sir," they said. Jake sat straight-backed at the conference table. "The partners are so pleased with the speed and efficiency of the hotel's construction," one of them said. "We wanted to give you a Christmas gift as a token of our appreciation of our thanks for all that you have done on the job. And, you have managed to do so with a smile and good will." They presented Jake with an intricately carved side table with a polished marble top and made in Belgium imprinted on the bottom. "Oh, and this," another man said as he handed an envelope to Jake, "is a more comprehensive token of appreciation that I'm sure your family will enjoy for the holidays. On top of that, whatever you may decide to do in the future, I insist that you please list us as a reference. Our board has many of the most powerful men in New York." Jake was overwhelmed and shook their hands vigorously. An office staffer carried the table to his car. Jake Debus smiled all the way home.

Mamie met her husband at the front door when he arrived home. "Wait right there," he said. Jake went to the car and retrieved the ornate table. "Mamie, look what the hotel owners gave us for Christmas!"

"Oh my, it's beautiful!" she replied. "I'm so proud of you. I will keep it beside my chair in the parlor forever!" She hugged him.

"But hold on a minute, they also gave me this..." Jake had already seen the check and knew its amount. He held the envelope to Mamie with both hands. She opened the envelope. Her eyes widened.

"I don't know what to say, "she said. "That's quite a bonus!"

"Yes, isn't that the bee's knees? Let's just say Merry Christmas and celebrate with the kids tonight," he said. "Better, yet," he added. "Let's load the kids into the Packard tomorrow and take a ride out on Long Island after church. We'll find a nice restaurant and all enjoy this bonus together."

With the hotel construction completed, Jake's work at The Piere was finished there. But there were more projects to come for him in the future that would also become famous.

An incredible, lavish grand-opening was held at The Pierre in October 1930. Jake and Mamie were invited, they attended and danced in the grand ballroom.

Throughout the years The Pierre would be host to royalty, Hollywood elites, sports stars, US Presidents, and business leaders. Its guests have included Queen Elizabeth II, Grace Kelly, Jackie Kennedy Onassis, Frank Sinatra, Warren Buffett, and many other dignitaries.

Jake rolled up the blueprints and tucked them under his arm and headed out the door. He gave all his kids a hug as he told them he would see them at dinner. A drab olive-green US Army staff car was waiting in front of the house at 219-01 133rd Ave, Queens, NY. It was driven by a young corporal. "Good morning, Corporal," Jake said. "I trust you had a good weekend?"

"Indeed, Sir. I'm ordered to take you to Flushing Meadows, again today." The driver opened the rear door for him.

"Correct, Corporal. Let's see what the progress is. Things have been moving along quite well."

The Great Depression was at its peak. America was reeling. One in four Americans lost their jobs, and millions lost their homes, wages were cut, and many went hungry. Jake and Mamie were thankful that Jake was taken on by the US Corps of Army Engineers for projects around New York City. They wondered if one of the board members from the hotel had put in a word for him. Then again, Jake could stand on his own merits.

President Franklin D. Roosevelt enacted The New Deal, which was a series of programs -- public works projects, financial reforms, and regulations enacted by in the United States between 1933 and 1939. One of those projects was converting what was an ash-dump in Flushing, Queens New York into a world-class venue for the World's Fair scheduled to open in April 1939. It was conceived by a group of New York businessmen who figured that a huge international exhibit would help pull New York, and all of America, out of the financial wreckage of the depression. It would create jobs and give business to building materials suppliers. New York City Mayor Fiorello LaGuardia was on the committee. Permits and plans were approved quickly. Work began in 1935 at the 1,216-acre site. "Building the World of Tomorrow" was the New York World's Fair theme. A futuristic theme rose like the mythological

Phoenix from the ashes from the surrounding swampland. Among the exhibits constructed by the US Army Corps of Engineers were the iconic Trylon, Perisphere, and the New York State Pavilion. Jake was there to help build the "World of Tomorrow." He was excited about his assignment to help with the design plans and oversee the construction of New York City Pavilion. Although it seemed a smaller project than some of the others, he was thrilled to have the work, given the state of the economy, and that he was a native of and educated in New York City's Brooklyn borough. His boyhood home was a mere 10 miles away and his current address was only a 15-mile commute to the Queens job site. And, with the arrival of their seventh child, Ann, who was born in August of '32, he had a big family to feed.

Although the World's Fair followed an ultramodern theme, the New York City Pavilion's architect, Aymer Embury III, (who was one of the favorite designers of renowned visionary Robert Moses) decided on a modern classical style. It had vast expanses of glass brick fronted by colonnades with limestone pilasters trimmed with dark polished granite, and solid limestone corner blocks. It didn't matter to Jake. Whatever the plan was, he would work to make it happen on time and under budget. He figured the future was going to happen no matter what the New York City Pavilion looked like. It was located directly beside two of the great icons of the Fair, the Trylon and Perisphere. It was one of the few buildings created for the Fair built to be a permanent structure. Knowing that, he also figured that future New Yorkers should have a glimpse of classical design from the past.

Sadly, Jacob John Matthew Debus went to heaven on February 18th, 1939, two months before the World's Fair opened on Sunday, April 30, 1939.

Years after the Fair closed, Jake's beloved Pavilion was used as the temporary headquarters for the United Nations General Assembly from 1946 until 1951 when the UN moved to its permanent, current location in New York City. The '39 World's Fair New York City Pavilion nobly served again in the same role in the 1964 World's Fair in Flushing Meadows, but now featured a Panorama model of the City of New York. Measuring 9,335-square-feet (867.2 m2) and commissioned by Robert Moses as a celebration of the City's municipal infrastructure, it included every single building constructed in all five boroughs of New York. Built at a scale of 1 inch equaling 100 feet, the huge model of the entire city was built by a team of 100 people. The magnificent Panorama remains to this day and receives occasional updates.

You can still see the New York City Pavilion building today from the Grand Central Parkway, just before LaGuardia airport, and it sits aside the Arthur Ashe Stadium, a tennis arena in Flushing Meadows – Corona Park in Queens. The almost 100-year-old historic Pavilion housed the *Queens Center for Art and Culture,* which was later renamed the Queens Museum of Art, and is now called the Queens Museum.

Mamie, now the widowed mother of seven, ranging in age from seven to 19, kept her family together and hop-scotched to different rental addresses around Queens over the years until her children were grown, married, and moved out. Living through the end-years of The Great Depression and during the rationing of World War II as a single mother and widow was not easy. But, being rich in family, she felt wealthy. Edwin, the oldest, left the seminary and became extremely successful in business. All the daughters married respectable men who were successful in their own careers. Marie married an artist who excelled in fine art and commercial art with a firm on Madison Avenue. Jane married Harry, a chemical engineer who served in the US Army and landed at Normandy on D-Day. Agnes, called "Jimmy" by her siblings, married Charles "Chaz", a textile executive from North Carolina. He served in World War II in the Navy. They married in St Patrick's Cathedral in New York City. Eileen married Jim, an executive in the mining equipment industry. Dolores, who became a Registered Nurse, married a NY City firefighter, with a law degree. Ann worked at NBC – TV Corporate and married Jack, an electrical engineer, who was a key person with NBC Sports and NBC studios. In all, Mamie had 23 grandchildren. They all continued the family traditions of the holidays... especially at Christmas.

Mary "Mamie" Dooley Debus kept her promise. The marble-topped, exquisitely carved table given to Jake so many Christmases before sat beside her chair at all the addresses her family lived at and for all Christmas celebrations. She had it until her final days. The table is still in the family. It was given to her grandson... who wrote this book. It sits in my home to this day.

FIFTEEN

Austin, Texas

Will's carriage clattered up to the curb. "Lohta, let me drop you off here to avoid the mud," Will said. "I'll circle back here in an hour to pick you up." "No, no," Lohta replied. "Please meet me up on the corner of Congress Avenue. I have another stop to make at the Driskill Hotel."

Will raised his eyebrows and glanced towards Lohta. "The Driskill?" questioned Will. "What are you doing at that fancy place?" Will was jealous.

The couple wasn't far from their home at 308 East Cedar Street, but as Lohta had been ill, Will insisted on taking her. Lohta had told him, "Will, getting ready for Christmas is of utmost importance no matter how I feel." He would have taken her by carriage in any event.

"I'm meeting the spinster dress shop owners Mary Hatch and Violet Bick there for tea. They are treating me."

A stunning 13-story Victorian masterpiece, the Driskill was the finest of fine hotels. Its red brickwork was accented by arched windows and intricate, carved cornices and corbels. Impressive balconies decked in wrought iron railings enhanced with floral and geometric patterns graced its exterior. A Grand lobby with marble floors, Texas-theme stained glass windows, and elaborate chandeliers led the way to an impressive Texas limestone staircase to the second floor.

Lohta made extra money through dressmaking and giving music lessons in their home. "Yes, Will. They want to place orders for quite a few new dress styles to appeal to some of the new, affluent women moving into Austin. You know, the wives of ranchers, and politicians over at the Capitol, and of course, wives of professors and administrators at the university."

During 1883 the University of Texas at Austin started and began to draw faculty, staff, and students to the city.

Construction of the Texas State Capitol began in 1885 when it had its cornerstone laid on March 2 and attracted construction workers to Austin. By September 1888 the Capitol building was completed and received its first government employees. The expansion of the railroads within Texas made it easier for people and goods to move in and out of Austin. Moreover, the largest driving force for growth in Texas was the discovery of oil there in 1894. By 1895 Austin was a good place to be. Austin was booming. Although, the population was only a bit shy of 15,000 in 1895. Will and Lohta didn't work at either the university or the State Capitol Building, and they did not rely on the railroads, and certainly didn't share in the gush of wealth created by the oil industry. They were just ordinary folks.

As a teenager Will worked in his uncle's drug store as a pharmacist's apprentice. He did well at it, but his thoughts of adventure and the Wild West pulled him away from his hometown back east back in North Carolina. His family had friends in South Texas who owned the Diamond Hoof Ranch, and he went there as a teen to try something new. Will grew tired of working as a ranch hand. Long days under the hot Texan sun herding sheep and cattle didn't align with his yearning for something more intellectual. He read every and any book he could lay his hands on, including the dictionary, which he read from cover to cover.

Will and Lohta met in Austin in 1885 at the cornerstone laying of the State Capitol building. Lohta was her class valedictorian and was asked to give a speech at the ceremony. Will was smitten instantly with her. Lohta was only 17. He was 25. Her father was furious and disapproved of their relationship, so the young couple decided to elope in 1887. After giving up and throwing in the towel for herding sheep and cattle he moved into Austin and was able to get a job at the land office as a draftsman drawing maps. Will worked his way up to chief clerk of the Spanish Archives. He oversaw documents related to land grants from the Spanish colonial era. His boss, the land commissioner, lost his politically appointed job after an election rearranged his, and therefore, Will's career. Will was well liked at the land office. He was quick with a joke or a fictional story, generous with compliments and thrifty with criticism. He took it upon himself to add drawings and sketches in the margins of the maps and was a good storyteller. After leaving the land office, he got a job as a bank clerk. First as a teller, then juggled the teller position along with being appointed the bank's accountant by the bank manager. Will had a little accounting experience from working at his uncle's pharmacy, although he was far from being an accountant.

"Take your time," Will said to Lohta. "I want to stop by the bank and see if I can figure out some of the mismatches in the balance sheet. You'll have plenty of time to get ready for Christmas, I hope Mary and Violet don't inundate you with too much work."

"Well, Will, I hope they do. We could use the extra money for some new furniture. I hope you can find the discrepancies in the ledgers, Will. I know how hard you work at it and how frustrated you are. "Will helped her down from the carriage in the light autumn drizzle, climbed back up to the buckboard and flicked the reigns.

Will knew what the basis was for many of the problems at the bank. It was primarily owned by wealthy ranchers who borrowed or lent money on a handshake. All honorable, but most times transactions were not written down. Sometimes the loans got paid back…and sometimes they did not. There was no way to be sure what the agreements or the amounts were. Will would tell anyone who listened that numbers were not his main interest. He was a word guy and considered himself a man of letters. He would write short stories, and once in a while a poem, and give them out to friends. Will sent a few manuscripts off to a newspaper in Houston. They paid him a small amount for his work they used. He considered himself lucky. In his heart he wanted to be an author. He had told Lohta, "That scoundrel Charles Dickens is tearing it up in London, and around the world for that matter. That piece he wrote about Christmas, A Christmas Carol, was an instant bestseller. And it still is. I want to do that."

Will pulled the hack up in front of the bank at 300 North Main Street, the corner of Main and 2nd Ave NE, just north of the courthouse square, and tethered the horse to a post. He swung the front door open, and his good mood changed quickly when he saw the heated confrontation in front of the bank manager's office.

The bank was typical of most banks in America at the time, which reflected wealth, power, and stability. Austin was growing rapidly, and the bank's investors decided they had to play the part of providing a bank that matched the latest Victorian architectural trends. It was built of brick and stone for a reason. The original bank built in 1868 burned to the ground. They wanted to extend a feeling of security to their depositors, and a sense of longevity to their borrowers. There were the usual vaulted ceilings and high windows, a marble floor, teller's cages with brass bars and heavy furniture. It certainly was fireproof, but what went on inside was not foolproof.

Mr. Mortimer Welch the bank manager and wealthy rancher, key bank investor, and a bank board member Henry Rettop, were engaged in a loud argument. It seemed neither disagreed with the other, and neither was accepting any blame for the root of the argument. Money was missing.

Will did not like Mr. Welch. He was shrill and could be mean. Mr. Rettop was mammoth of a man who was always loud, and let his feelings be known in a deep drawl. Rettop was beyond cheap. He was as miserly as Scrooge.

Rettop was a bully and told people what they were going to do, whether it was or wasn't the right thing to do. Mr. Welch usually did what Rettop told him to do, although most often with resentment. "Just exactly how much is missing," he yelled at Mr. Welch. "It's hard to say, Mr. Rettop. Some loans and their repayments were never entered in the ledger."

Rettop fumed, "Alright then, what is your best educated banker's guess?"

Mr. Welch recoiled with his back against the office door, which popped open inward from his weight, startling him. "You dang fool," Rettop continued and grabbed Mr. Welch by his long, four-in-hand-knot necktie. "Stand there like a man and answer my question!"

"We believe the discrepancy is about 1,000 dollars (Almost $40,000 in today's money)." Mr. Welch gulped.

Rettop snarled at the bank manager. "That's Grand Larceny. You get to the bottom of this, contact the police, and find out who did it. Start with that story-telling bank accountant, you know, Will Porter."

They hadn't noticed Will by the lobby door. He slipped out quietly. He wondered if Divine Provenance put him at the bank on his day off to hear the exchange between Welch and Rettop. Will knew he hadn't done anything wrong. If he found a discrepancy, he reported it to Mr. Welch. All a bank teller had to do was incorrectly write the wrong amount on a deposit or withdrawal slip for an error to occur on the books. Welch always told him, "Don't worry about it for now, Porter, and stop complaining. These things sort themselves out within the month."

On his way to his hack Will passed Mr. Harry Partridge. Mr. Partridge, like Henry Rettop, was a successful and wealthy rancher, He owned the Diamond Hoof Ranch where Will worked for a short time. Partridge was also on the banks' Board of Directors. Will liked Mr. Partridge. Unlike Rettop, Harry Partridge was jovial, kind, fair, and generous. When Will told Mr. Partridge he was leaving the ranch and moving to Austin, Partridge gave Will his blessing and a gift of some extra money on top of his pay to start over. "Hello, Mr. Partridge," Will said and tipped his hat. "Mr. Welch is tied up with Mr. Rettop in there. They seemed rather involved, and extremely upset, so I didn't want to bother Mr. Welch at the moment." "Oh, that miserable old rattlesnake Rettop. Let me get in there and straighten him out," Partridge said. "Will, I hope I get to see you and your lovely wife during the holidays. Matter of fact, I'll see to it that it happens."

Will picked up Lohta at the corner of Congress Avenue and West 6th Street at the agreed time. She was ecstatic. "My word!" she exclaimed. "The ladies have given me so much work. How will we ever get ready for Christmas for ourselves? I will be sewing right up until Christmas Eve."

Will pondered her comment. Austin was host to a variety of cultures, mostly consisting of German and Mexican immigrants and African Americans. And of course, there was always the cowboy culture. Depending on where you were in Austin during the Christmas season determined your holiday experience. He figured that he and his wife would work something out to celebrate Christmas.

During the mid-19th century scores of Germans had immigrated to Texas. They brought their Christmas traditions from the old country along with them to America. Most notable was the Christmas tree. Christmas trees were not common across the United States during that time, which made the Tannenbaum a special Texan Christmas tradition. German's trees were decorated with unique homemade Christmas ornaments that also included strings of popcorn and candles.

Christmas ornaments were hard to find, and if you could find them, they were expensive. Handmade and homemade ornaments and decorations came from pinecones, dried fruits, feathers, and ribbons. Gifts were also handcrafted. Women knitted items and sewed quilts. Wooden toys were hand carved. Home baked pies, cakes, and cookies along with jams and jellies were appreciated gifts.

The Mexican immigrants celebrated Christmas with the most flair compared to other ethnicities. During the 1890s Mexicans in Texas celebrated Christmas with a combination of festive traditions from their home country that were styled to fit Texan lifestyles.

During the nine days before Christmas Las Posadas (The Inns) were held. It is a key tradition with a nine-day long procession that reenacts the search by Joseph and Mary for a place to stay while Mary gave birth to Jesus. Each evening people would join together to sing carols and finish with a cheerful Posada with prayers, more music, and plenty of food.

Church attendance on Christmas Eve and Christmas Day was considered mandatory. Everyone wore their finest clothes to offer prayers to bless the New Year. Craftsmen made detailed and elaborate nativity scenes from local materials for the churches.

Posadas and Christmas Eve events were open to all, and everyone was invited. It created a greater sense of community, shared joyful traditions, and started new ones.

For the celebrations, festive Mexican food included a staple dish, Tamales. Made with corn masa and filled with a variety of ingredients, they graced the Christmas meal table. Recipes were shared between neighbors and handed down to the younger generations. Some dishes included local Texas elements like pecans or prickly pear cactus giving the dishes a Texan character.

A traditional festive punch called 'Ponche Navideño, was prepared for Christmas Holidays. Water, fresh and dried fruits along with tamarind, prunes, hibiscus, sugar cane, cinnamon, and piloncillo, a Mexican brown sugar are combined to make the punch, then tequila or rum was added. It kept the parties lively.

Sweet, crispy Buñuelos pastries sprinkled with cinnamon sugar were a common addition to the feast. Family and guests were served Buñuelos along with atole, a warm corn-based beverage or hot chocolate.

For holiday entertainment there were always Christmas carols, called Villancicos. Families sang them and the sounds filled their homes and spilled out into the streets. They were also sung during Christmas processions and gatherings by larger groups. Some local communities blended a religious theme with upbeat music and dance and put on a play titled Los Pastores. (The Shepherdesses). It is a traditional play that explains the shepherds' journey to Bethlehem.

To add even more excitement to the celebrations, traditional dances of different regions took place. Depending on where you immigrated from might determine the dances you did. It could be the jarabe tapatío (Mexican hat dance) or the baile folklórico (regional folk dance) that might be performed around Austin.

Cowboy influences created diverse ways to celebrate Christmas. Cowboy celebrations included elements like singing around campfires, telling stories and tall tales under the stars, or even cowboy carols with Western themes. With warm temperatures in December celebrating often took place outdoors. Envision Christmas carols sung under a clear, star-filled night sky, with the aroma of roasted pecans and mesquite smoke in the air.

For cowboys on ranches, Christmas may have included a hearty meal from the cattle they raised of barbecued meat and Dutch oven stew. Some cowboys would even hold mock rodeos or shooting contests, adding a bit of cowboy life to Christmas.

Will often thought about his early days on the Diamond Hoof Ranch and the colorful characters he met there. They influenced his stories. Will had a lot to work with when he developed the roles for his short stories. There were: the days in North Carolina until he was 19, his cowboy years of herding cattle and shepherding sheep, his work at the Land Office, and now the bank that helped him build caricatures in words. He tucked all those memories in the back of his mind and later spilled them onto paper through the tip of his pencil.

Will turned to Lohta as she settled in on the bench beside him. "That is all wonderful news. You got all those dressmaking orders. I'm so proud of you!" He put his arm around her. Will was hesitant to tell Lohta what he overheard at the bank. He took a deep breath, let out a sigh and unraveled the whole story.

"Dear God!" she exclaimed. "You of all people. Will, you are the most honest man in town. Besides that, Mr. Welch put you in that position to save money. He knew full-well you didn't have bank accounting experience. And… one more thing. Anyone can make a mistake, including Mr. Welch and Mr. Rettop. As you have pointed out repeatedly there have been shenanigans going on there for years. How dare they!"

"When I go to work tomorrow, I'll be ready to hear what they have to say and why I'm a suspect. They don't know that I know."

Will arrived at the bank early to check the ledgers to see if any recent changes had been entered. He was satisfied there were no new postings, and that he had done all the entries. In the following moment Mr. Welch stepped up to Will's desk with a police officer, and another man he didn't know alongside.

Mr. Welch cleared his throat and began, "Will, as you are well aware, the last couple of years there's been a severe drought and financial panic. Texas folks have faced an economic recession during this time. You see, it has affected many in Austin and around Texas. As you might imagine, it has created financial hardships for a lot of folks. Maybe for you and your wife, too? I hear tell she was at the Driskill doing business. That's a mighty extravagant place for regular folks. Rather expensive for a dressmaker, wouldn't you agree? You know how it is, these hard times can play a curious role in influencing politics and social developments, as well as business. Like here at the bank."

"What's your point, Mr. Welch?" Will asked.

Welch replied. "My point is…the bank's accounts are short. Wouldn't you agree that you are the only person making entries to the ledger?"

"Now hold on just a minute, Mr. Welch," Will blurted. "You can't possibly be accusing me of theft? That's preposterous!"

Welch peered over his spectacles. "I'm sorry, young man. If you cannot explain it, no one else can. You were in charge of all of the accounting."

"That may be so, Mr. Welch. But, I'm not your man. Every time I found an error in the books I reported it to you," Will fumed.

"Every time, hmm?" Mr. Welch smirked.

"I've been told to have the police handle this matter. If you can't come up with a verifiable explanation, there will be a warrant issued for your arrest. This is Officer Muldoon and Mr. Crowley from the District Attorney's office." Will recognized Clark from his time working at the Land Office. Crowley tried to bribe Will to change some documents, but Will wouldn't have any of it.

"How do you do, Mr. Porter…" Mr. Crowley said.

"I was doing just fine until a minute ago." Will said.

"There will be a thorough investigation by the Police Department and my office."

"Is that so? Well, I certainly hope you investigate everyone. And, you have a lot of nerve trying to involve my wife in all of this," Will stammered. Mortimer Welch glared at him.

"I would advise you to get an attorney. You will need one," Crowley said.

"Mr. Will Porter, you are permanently dismissed from this bank. Please leave immediately and do not step foot in here again," Welch ordered.

Will was devastated. He went directly home and told Lohta what happened. "This is absolutely ridiculous," she said. "Will there's no way you are guilty. I believe in you. Being wrongfully accused is a terrible thing. I just finished a dress for Mrs. Goodfellow. Her husband Clarence is a lawyer. I'm told he is an understanding and successful attorney. We should go see him."

"Lohta, we don't have the money for someone like that." Will shrugged.

"We should at least go talk to him and see what he thinks. I don't think there's any charge for that."

Will conceded and that afternoon they went to Clarence Goodfellow's office. "That's a mighty fine dress you made for Mrs. Goodfellow," the lawyer said. "My wife said she would have paid double for your workmanship alone."

"I charge what I think is a fair price, Mr. Goodfellow. It's what keeps the ladies coming back. I'm glad your wife was pleased," Lohta said.

"Well, the price is one thing, but your charm adds to the value," he said. "What can I help you with today? I don't know what might bring a fine young couple like yourselves to my office. Don't worry it's all strictly confidential."

Will unraveled the whole story. "I see," said Goodfellow as he furrowed his brows. "Will, I'm sure you understand that you are up against some powerful, contentious men. Since they offer no proof of a crime other than the money is missing, it's your word against theirs. It will be up to me to establish motive and opportunity. The police and Crowley will try to prove a case against you based on the same things. There may be multiple guilty parties. I will work to prove you're not one of them. You and Lohta live modestly, you haven't made any large purchases lately, and you don't have any hidden assets, correct?" Both Will and Lohta nodded in unison. "If I am representing you, the district attorney is required to share any evidence they have with me."

"Hold on a minute," Will said. "How much are your services going to cost?"

Goodfellow chuckled. "For right now, Will, pay me one dollar and you have legally retained me as your attorney." Lohta's hand covered her mouth as she tried to suppress her surprise. "As for you, Mrs. Porter…just keep on making my wife happy. On another note…I never liked Mr. Mortimer Welch one bit. And, Lohta, your father is an old friend of mine. This will be fun." He rubbed his hands together.

"I don't want my husband's good name, or reputation, dragged through the Texas mud, Mr. Goodfellow. We will do whatever we're told."

A few days passed and Mr. Goodfellow asked Will and Lohta to return to his office. "Here's what I found out. Crowley is preparing a charge of grand larceny and bank fraud with Will as the only defendant. I pressed him on full disclosure of evidence, but he waffled. Said it would be forthcoming. Balderdash, I say. I doubt that he has anything. On the way back I stopped by the saloon and bumped into Will's former employer, Mr. Partridge. He said he was in town for business about the Diamond Hoof. As you know, he's on the board of directors at the bank. Partridge heard about your troubles. He's concerned for the both of you. Seems they're looking for a scapegoat. He mentioned that he still wants to honor his promise to get together with both of you before Christmas. By the way. Like most everybody else, he thinks you're completely innocent. I told Mr. Partridge that you'd be happy to see a friendly face."

Will and Lohta took it all in. "What's the next step?" Will asked.

"We wait. In the meanwhile, I'm going to stop by the bank and call their bluff."

A few days before Christmas Will and Lohta received a letter. It was from Mr. Partridge inviting them to be his guests for a Christmas Eve lunch at the Driskill Hotel. Will shuddered at the thought of being seen in the Driskill and how some might misconstrue his reasons for being there, and the way he was paying for it. Being in the company of one of the most upstanding citizens of Texas would help. Lohta was busy finishing the last of the dress orders for Christmas, but she knew how important it was for Will's morale to see Mr. Partridge. They had been beside themselves with worry. Pleasant company would be especially welcome.

They arrived at the Driskall at one o'clock as the invitation letter instructed. Mr. Partridge was already seated at a table by himself. "So good to see you." he said and motioned to the waiter. "Please bring us a round to celebrate Christmas and the New Year ahead. I will have brandy. And for you, Mrs. Porter?"

"A sarsaparilla would be dandy," she said.

"I'd appreciate a brandy right about now. Thank you, Mr. Partridge," Will said.

With a wave of his hand the rancher said, "My pleasure. We have bully good reason to celebrate!" Will cringed. There was small, polite conversation and Will and Mr. Partridge exchanged memories from Will's days on the ranch. Will never realized that Mr. Partridge was the person leaving him a steady supply of books. Or, how much of an interest he took in Will. Partridge said, "I could see you weren't cut out for life on the range. I figured you'd have to discover that for yourself. I'm proud of you for what you have done with your life." Will gave a puzzled look and let his old boss continue. "Yes, and you never knew it, Will, but you helped me out in a big way when you figured out some boundary lines for my ranch that were in dispute. It had to do with land grants from the Spaniards centuries ago. You were chief clerk of the Spanish Archives, and I was battling that coyote Crowley who now, believe it or not, is the district attorney. You, Will Porter, saved me quite a large amount of money."

Will remembered the bribe offered by Crowley and his refusal to take it. "Ah, how the worm turns, Mr. Partridge. Yes, I remember Crowley. And now I am battling him, too."

"Yes, yes, I'm aware of that. Don't look so sad. We're celebrating Christmas and the shape of things to come."

Everyone finished their meal, and Will rose to his feet to leave. "Sit down for a minute and keep an old man company on Christmas Eve. I have another story to tell you," Partridge said and motioned to Will to sit down.

Partridge started slowly and chose his words carefully. "My friends, we don't always get the chance to do the right things for people who touch our lives. I was at a board meeting this morning at the bank to wrap things up before the holidays. I was already aware of the trouble you were in. Your attorney told me, and it came up in a discussion at the bank. It came up because I brought it up.

"Goodfellow told me that you shared all your bank error findings with Mortimer Welch. And… that he summarily rejected them. Therefore, it was presented by Henry Rettop that Welch should be fired at once. There was further discussion about the pending charges against you." Will leaned forward in his chair. Lohta looked down at her hands. Partridge continued. "With no clear evidence against you, we agreed that no matter who or what was responsible for the funds missing, if they were repaid, the case could be dropped. It would save the bank quite a bit in legal fees, and moreover public embarrassment. Our depositors don't want to hear about the scandal. Especially if their money is involved." Partridge clasped his hands, took a last sip of brandy and leaned back in his chair. He was smiling.

"Oh, please, Mr. Partridge. We don't have that kind of money," Will said as he planted his face in his hand. Lohta began to cry and dabbed her face with her napkin.

"I know you don't," Partridge said.

"I'm going to end up in prison." He reached for his wife and squeezed her hand. "I never should have been born."

"No you're not," Partridge countered.

"Not going to prison...How can you be so sure?" Lohta asked.

"I paid the entire amount. I figured it was a good investment. The bank withdrew its complaint with the District Attorney. All charges have been dropped. Merry Christmas."

Mr. and Mrs. Will Porter walked out of the Driskall in a state of euphoria. It was a balmy Christmas Eve afternoon. They walked home arm in arm.

The couple awoke on Christmas morning. "I'm sorry my dear," he said. "I don't have a Christmas gift for you."

"Well next year you will be celebrating Christmas with someone else." Lohta said and laughed.

Will raised up in the bed on one elbow. "How do you mean?"

"Mr. Will Porter all those stories and poems you have written for me are gifts in themselves. Nevertheless, as I said, in the future you're going to have to share Christmas with someone new. You're going to be a father. Merry Christmas."

"By Jove! I'm over the moon! That is the best Christmas present ever! For a moment I thought you meant that darn cat. Call him Let's get him up here and tell him the good news."

Lohta called out, "O Henry!"

Story Notes - I based this story on the early life of prolific short story writer William Sydney Porter, best known for his pen name, O. Henry, who lived in Austin, Texas for a few years in the mid-1890s. William Sydney Porter was charged in Austin, Texas, in February 1896 for embezzling money from the First National Bank. He had been employed there as a teller and accountant for several years before the accusations happened.

The charges against Porter were never fully proven. Exact details of the case remain somewhat murky. Some speculate he may have been framed or that the bank itself was involved in shady dealings. Porter eventually fled Austin before trial. He was later sentenced to five years in prison in absentia, but served only three years after turning himself in. It is believed that he coined the name O. Henry while in prison.

A popular explanation for the name O. Henry involves a night out in New Orleans. One evening, Sydney Porter was at a bar, and the patrons continually called out "Oh, Henry!" to the bartender. The phrase stuck with Porter, which he eventually used as his pen name. Some believe that the name O. Henry might have been inspired by Porter's childhood pet cat named "Henry." However, this story is less authenticated and might merely be a legend.

O. Henry is well known for his Christmas short story, Gift of the Magi.

I borrowed some of the character names from the Christmas classic, *It's a Wonderful Life*. For example, Mary Hatch and Violet Bick owned the ladies dress shop in this short story. In the movie, Mary Hatch (played by Donna Reed) who was George Bailey's (played by James Stewart) wife and Violet Bick was a character who had a girlhood crush on George. Henry Rettop, the rancher's name was an inverse spelling of Henry Potter, the villain in *It's a Wonderful Life*. I changed the name of Clarence Oddfellow, the angel who comes to earth to earn his wings in the movie, to Clarence Goodfellow, the attorney in this story. Mr. Welch is the name of the character who was the teacher's husband who punched George Bailey. His character contrasted with George Bailey, who was always trying to do the right thing. Mr. Partridge was the principal at Bedford Falls High School. It was a brief bit-part played by Harry Holman. Mr. Partridge's name was never mentioned in the movie, but it is listed in the credits without a first name, so I used Harry Holman's first name. Although it is a small role, his character represents a symbol of authority.

Will Porter's wife Lohta's name is an inverse spelling of Athol, which was the actual first name of William Sydney Porter's first wife.

The entire story was influenced by elements of *It's a Wonderful Life*, *Gift of the Magi*, and *A Christmas Carol* by Charles Dickens.

It's a Wonderful Life is a Christmas supernatural drama based on the short story *The Greatest Gift*, a self-published book by Philip Van Doren Stern in 1943. The story of *It's a Wonderful Life* was to some extent based on the Charles Dickens 1843 *A Christmas Carol* novella.

SIXTEEN

Boston, Massachusetts

Luigi Colombo shuffled out of Pieve di Sant'Agnese, the ancient Catholic church in Castellina that was built in the 10th century. He was married in Sant'Agnese years ago. He made his way to the small cemetery nearby to say his last goodbyes to his Angelina. Luigi had watched the political landscape change throughout Tuscany, and from what he was told, all of Italy. He feared the Squadristi, the Fascist Blackshirts, who had already threatened him many times. He feared their threats of imprisonment, exile, or worse. His shop was destroyed by fire, which he was sure they were responsible for. It was time to move on before it was too late.

As the leader of the village orchestra Luigi was looked up to by the townspeople. "Il maestro della musica!" they cheered at Luigi and his viola as the band played from the flower adorned gazebo. Today he knew that being the music master was a curse. The Fascists saw him as a threat. Luigi could lead the people. Being on a pedestal in the town square gave him power, or so they said. The Blackshirts claimed Luigi was hiding messages in his music to rile up the Anti-Fascists. He was falsely accused of being a ringleader for Giustizia e Libertà, the underground movement for justice and freedom. He never wanted any part of politics and knew he was innocent. He was humble, kind, and wanted to be left alone. He simply wanted to build and repair musical instruments, teach music lessons now and then, and play in an orchestra. He was never wealthy but always had enough. Now all Luigi had left aside from his memories of Tuscany…and his beloved Angelina were his viola, a steamer trunk that held a few valued tools, and a few clothes.

Luigi came from a long line of Italian woodworkers. His grandfather, Lorenzo, started as a cabinetmaker 80 kilometers west of Florence in Collodi. *"How appropriate,"* he thought. *Here I am in the same town that inspired a story about a woodcarver, La storia di un burattino, The Story of a Puppet, Pinocchio."* Lorenzo refined his woodworking skills and began to make stringed musical instruments – violins, cellos, and violas. An opportunity came up for him in Florence to work alongside one of the great violin builders. 17th and 18th Florentine luthiers such as Valentino Siani and Bartolomeo Cristofori, were remembered as master craftsmen. Lorenzo learned everything he could and passed what he learned on to his son, Francesco.

When Francesco became a young man he wanted to move north to Cremona, the world-renowned city of violin making that was home to the great builders, Stradivari, Guarneri, and Amati. While Cremona's focus was violin making, several shops turned out violas. He wanted to get away from the small family-owned shops of Florence and experience the vigor of the larger luthier trade in Cremona. Francesco loved the rich tone of the viola. He decided to specialize in making them. Once in Cremona he married and they had twin sons. As they grew up Luigi took an interest in his father's business, his brother did not. Francesco decided after a while that working at one of the big concerns didn't have the same feel or the hands-on interaction with musicians. He decided to open his own music store and deal directly with those who could appreciate his craftsmanship. Francesco taught Luigi all the tricks of the trade and his own secrets for making perfect musical instruments.

Luigi was a quick study. As a teenager he was already turning out instruments alongside his father that were sold in the family shop. The years went on and Luigi's skills reached a zenith of perfection that could only be matched by master craftsmen. On a sunny December morning a beautiful young woman with espresso hair, fair skin, and clear eyes came to the music store. Luigi was alone in the shop. He was at once struck by her looks and introduced himself. She responded in kind, "I am Angelina Bartolomucci of Chianti. Buongiorno a te, Luigi. I am pleased to meet you. My father sent me here to collect the violin he ordered from your shop. He could not get away to come himself. Accidenti! It was such a long train ride. But Papa didn't want to chance having it shipped. He had been saving for a long time to buy a Colombo made violin."

Luigi was in awe and started to blush. "I recognize the Bartolomucci name. I must humbly admit…I built this piece myself." He walked to the wall and removed a violin from the rack. "This is it. Listen." Luigi picked up a bow and sweet notes reverberated throughout the room. "I know that song!" Angelina exclaimed, "It is the Prelude to Act I in the Italian opera La Traviata written by the master Italian composer Giuseppe Verdi!"

Luigi looked surprised. "You know this music?

"Ah, sì, naturalmente, Luigi. La Traviata, the touching interaction of love, sacrifice, and the destructive consequences of family pressures. After all, you know who I am here for. Papa has taught us about musica very well. Indee, magnificamente. What an exquisite sound you and your violin produces. You both honor Verdi's work."

In that moment Luigi knew he had met the woman of his dreams. "May I invite you to lunch? There is a nice bistro down the street."

"I am old enough that I don't need my father's permission, and you seem very nice. Grazie, I accept your invitation. It will be nice to get refreshed before the trip back." Angelina said. Luigi flipped the sign in the shop window to closed, locked the door, and they left. "Please call me Gigi," he said. They talked for hours until Angelina finally said she had to catch the last train to Chianti. "I will write to you…every day," she said.

By Spring Luigi moved south to Castellina. In August he and Angelina were married in Pieve di Sant'Agnese. Life in the rustic and rural Chianti region was simple but good. Luigi and Angelina enjoyed everything the countryside had to offer. He loved the wine produced in the region. Luigi opened a temporary shop in the back of the wine barrel maker's storehouse until he could get a shop of his own. He made new friends and met musicians as word began to spread about his prowess in instrument making. Even performers who did not play the violin, viola, or cello came to see him for advice and to discuss musical scores. Angelina kept the house tidy and made sure there was always a good meal and a bottle of Chianti Classico Riserva on the table for him. After a scant few years of happiness

Luigi noticed her health beginning to decline. One night he came home to no dinner or wine on the table.

* * *

Luigi asked his friend Enrico, the drummer in the orchestra, to take him and his belongings to the train station. The musicians often relied on Enrico and his rickety truck from his family's vineyard to get their instruments to a performance. "Why?" Enrico asked. In a whisper Luigi replied. "I am escaping to America to live in Boston with my brother, Mario, and his wife Chiara. Times are tough there for people. I could help them with the rent. Things have grown to be too dangerous and ugly here. I hate to leave Tuscany. I will miss my friends, the wine, and everything about this place, but there's nothing here for me now. I am getting on in years and my heart is heavy." Enrico grimaced and answered, "Yes, caro amico, I will take you to the train. Where are you going on the train?"

"Livorno. My cousin Luca has a fishing trawler docked there at the seaport. He can take me over to Marseille where I know expatriate Italian musicians. They will help me. From there I can sail to America and a new life."

"I will drive you and your things to Livorno," Enrico said.

"Grazie. It's a long drive. What if we are followed? Mi capisci?"

Enrico chuckled. "Luigi, I make the trip all the time with a truckload of chianti to be shipped by boat." He jerked his thumb toward the truck. "We will put empty wine cases over your baggage and viola in the back. No one will be suspicious. If anyone asks, you are a worker from the winery helping me to unload. The Fascist are driving hard to promote agriculture. We won't be bothered. They're not going to stop a shipment of prized chianti that they are so proud of."

The two men arrived at Luca's fishing boat. Luigi turned up his nose at the fishy smell. *Well, this will only be for a couple of days. I don't like it, but I will live with it,* he mused. Luca helped him over the rail and Enrico lowered down the viola to the deck followed by the trunk. "Arrivederci, Gigi! We will all miss you, Amico mio! Don't worry so much about missing the vino. I will see to it that a case of the finest Chianti Classico Gran Selezione comes to you every year at Christmas." Luigi gave Enrico a questioning look. Luigi wasn't disagreeing about the fine quality of Enrico's family wines; they grew the best Sangiovese grapes in all of Tuscany. His concern was how such a Christmas gift would find him in America. The men hugged each other. "Farewell and Godspeed," Enrico whispered. Two days later Luca was docking the boat in Marseille.

Luigi enjoyed several nights in France enjoying the music, the wine, and the company of his fellow countrymen who were exiled to there. They helped him overcome his fears and worries about emigrating to America. "It will be good for you, Luigi," they told him "You will be with la famiglia."

Luigi arrived at the Boston waterfront on a blustery day. The East Boston Immigration Station at Jeffries Point was crowded and bustling with activity. A uniformed man directed him to the medical officers who screened new arrivals to identify any potential health risks. "Leave your baggage and banjo outside the door," the man mocked. A white jacketed doctor gave Luigi a cursory exam and told him he seemed fine and to proceed to the immigration inspectors for review. Luigi stood before a skinny, balding agent. The man sneered at Luigi and held out his hand. "Papers!" he ordered. Luigi trembled as he reached into his coat pocket. Despite the cold the luthier started to perspire. "What is the reason for your immigration?" the agent questioned. "Political asylum, Signore," he answered in a weak voice. "Tell me more... In English!" the skinny man barked. "Do I have to drag a translator over here?" "I speak English." Luigi countered. "Ask me whatever you want. I have nothing to hide. I have a professional trade, and I have family to live with here in Boston. I do not make any trouble." A thousand thoughts raced through the Italian's mind.

The man shuffled the papers on his desk and pushed his chair back. "You alone?" he asked. "Very," Luigi replied. "You don't seem like a threat," the inspector said as he slid back closer to his desk. He stamped Luigi's papers and said, "Welcome to America, Mr. Colombo. Next month you will have an immigration hearing on the date shown on your application at the address below. Try to become a good citizen and respect our country. Good luck to you." Luigi's shoulders heaved. "Grazie," he said as he reached for the papers. The immigrations inspector smirked in response.

Mario and Chiara were waiting for Luigi at the pier. They knew the day he was coming but didn't know the time, so they decided to get there early and wait for him. It was late afternoon when Luigi slung the viola over his shoulder and lugged his trunk behind him as he made his way down the ramp. The brothers hugged for a long time. Chiara was in tears. "Let's get out of here before we all freeze to death," Mario said. "We will have to change streetcars a couple of times to get to the North End. Let's be on our way. I will take the trunk." Luigi had grown accustomed to the mild winters in Chianti but accepted that this was his new home, and he would have to get used to it, and also buy a warmer coat. Chiara saw him shivering. "When we get to our place, I have a nice hot ragu and fresh pasta waiting for you," Chiara said. "I rolled the pasta out this morning. Luigi couldn't wait. He knew what a good cook Chiara was. Chiara looked forward to her good-natured brother-in-law staying with them until he could get a place of his own. It would be cramped in their tiny apartment, but they would work it all out. Luigi had written and insisted that he would contribute towards the rent. Mario was generous and proud and wouldn't hear of it. He finally relented after Chiara's urging. The Great Depression had hit them hard.

Despite Mario and Chiara's meager kitchen, Luigi's was treated like a king on his first night in America. "I'm so sorry," Chiara said to Luigi. "There is no meat for the ragu. It is hard to come by these days and when I can find it, the prices are very high. I made extra bread, and there is plenty of Pecorino Romano. And, yes, vino. We always have a good bottle or two on hand. I trade my knitting for it." They ate and raised a glass, "Salute!" Mario toasted. Luigi and Chiara answered, "Salute!" Chiara added, "Mangia, prima che si raffreddi!" Luigi did not need any urging to eat. He didn't mind the meatless dish. He would have eaten anything.

In Italy Mario went off to work in the Carrara marble quarries at a young age. He was a hard worker, but other than cutting stone, he didn't have much else in the way of skills. Unlike Luigi, Mario was political. He tried to organize Anti-Fascists at the quarry. His bosses wanted no part of it for fear of reprisals by the Fascist regime. Sure enough, someone let the word out and one morning the Blackshirts came to the quarry. They told Mario only Fascists are "true Italians, "and "Complete Citizenship" could only come through membership and full endorsement of the Fascist Party. If he did not swear allegiance to fascism, he would not be employable and be banished from Italy. Mario and Chiara fled to Livorno as Luigi would do several years later. They escaped to America and made a home among the Italian immigrants in Boston's North End, the location of the Boston Massacre, The Boston Tea Party, Paul Revere's house, and the Old North Church where lanterns were hung to warn of the British soldier's approach, one if by land, two if by sea.

Once he was in America Mario thought he could get work at the Quincy granite quarry that was only ten miles away. With the Great Depression affecting all the building trades, the quarry wasn't hiring. He got work at the Boston Harbor docks when work was available, worked as a night watchman on weekends, and he always had a side hustle.

Luigi's plan was to get as many instrument orders as he could and use the deposits to rent workshop space and buy the materials. Every day the luthier went to every music shop, music school, and orchestra he could find, trying to convince them to commission him to make stringed instruments. It was to no avail. Luigi took the streetcars when he had money and walked when he didn't. To get by he bartered music lessons for the things he needed most. Chiara could see the sorrow in his eyes and how frustrated he was getting. "Gigi, ascoltami,' she said. "Yes. I will listen," he said. "I hope you have kind words for me." Chiara continued in a soft voice. "I know how hard you are trying. It's not your fault that no one wants to place orders. They want to but they can't, except for the very wealthy. They just don't have the money right now. Here's what I think you should do." Thoughts ran through the luthier's mind. Was she going to ask him to leave? Get a job on the docks with Mario? It was all too overwhelming. "What are your thoughts, Chiara?"

She took a deep breath. "Most people don't have much right now. But they still love making music. I have to believe a lot of them need repairs or improvements to their instruments that will play well enough if they cannot afford a new one. Capisci?"

Gigi, you know Joe the Barber, yes?"

"Giuseppe, yes of course. I give lessons to his daughter," Luigi answered.

"Mario spoke with him. The barbershop has a large empty storage room behind it. Giuseppe told Mario you are free to use it for no rent. It has heat. Just continue with his daughter's music lessons. And, he says shaves and haircuts will be included, too."

Gigi thought about it for a minute. "So, the storeroom is for music lessons?"

"It could be for that, too. But there are large workbenches in the room. You could set up a nice repair shop there."

"How am I supposed to get customers in a barber shop?" Gigi questioned.

"Ascoltami attentamente, Gigi. First you must have faith. We will all pray for you. Then you must take action. Retrace your steps to all the music shops and schools you have visited. Tell them if they have any violins, cellos, violas, or contrabasses that needs repairs, you are the man for the job. Tell them you will charge only a very fair price, and you will guarantee your work or give them their money back if they are in any way unsatisfied. Nobody will be dissatisfied. You are that good. Eventually, in the future, when people have more money, they will come to you with orders for strumenti musicali. And perhaps word will get around about how skilled you are and orders may be placed. It will be il giorno di Natale in six months. I predict that you will have many successes by then. I want you to have a good Christmas, a buon Natale.

"If customers cannot get to your shop, Mario will help you pick up the instruments and deliver them back to the customer when you are finished."

Luigi gazed out the window and thought for a long time. "I have most of the tools I need. A few of them where handed down to me from nonno Lorenzo of Collodi. But now I don't have enough money to buy the woods and materials that I will need."

"Not to worry, Gigi. Mario knows all the people in the trades. I'm told that most of the fine woods needed grow in the forests of New England. Apparently like in the mountains at home, the colder climate suits them well. I'm sure he can talk to them about giving you materials on consignment and pay for them as you use them. Tell Mario what you need, and he will take care of it. Funzionerà."

"I can see that you and Mario have thought this out well. The rest is up to me. By Christmas, you will be proud of me."

"We are already proud of you, Gigi. Now we want you to be happy. Tomorrow morning I will pack you a lunchbox to take on your travels. Dio ti guiderà."

"Infatti, I must leave it up to God to show me the way."

The next day after a brief breakfast of bread, cheese, and coffee Luigi was headed out the door. Chiara thrust a lunchbox into his hands. "You will be okay, Gigi. I don't expect you back until dinner. I will want to hear how the day went," she said. Luigi made his way to the streetcar stop and set off to visit all the shops and places he had before. He wrote down the address of Joe's Barbershop clearly in block letters in case there was a language issue. So many inhabitants of the city were from foreign countries. Of course there were Italians like himself, but moreover the Irish. There were also French speaking Canadians from Quebec, Jews, Poles, Portuguese and Lithuanians, and other nationalities, who all spoke English as a second language. To be clear he also sketched a picture of Joe's storefront including the striped pole, awning, fire escape and the small statue near the front door of the patron saint of barbers, Saint Martin de Porres. He also wrote down Mario's phone number. Chiara agreed to take any messages.

Day after day he roamed the streets of Boston emanating from the North End to East Cambridge, past Fenway Park, the Boston Common and any street where he thought he could drum up business. Again, Luigi Colombo was feeling defeated. He kept the faith. His family prayed for him. He kept going. Luigi arrived home one day and Chiara met him at the door, "Good news, Gigi! You got a phone call from a schoolmaster this morning. It seems there are student instruments that need repair before the start of the school year. I already sent Mario to get them. You did it!" she exclaimed. The next day Gigi once again returned home to good news. "Gigi! There is a music shop in Lower Roxbury that no longer wants to fix stringed instruments," Chiara told him "They are willing to give you all of their repair business if you can provide a small percentage of the repair bill to them for the referral." For the first time in a long time Luigi's heart felt light. Although, he was growing concerned about how he could make his sales calls and still have enough time in the workshop. *I am so grateful for this opportunity America has given me I will work all night, every night, if I have to*, he told himself. It was not unusual for him to arrive at the barbershop and several repair jobs would be waiting for him that were dropped off by customers or Mario. The tides had begun to turn for the widower from Castellina.

The New England nights began to grow crisp as the leaves changed color from green to orange, crimson, and brown. Mario was able to find several suppliers of hardwoods that Luigi needed. Gigi had most of the tools he needed but learned to use mail order and was able to have whatever he needed from anywhere in the country delivered to the barbershop. Things were going well. As usual, he set out in the mornings to either deliver a repair, pick up a new job, visit one of his accounts or try for new ones. One unusually cold evening he stood at the streetcar stop on his way home and noticed a woman clutching a violin case. It seemed she had been crying. Gigi supposed that she was about his age. She had large expressive eyes and dark hair. And like himself, a little on in years and slightly graying. "Excuse me," he said. "Are you alright?" She replied, "Yes, I am fine. Just a little sad."

"Is there anything I can help you with? Let me carry your violin for you." The woman pulled the violin case closer to her chest. "I can see you are very attached to your violin. Such a fine instrument." Tears began to well in her eyes once more.

"It was a fine instrument until yesterday. I am so careless and clumsy. I was on the davenport in my parlor practicing. There was a knock at my door. I jumped up and in that instance Dora my cat got between my feet, I fell over the ottoman and landed on my violin. It shattered into several pieces. I am heartbroken. It was handed down to me from my nonno, excuse me, my grandfather. It had such a sweet voice. I treasured it so much. Good grief, it turned out the visitor was my landlord looking for the rent."

"Non scusarti," Luigi said. "As you can probably tell from my accent I speak Italian. Although, at times I struggle with the English. May I see your violin? I know a little about these things. Please allow me to introduce myself. I am Luigi Colombo of Castellina until recently. My friends call me Gigi."

The woman hesitated then handed him her violin. "I don't suppose much else bad can happen. Feel free to see what I've done. My name is Silvia Fiorentini. I am American now, as my husband was an American. I came to America as a little girl. My family was originally from Prato, Italy. It is just above Florence. They were textile merchants who first settled in Lowell Massachusetts, the textile mill town. When the industry began to decline in Lowell because of competition from Southern mills with lower labor costs and more modern technology, we moved to Boston.

Luigi smiled at the mention of Prato and Florence. "I know Prato well," he said. "I always loved the culture there, its rich history, and splendid medieval architecture, such as the Gothic-style palace Palazzo Pretorio adorned with frescoes. And of course, I know Florence well. Mio padre was from Florence.

Luigi took the case and sat on a bench. He opened it and cleared his throat. The soundboard and back plate were broken clean through across the f-holes and the sound post rattled around in the wreckage. "Mmhmm. Yes, accidents happen. How is your cat?" Silvia didn't answer. Luigi cradled the pieces in his hands and felt a closeness to the violin. He continued, "There is good news, though. This is an extremely well-made piece. The neck, scroll, pegs, fingerboard, and bridge are fine. Where were you going with this?"

"Good news? You can't be serious! As crazy as it sounds, I am taking it to a barbershop in the North End. My neighbor told me about a man there who is said to be a miracle worker with wooden instruments. Maybe he will be willing to give me a small amount for the parts that still work. The rest he can put in his fireplace to stay warm. I could never afford such a large repair, and besides, Christmas is next month. Times have been hard enough for everyone. President Roosevelt introduced the Second New

Deal this year. If the first one didn't work, I don't know if I can hold on if FDR's second one doesn't work either. Maybe in the future if the economy improves, I will be able to buy a new one."

Luigi couldn't hold back his laughter. Silvia glared at him. He smiled as he said, "I know exactly the place you are talking about. I'm heading in the same direction myself. I will show you the way." During their travels they shared their histories. Silvia told Luigi that she was a widow, and her three adult children moved away to find work. It was just her and her cat Dora now. Gigi talked about living in rural Tuscany with Angelina and losing her, being wrongfully accused of being a political radical, and that he had no one other that Mario and Chiara.

They got off at the streetcar stop two blocks away from Joe's barbershop. It occurred to Luigi that he was growing fond of her. When they arrived at Joe's the barber was getting ready to close for the day. Joe greeted them. "Ah, Gigi! Two more pieces were delivered by the school and Mario brought in a viola to fix. Business is good for you!" Gigi laughed as he answered, "Sì Beppe. And it looks like I have my most challenging work to come in this case." He held up Silva's violin case as confusion swept over her face. "Whoa!" Silvia shouted. "You tricked me. Gigi, you are the master craftsman! You had me fooled. I feel so silly. I am very embarrassed."

"Oh my. I was only trying to lighten your spirits," Luigi said. "I am sorry if I hurt your feelings. Let me show you my workshop." He then told Giuseppe to go on ahead and that he would lock up when they left. Gigi opened the door to the workroom and flipped the light switch. The fluorescent lights flickered then reached their full potential bathing the room in cool light. Silvia was impressed. The workbenches, floors and shelves were immaculate. Saws, chisels, clamps, and tools she didn't recognize were neatly aligned in racks on the wall. One end of the shop was sectioned off into places for incoming and finished work. Silvia saw instruments in the in-box that didn't look much better off than her own heirloom violin. She pulled her violin away from Gigi and placed it gently on a shelf of the incoming section.

"I must say," she said. "I am impressed. Your shop space is so clean and well organized it tells me that you care very much about what you do. If any of the instruments in the finished area looked anything like those awaiting repair, then yes, you are a miracle worker with wooden instruments. I will be honored beyond words if there is anything that can be done with mine. If you think there's a chance, I will pay you a little bit each month. Once the bill is paid in full, I will take it home."

Gigi felt humbled and began to blush. "I welcome the challenge but let's both be patient," he said. "There's no need to make monthly payments. Hold onto your money. We can always work it out later after the reconstruction is finished...if it can be finished. Yes, it will be a challenge, but I will try my best."

"Grazie millie," she whispered. After what seemed like a contentious start to their relationship, she felt pulled to him. She liked his calm demeanor, kindness, and his willingness to laugh.

"I have a thought," Gigi said. "It's getting late. Let me make a phone call. Have a look around. I will be right back." Gigi felt bad about leaving Silvia by herself in the workroom, but he didn't want her to hear his phone conversation. He stepped up to the pay phone and dropped a nickel in the slot. Chiara answered the call. Gigi asked if they had sat down for dinner yet and if he could bring a guest. Chiara told him they were waiting for him, there was plenty to share, and that there was a large crate for him delivered to the apartment earlier in the day. He told her his plan.

Gigi heard the melodic strains of a violin coming from the workshop. He recognized it at once. It was Franz Schubert's *Ave Maria*, the Latin prayer to the Virgin Mary and a core part of Catholic devotion for centuries. The ancient prayer traced its origins back to early Christianity. Gigi went back into the shop with a broad smile. Silvia had borrowed a violin from the finished work bin. He picked up his own viola and accompanied Silvia. "You play beautifully. Impressive finger vibrato. You are very talented. My grandfather taught me the song years ago," he said. "It's getting late. The streetlights have already been on for hours. "May I invite you to the home of my twin brother Mario and his wife for dinner? Chiara is a fantastic cook. It is always authentic Italiano. It's the bees-knees as they say here. You won't be disappointed."

Silvia touched a finger to her lips and was slow to respond. "We've only just met. But I must admit, I am not fond of dining alone. I am old enough that I don't need anyone's permission, and you seem very nice. Grazie, I accept your invitation. It will be nice to get refreshed before the trip back home."

Gigi froze. He recalled that Silvia's words were almost exactly the same words that Angelina had said to him when they first met decades ago. His head was spinning. Gigi flipped the sign in the barbershop window from open to closed and locked the door as they left. A light snow was falling for their short two block walk to Mario and Chiara's address.

"Please allow me to introduce Signora Silvia Fiorentini, originally from Prato," Gigi said as he dusted the snow from his coat and hung Sivia's coat on the coat tree.

Silvia greeted them graciously. "Grazie per la vostra ospitalità," she said as she extended both hands then gave her hosts a peck on both sides of their cheeks. First the right then the left in the Italian custom.

Chiara said, "Gigi. Come see. There is this big package here for you. It's heavy." There was a crate sitting by the door. Mario helped him pry the lid off. Within the crate was a box with a card taped to the top of the box. Chiara handed Gigi a kitchen knife to cut the tape holding the box closed. He opened the card and read it aloud, "Gigi, Buon Natale a te! Warm regards from your friend. Enjoy! Enrico."

"He kept his promise," Gigi said as he pulled the top off the box. It held a full case of Chianti Classico Gran Selezione from Enrico's vineyard. "This is Enrico's very best. Let's celebrate our new friendships!" he shouted. We will have a bit tonight, save some for the American Thanksgiving holiday, the Feast of the Immaculate Conception on December 8th, and later for La Vigilia di Natale. Silvia, I hope you can join me for those celebrations."

"How lovely," Chiara said. "I have gabbagool and sugo al pomodoro on the stove. The Chianti will go nice. I will start the pasta water now. I wanted to wait until you got here." With the additional household income from the successes of Gigi's business she was now able to buy meat when it was available. The four spent the evening laughing, eating, and sipping the wine. As the evening came to a close Gigi said, "Silvia, it is late, and the weather is bad. I am calling a cab. I will escort you home and see to it that you arrive at your door safely." Silvia was impressed.

The next morning Gigi was up earlier than usual. He went to his shop and at once picked up Silvia's violin. After closely examining the break, he realized it needed a whole new body. The back, bouts, and sound board where beyond repair. Gigi went to a rack and carefully selected a slab of dried maple for the back and bouts and after changing his mind back and forth about the pieces for the top he finally chose a sheet of Engelmann spruce for the sound board and sound post. Gigi knew the North American Englemann spruce was lighter in weight and had a softer, more nuanced sound and the ability to produce a warmer, more complex tone compared to Norway spruce. Soft, warm, and complex is how he thought of Sivia.

He deftly put the broken pieces back together and held them in place with large gum bands then arranged the instrument on the select maple and traced its outline leaving enough space in the margins to make the bouts. Next, he flipped it over and placed it face down on the spruce and repeated the process of tracing the curves. With all of the tracings and measurements done Gigi started the delicate process of removing the good parts from the damaged ones. Following the application of moist heat using Giuseppe's steam towels to break the glue joint he used a thin-kerfed saw to cut along the sides of the mortise neck joint to release it from the body. To avoid cracking the wood, separating the sound board from the ribs is usually a tedious job but Gigi was not concerned about this as the parts were unsalvageable. He wanted to disassemble it and remove the bridge and other parts later. Nonetheless he applied the moist heat of the barber towels to loosen the glue and then inserted the thin blade of his specialized tool that resembled a narrow chisel, then a scraper, between the between the soundboard and bouts and gently lifted the top off. After flipping the soundboard over and placing it on the bench he noticed a small label glued to the underside beside the bass bar. Gigi didn't think much of it since this was a usual practice of luthiers who often imprinted their name, the town where the piece was made, and often the date on a slip of paper and pasted it beneath the soundboard. The only way to read it was disassembly. The ink on the label was faded but something caught his attention and he held it up to the sunlight pouring through the window. His hands trembled as he made out the words and said them aloud. *Lorenzo Colombo, Collodi Italy, 1855.*

Luigi Colombo paled as he realized the broken violin in his hands was built by his grandfather Lorenzo, and it was made the same year Gigi's father Francesco was born. *This must be a message from the Holy Spirit*, he thought. *I must honor this family masterpiece. And...Silvia is the angel who delivered it to me!* The luthier drummed his fingers on the work tabletop. *I've already selected the best wood New England has to offer.* Now *I must put the very soul of Italy into this violin.* Gigi smiled as he hopped off his seat and went to his supply shelves. He reached for the Mason jar of fine metal shavings from a local machine shop that he used to polish frets and clean brightwork. Then he selected a half empty bottle of white vinegar that he used for cleaning unfinished wood to remove dirt and grime and returned to his bench. After unscrewing the Mason jar lid and uncorking the vinegar he slowly poured half of the vinegar into the metal dust and swirled it around. Gigi said aloud, "Scusa, Nonno," as he reached across the bench for a steel card scraper that belonged to his grandfather and dropped it in the jar, left the jar lid loose and put the concoction aside. "Your scraper will once again visit this piece," he added. Gigi was now on a mission with a self-imposed deadline and vowed to get the rebuild done in record time. With the tracings and measurements of his grandfather's original work he knew exactly what to do. He cut the spruce from the pattern, saved the sawdust and scraps, and did the same with the maple for the back and sides.

Using chisels and gouges he began to carve the maple to create the basic outline and thickness. Next would be the arching, a process of precisely carving the distinctive arch of the back with a curvature that would provide the desired tone. The entire process would take him many days. His hands flew over his work. He knew there wouldn't be much time at the moment to give music lessons, and the other repairs would be delayed, but he would do what he could.

At lunchtime he ran home and bounded in the front door. "What is your hurry, Gigi?" Chiara wanted to know. "Sit and have a nice lunch." Without answering he grabbed a panini roll and a bottle of Enrico's Chianti from the rack. "It's a little early for that. Don't you think?" Chiara questioned. Gigi answered, "I don't have time to dilly-dally!" and ran back to the shop.

Silvia and Gigi spent Thanksgiving, the traditional start of the Italian Christmas season on December 8th, and Sundays together. After Sunday Mass Gigi said, "The pastor and the music director here have asked me to take charge of the Church String Ensemble for Christmas Services and other special occasions." Silvia and Gigi had been attending the church together since they met. They both loved Saint Leonard's Catholic Church founded in 1872 at 320 Hanover Street, and only 350 yards from the historic Old North Church, with its beautiful stained-glass windows and one of the oldest Italian American Catholic churches in Boston. "How wonderful!" Silvia said. "You are the perfect man for the job!" He took a long pause and gazed intently into Silvia's eyes and said, "Thank you for saying that but there is something else. I want you in the violin section." Silvia began to blush. "I'm honored, Maestro, however I don't have a violin at this time. How will I practice? May I borrow one of the repaired ones from your shop?" Silvia looked perplexed. Gigi chuckled. "Well, those instruments don't belong to me. It wouldn't be right for me to loan one out. You can come by my shop and practice there. Actually, we can practice together."

Gigi smiled. "Silvia, do you know Tu Scendi Dalle Stelle?" Of course I do. *You Come Down From the Stars*. It's an Italian Christmas classic." "That's good," Gigi said. "You and I will perform it as a duet at the start of Mass. And do you know Adeste Fideles?"

"O Come All Ye Faithful! I know it by heart."

"Eccellente. That will be the second song performed by the string ensemble. The organist will join in on the second verse. I'm sure you will be familiar with the other music. They are all traditional master works.

"We still have a number of weeks until vigilia di Natale. Let's see what we can do. Let's take a walk. They left Saint Leonard's and Silvia said, "Yes. It's a beautiful day. I know exactly where I want to go. She grabbed Gigi's hand and led the way. The couple headed down Prince Street toward Hanover Street and turned right. Then a left on Congress Street followed by a right turn onto Tremont. In less than 30 minutes they arrived at Frog Pond in the Boston Common. It was frozen over and lightly dusted with snow. "Pretty, isn't it?" Silvia said. "There's another spot I want to show you. It's a short walk. Come this way." Gigi and Silvia crunched over the frozen grass to a small structure. Silvia told him the history of it. "This is the Parkman Bandstand. It was built more than 20 years ago. I remember it well. The architects modeled it after the Versailles' Temple d'AmourIn in France and it was named after George F Parkman who was the last remaining member of an extremely wealthy elite family in Boston's high society. On a gruesome note, his father, Dr. George Parkman, who was a surgeon, was murdered in 1849 at Harvard's Medical School by a Harvard chemistry professor, Mr. John White Webster, who had a lavish lifestyle and a lot of debts. It seems that Webster couldn't pay Dr. Parkman the money he owed him, so he murdered him and placed the body inside a brick wall. It was discovered by a janitor at Harvard Medical School a week later." Silvia turned to see Gigi shudder. "è orribile," Gigi uttered. Silvia finished the story. "The murder shook Bostonians to the core. The trial became a circus and a national obsession. It was reported in every newspaper in America. Webster was hanged in Boston's Leverett Square in East Cambridge the following year."

"Mi scusi," Gigi remarked. "Let's change the subject. When I arrived in America the immigrations man said to me, 'Try to become a good citizen and respect our country …' I have tried. I love this country. I can do and say as I please. It is a freedom that I didn't always have at home. Maybe Fascism will go away one day but America has given me the opportunity to start a business, and I want to be a good citizen and repay the favor. The city pf Boston was the birthplace of a movement, like those who battled against the Fascists. The Boston Massacre, the Boston Tea Party, the Battle of Bunker Hill all took place here. I want to honor all of those who took part."

"Luigi Colombo, listen to me. You are a good man and a good citizen, in fact, better than most others," Silvia said. "What did you have in mind? Hmm?"

Gigi drew a deep breath then spoke, "I have an idea that I think some people in Boston might appreciate. They might want to go to the Boston Symphony but don't have the money. As we both know, the economy is bad right now. Not even enough money for some to buy food. Mabe that will change. Listen to what I have in mind. I have met several other musicisti, musicians, here in Boston. What I want to do is organize a volunteer member orchestra and give free concerts here in this pavilion. It will also help keep them sharp and give them something to do as they try to find work. Maybe the Boston Pops will hire some of them. Do you think it is good idea?"

Silvia beamed at him, "Gigi I don't think it's a good idea...I think it's an excellent idea. I am so proud of you!" The couple left the park. Gigi walked Silvia home. He felt light on his feet as he made his way back home. It was his custom to not work on Sunday, but for now he was going to make an exception. He went straight to the barbershop.

With the cutting and carving completed Gigi could now concentrate on assembling, staining, and finishing Silvia's violin. Before gluing and clamping the parts together he replaced his grandfather's original label next to the bass board, then carefully added a new one that said, *Luigi Colombo, Boston MA, USA 1935.* Then Gigi mixed the spruce sawdust with rubbing alcohol from the barbershop and rubbed it into the wood scraps to help seal the grain to reduce blotching before testing the coloring. The next step was to blend the color for his wood and evaluate the finish. He got out the bottle of Chianti Classico Gran Selezione, opened it, and pulled the lid off the Mason jar. An acrid smell of vinegar carried by hydrogen gases filled the room. The acetic acid in the vinegar had caused a chemical reaction with the metal shavings and steel card scraper to produce iron acetate. Gigi poured a small amount of wine into a dish, dipped a rag into it and wiped it over the spruce giving it a warm reddish color. This process was repeated several times. The red color deepened with each application. He dipped a clean rag into the vinegar solution and smeared it across the wood then quickly wiped it off with a dry cloth. The iron acetate reacted with the wood's tannins adding dark hues to the wood, the vinegar would eliminate any mold spores in the wine. Being satisfied with the results, he applied his unique stains to the assembled violin parts with each layer being smoothed with a card scraper to remove wood fibers raised by the liquid. Gigi drained the rest of the wine bottle into a pail. What he wanted were the dregs in the bottom of the bottle called "wine diamonds," a natural byproduct of the winemaking process. They are often seen as a sign of a high-quality wine. He rubbed the crystals into the finish after the final coat. As the final step he applied several thin coats of varnish and buffed them to add a rich glow. His oil-based varnish would take two or three days to dry for each coat. Gigi turned up the heat in the shop and placed the new violin in front of the fan to speed up the process, the winter humidity was already low, which would help, too. There was enough time. His deadline was still a couple of weeks away. On the evenings he knew Silvia would come to rehearse he hid it under a box. Whenever she asked about her violin, he would tell her that it was a long and tedious process, pray to Saint Joseph, the patron saint of carpenters, and to please be patient. She agreed but continued to ask how she was to perform at Midnight Mass without an instrument. Gigi said, "I will come up with one. Don't worry so much."

The morning of Christmas Eve arrived bright, clear, and beautiful. Snow the night before covered the streets of the North End and all of New England. Gigi called Silvia early from the barbershop pay phone. "Good morning, Silvia. Buon Natale! At one o'clock please meet me at Cantina Italiana at 346 Hanover Street in the North End. Their chef quit this week, and they have hired Chiara to cook. Because of her work they cannot have dinner at home today. She and Mario have invited us to lunch there. It's only a block from Saint Leonard's, we can walk there later. The snow will be gone by then. We can all go to Mario's after church tonight. Bring your bow. Ci vediamo!"

Gigi was already at the restaurant when she arrived. He sat alone at a corner table then stood and greeted her with "Buon Natale!" when she arrived. They exchanged hugs. "Today is going to be beautiful. I have something for you. I'm sorry that I did not gift wrap it." He reached under the table and pulled out her violin case. "Oh, you borrowed a violin for me to play tonight! Grazie!"

"Not quite. Please open it."

Silvia undid the latches and her eye widened. At first, she was speechless then spoke. "Oh my, it is beautiful! How where you able to repair it and get such a beautiful, warm red finish?" Gigi recounted the story of finding out it was made by his grandfather, selecting woods that grew in the New England forests, and how the soul of Italy itself was represented in the finish through his use of Chianti. "Truly it is a united effort of America and Italy," he uttered.

She removed her bow from its case, placed the violin under her chin, and drew it across the strings. "What a fabulous sound! The tone is so rich, so warm, so full!" Now with moist eyes she added, "Maestro... you are amazing. It's as if you came down from the stars. This thoughtful, united effort was made possible by you. Magnifico! I have a surprise for you tonight at church. There are people I want you to meet."

At the stroke of midnight together they played the opening stanzas of the cherished Italian Christmas song, Tu Scendi Dalle Stelle. Parishioners sang along or nodded their heads in acknowledgement. In the front row were Chiara and Mario and sitting beside them were Silvia's family. Her daughter and two sons, who Gigi had never met, had returned to Boston that day for a Christmas visit.

Everyone gathered at Mario and Chiara's after Midnight Mass, and together they enjoyed the last remaining bottles of Chianti Classico Gran Selezione from Enrico's vineyard. Luigi Colombo the luthier from Castellina and Silvia Fiorentini, who came to America from Prato as a child, played at Midnight Mass the following year... and every year thereafter as Mr. and Mrs. Luigi Colombo. Enrico continued to send Chianti every Christmas.

Story Notes - Thank you to Daniella Ronchi, a native of Milan Italy, for her input and influences on the story. Although I am not of Italian descent, I've always had a fascination with the country. Further, when I was in Boston's North End in the early 1990s, I was surprised to learn of the large number of Italian Americans there. This story is a salute to musicians, woodworkers, luthiers, and Italian Americans everywhere.

SEVENTEEN

Bayou Barataria, Louisiana

Marie Broussard was an oddity in her day. She performed her Cajun music live, despite what was socially acceptable in the deep south during the first quarter of the twentieth century. Her guitar playing and singing in saloons, honkytonks, and anywhere she could get a gig in public raised eyebrows.

Cajun music was not well known outside of Louisiana. A booming commercial radio industry that begged for content began to change that. In addition to her music, she was a storyteller.

"Good evening. Comment allez-vous ce soir? Joyeux Noël!" she said to the small crowd that had arrived at a Friday night fish fry. My name is, mon nom est, Marie Broussard. I am here to entertain you. A few hands clapped in appreciation, or approval, depending on one's point of view.

"Joe, my brother, will be joining in on accordion and washboard, please give him some applause." With her prompting, the onlookers offered a more boisterous applause than they had for Marie.

"Oui, oui merci. As I said, my name is Marie. And as you may know, in France, the name Marie comes from the Latin words 'stella maris,' which means, 'star of the sea.'" As you may also know, it is the French version of Mary, La Mère de Jésus. I can assure you, and Joe will attest, Holy Mary and I are not related." The group on hand chuckled. "I do have an interesting story for you tonight about a magical Noël, Noël magique, that took place not far from here a long time ago. We will get to that later.

"Let us play for you this evening as we prepare for Papa Noël and Christmas. Dansez si vous le souhaitez. We are deep into the Advent season. What a time to celebrate. Que la fête commence!"

Marie and Joe lit up the impromptu stage, merely the bed of a flatbed truck, with lively Cajun songs mixed with some traditional Christmas music. Their music was spot on. Marie knew what to play instinctively. People who were tapping their feet, breaking out with laughter and singing along when they knew the words, proved her to be correct. Plates of steaming crawdads, potatoes, onion, celery, and garlic heads were passed around the long tables. During autumn a steady decline in temperatures heralded the time to bring out the well-seasoned cast iron pots that produced flavorful Cajun seafood gumbo. Gumbo's flavors are the soul of Louisiana itself. The cooks started the gumbo hours earlier with a dark roux and spicy, smoked sausage. As the music intensified, and the beer flowed, oysters, shrimp, and crabs gathered from the Gulf waters were added. Of course, the ever-plentiful crawfish from inland ponds were tossed in, too. The delight of a good gumbo is in the mouthwatering herbs and spices used. Every Cajun had their own special blend. Depending on who was doing the cooking, different proportions of cayenne pepper, black pepper, dry mustard, paprika, sage, cumin, bay leaves, thyme, and parsley were added. The precise amounts and the timing of their addition to the pot were each chef's secret. Anyone who handled a roux spoon claimed their gumbo was the best. In most folk's opinions…they were all good. Beads of sweat were worn like badges of honor.

In South Louisiana celebrating Christmas began in the 1700s with the arrival of French Catholics in New Orleans. French Catholics from France and Northeastern Canada brought their Christmas traditions of lively feasts and parties to Cajun country. They transformed the French name for Santa Claus, Père Noël, to Papa Noël. He would arrive with toys for children after Christmas Eve Catholic Mass. Rather than a sleigh and reindeer, local Cajun legends say that Papa Noël would arrive on a small boat called a pirogue pulled by a crew of alligators. For hundreds of years

Cajuns lit bonfires on the levees during Christmas Eve to guide Papa Noël through the bayou to their homes. Some of the children left their shoes outside the door, a Christmas tradition in other cultures as well, for Papa Noël to fill with toys, candy or money.

"Reveillon" was the traditional meal served after Midnight Mass on Christmas Eve. It comes from French word for "awakening." In the early days New Orleans was mostly Catholic, and nearly the entire community participated in this custom.

Marie and Joe took a break to enjoy some of the traditional local fare. Afterwards, Marie took to the stage, cleared her throat, and shouted out to the gathering. "Okay, it is Cajun story time, A little lagniappe!"

Marie lowered her voice and started slowly. "Many years ago, Louisiana came under attack from the British. Most people call it the War of 1812. Here we call it the 'Second War of Independence.' Our American forces were led by General Andrew Jackson, which included almost 5,000 men, and perhaps a few women, but don't quote me on that. But… as y'all know, don't ever mess with a Cajun woman!" The crowd chuckled. "Jackson's crew was made up of about 1000 Army regulars, 58 Marines, 106 Navy seamen, over 1,000 Louisiana militia and volunteers, of which 462 were Black, plus Tennessee militia, Kentucky militia, Mississippi militia, and 52 Choctaw warriors filling out the ranks. Oh, and another thing, there was a force from pirate Jean Lafitte's Baratarians. And, I must say, they were a force to be reckoned with! My great, great granddaddy was one of them Baratarian pirates. I'd also have to say; Andrew Jackson's krewe was the all-time krewe of krewes!" A round of applause followed.

Marie continued, "British General Edward Pakenham arrived to fight on Christmas Day. Within two days he received nine large naval artillery guns to silence the two U.S. Navy warships that had been harassing the British army around the clock for the past week from the Mississippi River. Those ships were the schooner USS Carolina and the pride of our state, sloop-of-war USS Louisiana. Pakenham's troops sank the Carolina in a gigantic explosion, but thanks to the Baratarian pirates, including my great-great grandpa Joseph, who my brother is named after, the Louisiana was rescued from the battle. Although her sails were damaged beyond usefulness."

What happened next was truly astounding. Laffite's pirates, as unsavory as you all might think pirates are, had a place in their hearts to help America win. Some boarded the Louisiana and tied lines to her cleats. They tossed the lines to other Baratarians waiting below in rowboats. Joseph and his mates tied the lines to their boats and leaned hard into their oars! Despite being fired on by the enemy they towed the damaged Louisiana farther north up the Mississippi and out of range of the British artillery."

What most folks don't know is that Laffite's band of pirates helped General Jackson in other ways. In the dark of night, they would deliver ammunition with their boats to waiting American forces hiding along the river. Another unknown part of this story is that the Baratarian pirates manned firing posts among the low hanging moss in the bayous to snipe at the enemy. It harassed the British so much that it delayed their advances and gave Jackson more time to organize his men. So, I guess the moral of this part of the story is that you can even find good in the heart of a pirate, and...the magic of Christmas can happen in a lot of ways."

For many years the pirates of Barataria Bay had made the Gulf Coast the stage for their illegal mischief. They resisted and outfoxed the authorities and found an underground and ready market for their stolen wares, furs, and smuggled rum in New Orleans. In mid-December of 1814 Andrew Jackson met with Lafitte. The pirate leader asked Jackson if the US would pardon those of his men who agreed to defend the city and who offered to serve. Lafitte reminded the general about the Baratarian's covert efforts to help Jackson's effort. Jackson agreed to the pardon. On December 19, a resolution was passed by the Louisiana state legislature for a full pardon for all former residents of Barataria. Lafitte encouraged a lot of his men to join the ranks of New Orleans militia or as sailors aboard the US ships, which they did. On land and sea, it had been well recognized that the artillery skills of former Barataria pirate gunners was greater than that of the British. So, some of the Baratarians formed artillery companies."

Unfortunately, as Christmas 1814 approached, on December 23, 1814, the battle was still going on in New Orleans. It was a woeful Christmas for both sides. There were casualties, much more so for the British. Our American troops, made up of all those different people I told you about prevailed. I might add, it also gave way to raising General Andrew Jackson up as a hero, an honor I'm sure we can all agree on, that helped him become our seventh president of the United Sates!" The crowd cheered and began a rousing chorus of *For He's a Jolly Good Fellow*. Marie laughed and continued.

"But wait, there's more to this little-known Christmas story. As luck would have it, On Christmas Eve 1814, even though the British were trying to occupy Washington and take over New Orleans, diplomats including nonother than Mr John Quincy Adams, who later became our sixth president in 1825, and future presidential candidate Mr. Henry Clay, were meeting thousands of miles away from Louisiana in Ghent, Belgium to negotiate an end to the war. The Treaty of Ghent was signed Christmas Eve, 1814 ending the War of 1812. On Christmas Day all of those involved in the peace talks sat down to a Christmas dinner of beef and plum pudding brought from England. Glasses of fine spirits were raised, and toasts were offered to the health of King George and President Madison, alike. An orchestra played *God Save the King* and *Yankee Doodle*."

Louisiana government's resolution was passed on February 6, 1815. A full pardon was granted to all the Baratarian pirates, including Grandaddy Joe."

So here we all are today. Once again, the magic of Christmas came through with peace for the world.

Let's all remember the magic of Christmas, no matter where and no matter with who. Let us all prepare our hearts for Papa Noël and Christmas Louisiana style! Let the good times roll, Laissez les bon temps rouler!"

Marie tuned her guitar and motioned to her brother to step up with his accordion. "Okay, here's Cajun party song I wrote. It's new. I hope you will like it. It's a great beat to dance to. Grab your sweetie and get up and dance. Se lever et danser!"

Marie and Joe restarted the party with a stirring version of *Allons à Lafayette – Let's Go to Lafayette*. She sang the lyrics in French then English.

Allons à Lafayette, c'est pour changer ton nom.
On va t'appeler Madame, Madame Canaille Comeaux.
Petite, t'es trop mignonne pour faire ta criminelle.
Comment tu crois que moi, je peux faire comme ça tout seul.
Mais toi, mon joli Coeur, regarde donc ce que t'as fait.
Je suis si loin de toi, mais ça, ça m' fait pitié
Petite, t'es trop mignonne pour faire ta criminelle.
Observe moi bien mignonne, tu vas voir par toi même.
Que moi je n'mérite pas c'que t'es en train d' faire.
Pourquoi tu fais tout ça, c'est bien pour m'faire fâcher!
Let's go to Lafayette, to change your name.
We will call you Mrs. Mischievous Comeaux.
Honey, you're too pretty to act like a tramp.
How do you think I am going to manage without you?
But you, my pretty heart, look at what you've done.
We are so far apart and that is pitiful.
Honey, you're too pretty to act like a tramp.

Look at me honey, you will see yourself
that I do not deserve what you are doing.
Why are you doing all this, clearly to make me angry.

Story Notes – This story is loosely based on Cléoma Breaux Falcon, a pioneer of Cajun Music. Born in 1906, she was a groundbreaking guitarist and vocalist, and a trailblazer for women in music. Despite the public scrutiny, criticism, and social limitations of the era, Cléoma was one of the few women to sing and play live and record music. *Allons à Lafayette* was recorded by Cléoma Breaux and her husband, Joe Falcon, in 1928. It is considered one of the first commercial recordings of Cajun music. Cléoma Breaux, along with her husband, helped lead Cajun music to national recognition.

EIGHTEEN

Riverhead, New York

The Town of Riverhead, situated between the Long Island Sound and the Peconic River, and just to the east of the Long Island Pine Barrens on eastern Long Island sits. In 1909 the bucolic hamlet was a bustling place surrounded by agricultural acres and bays teaming with fish. That year William Howard Taft was inaugurated as the 27th president of the United States, he succeeded Theodore Roosevelt who was president until March. As president, Roosevelt spent a lot of time on Long Island at his summer home in Oyster Bay, which is 50 miles west of Riverhead. That year Roosevelt left New York City on a year-long hunting and scientific expedition to Africa that was sponsored by the Smithsonian Institution and the National Geographic Society. One of the world's most prestigious bicycling races, the Tour de France, was held for the first time in 1909 and the Pittsburgh Pirates defeated the Detroit Tigers to win the World Series that same year. By 1909 Riverhead was unique. It would also be the first and only time an automobile race, the Long Island Stock Chassis Derby, would be held on public roads in Riverhead.

Riverhead became the Suffolk County Seat in 1727. It happened because the courts only met twice a year. Once in the spring and once in the fall. One took place on Long Island's south fork, the other on the north fork and people didn't want to travel from one fork to the other for court business. Riverhead, located between eastern Long Island's forks, became the logical location for the new County Seat.

The Suffolk County Agricultural Fair had been taking place in Riverhead since the 1840s and continued to the 1930s. By 1868 20 acres had been bought for $1,650 to hold the Fair on Pulaski Street near downtown Riverhead and only a few blocks from the train station. Its proximity to the Long Island Railroad station made it easy for people to come from all over Suffolk County and beyond to attend. On the west side of the grounds were stalls for horses and cattle, and poultry coops. On the southern and eastern portions exhibits were held of carriages and the latest in agricultural implements along with carnival barker tents. On the north side of the layout a half-mile track was featured. The center of the track was leveled for playing exhibition baseball games. The annual County Fair became a major event. On the west side of the track were grandstands that held thousands of people who came to watch the horse races. There were more than agriculture exhibits to be seen. People came to watch not only horse racing, but bicycle races, baseball games, fireworks, and other entertainment activities as well. At the 1898 fair, future president Teddy Roosevelt, who was the Assistant Secretary of the Navy, was there as a guest speaker and was campaigning for governor of New York State. In 1899 he won the election and became governor of New York State. In September 1901 he became Vice President of the United States and following the assassination of President William McKinley, Roosevelt became President.

Dave grew up in town. His grandfather was a carriage maker with a shop on Bridge Street, which later became Peconic Avenue. It was flanked by the Vail-Leavitt Music Hall that was built in 1881 and modeled after the Ford Theater in Washington, D.C., which unfortunately, was better known as the place where Abraham Lincoln was assassinated in 1865. Dave's father inherited the carriage business and taught Dave the trade. Over the years the family built handsome carriages for the attorneys who visited the nearby courthouse and local businessmen, and more so, wagons for the booming agricultural business that surrounded the town. At a young age Dave learned quickly how to work with tools. Meanwhile, automobiles were beginning to take over the horse and buggy for transportation.

Dave could see the change coming. He was fascinated by the gas-powered vehicles and hoped to own one himself one day. He didn't really need one; he wanted one. He could walk to work from his home and walk to everything he needed in town. If he had to move supplies for the shop, there was always a horse and wagon available there. If he wanted to venture out to go hunting or fishing, he would go to the saddle shop on West 2nd Street and borrow a saddle for the day and throw it on a carriage horse.

By the age of 18 Dave had his own workshop in a barn on East Main Street. He figured if automobiles were becoming all the rage, he should change with the times and learn to repair them. He became an expert on the Ford Model A with its horizontally opposed, air-cooled, two-cylinder motor, called the "flat-two" engine, mounted under the front seat. Its 100 cubic inches produced only eight horsepower. Typically, the cars only had a top speed of 25 to 30 miles-per-hour due to the small engine's output. Dave became well-known for tweaking the Model A to get top speed and a little more. He would take the customer's cars to the long, straight, Roanoke Avenue to test them. He waved to the farmers as he sped past at a startling 30 mile-per-hour clip. The only thing that held him back was the condition of the road. The Ford factory only turned out the Model A in red. It proved to be a little too flashy for some. For example, the local undertaker thought being seen in a black Model A would be more befitting of his profession. Likewise for the judge. Dave also turned a tidy profit by repainting the cars. He had a lot of experience painting the handsome cabs that his father built and followed the same painting techniques on the red Fords. Only the wealthy could afford automobiles, so Dave's customer list was short. Nonetheless, word spread that Dave was a young man who could fix anything with wheels.

Motorcars were expensive and the roads were not good in the early 20th century, but because of his reputation Dave saw a steady flow of Oldsmobiles, Buicks, Cadillacs, and Packards in addition to the Fords that were available at the time. Assembly line auto production was still in the future and models that were available were in limited supply. Being a quarter mile from the county courthouse it was easy for him to attract the attorneys and businessmen coming there to his shop. The lawyers always tried to haggle Dave's fee. In return Dave would politely remind them that he would never question their fee if he needed them to fix something, and if they felt there was anyone around who could fix or improve their automobiles better than he could, they could let him know.

Dave read in the Long Island Traveler Newspaper that Henry Ford was now producing a Model T with a top speed of 42 miles-per-hour for 1908. Dave was sure he could coax a little more out of the front mounted 20 horsepower 177-cubic-inch inline four-cylinder engine. Ironically, they were only available in black. Henry Ford was quoted as saying about the Model T, "You can have any color you want as long as it's black."

He also read about the Vanderbilt Cup Race taking place in Nassau County to the west on Saturday, October 24th, 1908. It would be held on public roads that included nine miles of newly paved Long Island Motor Parkway that was created for the event and 14.46 miles of existing public roads for a total of 23.46-miles for the road course. Motor Parkway was the world's first concrete paved roadway. Dave dropped the broadsheet newspaper on the workbench. *That sounds fantastic*, he said to himself. *I have to go.*

Dave walked to Griffing Avenue and turned north to the train station. He asked the station master for a schedule. He wasn't sure if the early train on Saturday would get him there in time for the start, or the finish for that matter. He bought a ticket for the last train on Friday and to return on Sunday. If he could get to the train station for the last train on Saturday, and there was a seat available, he would catch that train since it would be dark by 5:30 and the race should be wrapped up well before then. He figured he'd sleep on the train if he had to.

Dave finished his work on Friday and hung a sign on the barn door, Closed until Monday. He boarded the train to Westbury. He figured from the racecourse map printed in the newspaper that from the train station there to the Westbury Turn that would send the racecars from Jericho Turnpike onto Ellison Avenue it would be about a half hour walk.

It was cold and crisp when he arrived it was too cold to sleep outside until morning when the race started. On a tip from a local he learned there might be a room available at Luessen's Hotel a half mile up Union Avenue. He decided to walk to Luessen's Hotel, which stood on the corner of Post and Union Avenues. Luck was with him. The clerk told him they had a cancellation despite the area being overrun with those attending the Vanderbilt Cup Challenge. Dave dug into his pocket and paid the man. He made his way to the tavern across the street, sat at the bar and ordered beef stew. The place was full of race fans and Dave was quick to chat them up. In a mist of cigar smoke, men placed their best predictions and argued about who would be the winner. Some made bets.

Would it be one of the American built motorcars? The Thomas Flyer? The Locomobile? The Matheson? A Knox. Chadwick or Acme? Or would it be one of the European challengers? The Mercedes team from Germany, Renault or Hotchkiss from France, or the Italian Isotta-Fraschini? There were 17 entries, and it wouldn't merely be a question of which one had the most horsepower, but also, what car could endure the grueling demands over such a long distance, and at times, on less than perfect racing surfaces.

Dave sat amazed. He was affable and neither smoked cigars nor gambled but he was in his element. Although he never had the chance to work on any of the brand's hybrids, he was well-spoken on motorcar topics and held his own in the debates. Dave was flattered when older men asked his opinion about mechanical issues with cars they owned.

Dawn arrived and Dave started his walk to the Westbury Turn. He was shocked by how many people were already lining the roadway at the early hour. The officials started the race at first light to reduce disruptions to public roads and to avoid spectator-related issues encountered in earlier races. Cars competed against the clock unlike modern races with a mass start. The 1908 Vanderbilt Cup used a staggered start format. Cars were sent off at 30 second intervals. Dave was amazed as the racecars with their goggled drivers and ride-along mechanics flew by sending up clouds of dust. Dave wondered what it would be like to be in one of those automobiles.

In 1908 the Vanderbilt Cup Race had a historic finish since it was the first time an American car won the event. George Robertson, driving the number 16 Locomobile, won the race by completing the 258-mile distance at an average speed of 64.3 miles per hour in four hours. All the American spectators, and Dave, were proud that the Locomobile built in Bridgeport, Connecticut won, outshining the European competition.

Dave was excited beyond words. He ran to the train station to catch the next train east. It was estimated that more than 250,000 people attended the Vanderbilt Cup...including Dave from Riverhead. He knew he had to have an automobile. He couldn't afford one, but with Christmas not far off it was on his mind to start saving for one. Maybe by next Christmas he might have enough for one of the new Model Ts that were coming out. On the train ride home he kept thinking about the racecars flying past him and the excited crowds.

The following weekend he went to the Suffolk County Agricultural Fair on Pulaski Street. The exhibits of horses, cows, and farm tools didn't hold his interest. He kept thinking about the new technology of the automobile. However, he thoroughly enjoyed attending the exhibition baseball games between regional teams.

Molly, a friend from their school days, approached Dave. "Nice to see you here, Dave," Molly said. "What brings you to the fair?"

"Oh, just having a look around," he said.

"Find anything interesting?" Molly asked.

"Nothing nearly as interesting as what I saw at that Vanderbilt Cup Race up island last week. I really think some of those automobiles should be on exhibit here along with the same old horse buggies."

"Well, maybe next year you can do that. I hear you've become rather popular with the highfalutin' folks who own motorcars. It could be good for your business to run a booth dedicated to the automobiles. You know, all of that new stuff," she said. "I'm being on the level with you. For you it would be duck soup."

Dave raised his eyebrows. Molly made a good point. Her idea began to grow on him, and so did Molly. She was attractive, witty, and smart. "I suppose I could line up a Tin Lizzie or two," he said as he pushed his hands deep into his pockets. "Say, Molly. There's that harvest square dance up at the Hallock Farm next Saturday, I thought maybe if you didn't have plans you might like to go with me?"

Molly twisted the ends of her long brunette curls. "Well, sir, I'd be delighted. Invitation accepted. I'm still living at my folk's farm on Church Lane. You can pick me up there. It's on the way."

Dave walked home in the autumn colors feeling better than he had in a long time. His thoughts turned to the square dance and the holidays ahead. Molly was shocked when Dave arrived the following Saturday in a Model K. "Did you steal this auto," she said with a laugh.

"Nothing of the sort," Dave replied. "It belongs to Mr. Carruthers the restaurant owner. His Model K was in for a fix and we got to talking. I mentioned that I had the momentous opportunity to take you to the square dance. He told me a fine young lady such as yourself should arrive in style. He loaned his horseless to me and told me to just bring it back tomorrow."

"Well, thank you Mr. Carruthers and thank you Dave," she said.

Dave and Molly went to the dance held in the barn. Then spent the following Sundays together. She worked at Riverhead Savings Bank on

West Main Street and would sometimes walk to Dave's shop at lunchtime if the weather allowed. In early December she came by the shop with a basket filled with homemade bread she had baked, strawberry preserves from the family farm, and kroschiki, a traditional Polish pastry that Molly baked with her mother, which is enjoyed year-round but especially popular during Christmas and other holidays. "Dave," she began, "Today is December 6th. It's St. Nicholas Day and the time for gift-giving in the Polish tradition. So, I brought you these gifts. And I would like to invite you to our family home for Christmas Eve dinner. It will be a customary Polish meal. We call it Wigilia. There is no meat, only fish, I hope that's okay. We get carp from Mr. Saxstein who has those fish pens on the Peconic River. We will also serve: Barszcz Czerwony z Uszkami, which is a bright red beet borscht soup made with vegetables and dumplings, Pierogi with Sauerkraut and Mushrooms, Kapusta z Grochem Salad made with cabbage with peas, and other dishes, and for afterwards -- pierniki gingerbread cookies that we cut into Christmas shapes and decorate with icing. In all there will be 12 dishes, each one representing one of the 12 Apostles. We will then attend, Pasterka, a special Christmas Eve Midnight Mass. I understand if you don't want to come with me. It's all in Polish. It will be at St. Isidore's that opened last year on Pulaski Street."

"I'm honored, Molly. I'm looking forward to it. It sounds terrific. And, yes, I know St. Isidore's. It's the church with two steeples."

For Dave, the days came and went repairing and repainting automobiles, and an occasional harrow, plow, or other farm implement in the barn. He went about his business and continued to save what he could for a car of his own. With Christmas only a few days away, he tried to think of a way to reciprocate Molly's invitation.

Christmas Eve arrived. Dave borrowed a wagon from his father's shop and picked up Molly at the Riverhead Savings Bank Building at the end of the day. A light snow was falling. He brought along extra carriage lap robes to keep her warm.

They enjoyed Christmas Eve together and little did they know that their life together was only beginning. Dave found the traditional Polish foods to be delicious and Molly's family warm and hospitable. He got along well with her mother and father, aunts and uncles, and cousins. And, he found the Midnight Mass at the Polish Church interesting to say the least since he didn't understand a single word but felt the emotions of Christmas. As Christmas presents for Molly, Dave bought a book of poetry, a pair of tickets for a musical production at the Vail-Leavitt theater, and dinner afterwards at the town's best restaurant, which happened to be owned by Mr. Carruthers.

A hard winter gave way to spring. Spring weather could be unpredictable on eastern Long Island, which relies on the warming of the surrounding ocean waters to bring up the temperatures. The oceans were a blessing to the farmers, though. It was believed that as the ocean waters evaporated and ascended to the heavens, the winds that carried the clouds over the farms would deposit enriched rain to the fields. The result was rich soil that produced some of the best produce in the country.

Summer of 1909 arrived. On a Thursday Dave bought a copy of the Mattituck Watchman Newspaper. He read the headlines and broke out in a wide grin. It said, *"Automobile Race to Be Held On Public Roads in Riverhead and Mattituck... Long Island Stock Chassis Derby to Happen Sept. 29th."* He let out a low whistle as he read. A road course would be laid out over 22.7 miles. Racecars would take ten laps around the course on September 29th. A grandstand would be erected on Roanoke Avenue for spectators just north of Main Street and his shop. Motorcars would race east on Main Road to Mattituck where they would make a sharp hairpin turn at Love Lane in front of Mattituck Presbyterian Church and then continue back west on Sound Avenue. Once past Northville, they would race to a sharp left-hand turn in Centerville, a turn on to Roanoke Avenue, heading south to the start finish line.

"This is really going to be something big," he said to Molly.

"Well, if you say so, I'm sure it will be spectacular," she said.

Dave watched the calendar almost as if it would help the days until September pass more quickly. He didn't get to see Molly as much as he would have liked to in the summer. In addition to her bank job her parents kept her busy on the farm with what seemed like endless chores in the evenings and during the weekends. They did manage to spend July 4th together. First, attending the parade in town, then a picnic at a small beach on the bay in South Jamesport. The big race was becoming the talk of the town, and everyone asked Dave's opinion about the event.

By the end of the summer Dave had learned that there were 13 different makes of cars entering the Long Island Stock Chassis Derby. They ranged from 18 horsepower to 90 horsepower. Well-known racing drivers would drive some. The lineup would include Ralph DePalma driving a Fiat, Herb Lytle in an Apperson, Louis Disbrow piloting a Rainier, Frank Lescault was listed to be behind the wheel of a Palmer-Singer, and Louis Chevrolet and Bob Burman both would drive Buicks. Prices of the cars competing in the race ranged from $851 to over $4,000. There were five different classes that could be entered. Eligibility for each class was decided by the selling price of the cars, which had to have at least 25 production models built. Higher horsepower models typically had higher price tags, which kept the classes in line. This eliminated the hybrid racecars that competed in the Vanderbilt Cup Race. Although automobiles specifically designed and built for racing were eliminated, alterations including the removal of lamps, fenders, running boards, and most of the body were allowed for competition. Many teams took advantage of the rules as they tried to squeeze out a few extra miles-per-hour around the racecourse.

By the third week of September the entries began to arrive in the Riverhead area. Most teams made arrangements with local farmers to store their racers in the barn. Dave approached Molly's father with the idea, but he declined saying he was afraid it would scare his horses.

Molly said, "Dave, why not put up one of the cars in your shop? It would be newsworthy and good for business."

Dave was in luck. Louis, a young man born on Christmas Day 31 years earlier and emigrated from France in 1900 sauntered into Dave's barn. With a strong accent he asked if there was a mechanic around.

"You're looking at the best mechanic east of the Vanderbilt Cup," Dave said.

"I see," Louis said and paused. "You seem young. How much experience do you have?"

"I've had them all here in my workshop. Fords, Oldsmobiles, Cadillacs, and Buicks. I'm not a stranger to any of them. And they run better, and sometimes look better, than when they rolled in here."

"I like your confidence, my friend. It is the Buick I'm most concerned with. Oh, and I am looking for a garage until the Stock Chassis Derby on the 29th of September."

Dave's heart jumped. "My shop could be available to you. There's plenty of space. And...why do you need a mechanic?"

Louis folded his arms and looked down. "Unfortunately, my brother Arthur, who often works with me as mechanic, could not make the trip all the way out here to the end of Long Island. And it is a requirement that I have a ride-along mechanic for the Derby."

"Look no farther, sir. I'm your mechanic, shop proprietor, and guide to everything around here."

Dave still wasn't sure who he was speaking with. "Have you raced before?" Dave asked.

"Oui! My passion for speed began with bicycle racing in my hometown of Beaune, France, in 1895. I had several successes, winning many races and titles over the next three years before coming to America in 1900. I began to learn a lot about the automobile, how they worked, and how to improve them. In my first automobile race, I defeated the renowned American driver, Barney Oldfield. In 1905 I won the Morris Park Race in a Fiat, and I set the record for the measured mile that year with a time of 52.8 seconds. Some still say it was remarkable. In 1905 and 1908 I raced here on Long Island in the Vanderbilt Cup. Last year I drove the Matheson. Over the years I have set records on every key track in the United States. I am entered in a Buick for the Long Island Stock Chassis Derby. The Buick will be in class 4 with 30 horsepower."

Dave was in disbelief. "Jiminy Cricket!" I saw you race at the Vanderbilt Race last fall Dave exclaimed!

"My name is not Jiminy. It is Louis." he said with a strong French pronunciation of Louis.

"That's not what I meant. Of course you're not Jiminy Cricket. You are non-other than the famous Louis Chevrolet!"

Dave extended his hand. "Welcome. There will be no charge for keeping your car in my shop or for my services. And I do believe I can help you get a little more power for maximum speed in that Buick."

"I am driving a Buick Model 16A that has the big 318 cubic-inch motor. Are you ready for a wild ride Monsieur?" Chevrolet asked.

"You can't change my mind," Dave retorted.

Dave told Molly the next day. "Are you insane?" she said. "You could get hurt or killed riding with that wild Frenchman."

"He will be in complete control and the Buick 16A has a long wheelbase that will keep it steady around the bends," Dave countered. "I will get tickets for you and your family to sit in the grandstand for the best view." Molly sighed.

Dave and Louis worked on preparing the Buick for the race. Chevrolet was an automobile designer, and he shared his thoughts with Dave about a concept for a new brand. Already an established engineer, Chevrolet had previously designed cars for other manufacturers.

As they worked Chevrolet explained his plan. "I think the new motor carriage should have a six-cylinder motor of at least 40 horsepower, a wheelbase of at least 120 inches, and other features such as electric headlamps mounted on the front fenders for nighttime driving, a horn for safety and a speedometer so the customer can understand how much speed it takes to give a thrill. I think it should have four doors as opposed to the standard two for more passenger space and ease of entry. Also, a fold-down top. Oh yes, and an electric starter motor!"

Dave then told Chevrolet some tricks he had learned while working on other motorcars to improve their performance and stability. Chevrolet liked what he heard. Dave adjusted the magneto for a stronger spark and the spark plug gaps for smoother running, these were often issues among autos of the day. They then made other changes to the Buick including removing the acetylene headlamps, oil burning taillights, running boards, doors and bumpers.

The next day Dave and Louis took the Buick out for a road test. Dave had studied the course map and was familiar with the roads they would take. They turned out of his shop and headed east on Main Street. Once out of Riverhead on Main Road they hurtled through the town of Aquebogue, then Jamesport and the village of Laurel before reaching Mattituck and the sharp U-turn in front of the Presbyterian Church, which was preparing for their 200th anniversary. Dave hung on as they rocketed over the sand and gravel roads at break-neck speeds. They sped along Sound Avenue and passed the homestead of Patriot Jonathan Howell who was taken captive by the British troops during the Revolutionary War, tied to a tree and flogged almost to death, then past the homestead of Capt. Zachariah Hallock, who was in the Suffolk County Militia's First Regiment of Minute Men during the American Revolution. He lived there until his death in 1820, a mere 89 years before the Stock Chassis Derby. The unlikely duo buzzed through the cornfields and past dairy cows on the way to their next turn on to Roanoke Avenue to complete a full lap of the 22.7-mile course.

Chevrolet noticed the improved power and responsiveness of the Buick's motor and that it ran much smoother. He removed his goggles, thanked Dave, and shook his hand. "This auto car is now magnifique! Monsieur, you are a fine mechanic. We will do well together in the Derby!"

Louis Chevrolet and Dave did indeed do well. Although he did not have an overall win, he did win his class, Class 4 for cars between 30 and 40 horsepower. Moreover, the automotive press reported that "there was an exceptional demonstration of speed." The Automobile Magazine for September 30, 1909, noted "Louis Chevrolet in his victory in class 4 with the 30 horsepower Buick traveled at a speed which was close to 70 miles per hour, this being the greatest sustained flight ever accomplished in an American road race." An extraordinary feat for the time.

Molly watched from the grandstand as the Buick rolled to a stop past the finish line. She ran to hug Dave. "I was scared to death, but I am so proud of you!" she blurted. Chevrolet was grateful and told Dave so.

Unfortunately, the Derby was a financial failure and was never held again. The promoters didn't take into account that spectators would watch from the sidelines and the farm fields rather than buying grandstand tickets. The drivers were given a trophy, but no prize money. Chevrolet apologized saying how important Dave's work was for their success and Dave hadn't accepted a dime in payment. Although, Dave couldn't believe his luck. In the days following the race, strangers began to bring their motorcars to Dave with instructions to do what he did to Chevrolet's Buick. Dave obliged. Life was good.

With the sudden surge in business Dave's savings account began to grow. He felt an automobile of his own was getting closer... and, so was Christmas. In mid-December Dave received a telegram, it read, "Expect a large delivery coming to you by rail freight due to arrive next week STOP. You will be contacted by the freight agent on its arrival. STOP." He didn't know what to make of it. He hadn't ordered anything. A few days before Christmas a messenger knocked on Dave's door. The man at the door handed Dave a bill of lading. It listed: the origin of a shipment – Flint, Michigan, the destination – Riverhead, Long Island, New York, description of the goods – Buick Model 10, Roadster, charges and payment terms – Free of Charge.

Dave was puzzled. He figured a customer who he did not know was sending him the auto for modifications. Flint Michigan seemed like a long way away to send a car for some minor improvements. He was familiar with the Model 10, which was considered a reliable and affordable car, with a 4-cylinder, side-valve 22 horsepower engine and two-speed planetary transmission. It led to establishing Buick as a major player in the early motorcar industry.

By 1911 Louis Chevrolet had partnered with William C. Durant to set up a car company, which later became the iconic Chevrolet brand under General Motors, producing the best-selling autos in America.

"Ain't you going to come over to the rail siding and pick it up?" the courier wanted to know. "I suppose I should find out what this is all about," Dave replied. Dave went to the rail siding and there it sat. A brand-new Buick. He got it started and drove it to his workshop. He didn't know who it belonged to, so it would be best to keep it inside until he found out.

The next day a telegram was delivered to Dave. He read it aloud, "Due to our success in the Stock Chassis Derby factory orders for Buicks have soared STOP. Likewise, my fortunes have grown as well STOP. Monsieur Dave, please accept this auto as a token of my gratitude STOP. Merry Christmas STOP. Louis Chevrolet STOP.

Dave was stunned. He never could have imagined such a generous Christmas gift. He decided to wait until Christmas to tell Molly.

Once again Dave had Christmas Eve dinner with Molly and her family. They were all amazed when he arrived in the Buick. "Oh, did someone loan you an automobile for the holiday?" she asked. "Not quite," Dave said and told her the story. After dinner Dave asked Molly's father to come out to the barn and take a closer look at his new roadster. While the two were alone in the barn, he asked for Molly's hand in marriage. Her father agreed.

After Pasterka at St. Isidore's Dave said, "Molly, I have quite a bit of money saved that I was going to use to buy an automobile."

"I know," she said. "I've been making your deposits at the bank."

"Molly, will you marry me? We would have enough to make a proper start with a place of our own."

"Yes, Davey! I don't care about the money. I would marry you even if you were a hobo."

That spring their wedding was held at her family's farm. All of their family, and friends, attended…along with a good number of automobiles and their affluent owners. They bought a modest house on East Avenue with a garage for their automobile and a small yard for their new dog named Rocky. They kept things simple. On paydays they would meet half way between Dave's shop and the bank building at Star Confectionery, or as most folks called it, Papa Nick's, for lunch. They would talk about plans for the upcoming week and their dreams for further into the future.

Seasons came and went. Early one morning in June of 1917 Dave scooped up the newspaper off the front porch. He and Molly had been following the progression of the war in Europe. The headline stated, "*All Eligible Men Required to Register for the Draft.*" America was entering into the war and Dave was eligible to be drafted. He folded the paper and called Molly. "Molly, come look," he said. "It says here I'm to go down to the courthouse and register for the draft." Molly's heart sank. By September Dave was enrolled in the U.S. Army and was headed to Europe.

He tried to make the best of things. Life was difficult, but it was tough for all of them. He wrote to Molly every day. He was never sure if she got his letters. The men did their duty and served gallantly. Their wives and girlfriends waited anxiously at home.

Towards the start of the following summer Dave's unit was sent to Belleau Wood, France. Dave learned it was less than 20 miles from Beaune, the hometown of Louis Chevrolet. He was glad he could try to help the people of the region. He hoped he was making a difference.

Along with the other American and French soldiers. Dave fought during the entire month of June in the Battle of Belleau Wood near the Marne River in France, roughly five miles west of the town of Château-Thierry. The fighting was intense and brutal, with heavy casualties on both the allied and German sides. The battle lasted a month. Dave survived. His commanding officer told Dave that he would have a lot of stories to tell his grandchildren. By Easter of 1919 he was back home in Riverhead.

Molly met him at the train station not knowing what to expect. She had a basket with preserves, homemade bread and kroschiki from their kitchen. Molly held up the basket. "I wanted to bring back warm memories," she said as she wept. They held each other on the train station platform for a long time. "Good grief!" Molly said. "You've lost a lot of weight. You're a bag of bones! Let me get you home and feed you a proper meal." Molly looked into Dave's eyes and could see he was a changed man. "I got all of the packages you sent me!" he said. "And I got all your letters. I kept every one of them," Molly replied softly. Dave was delighted to see that Molly brought their Buick to the train station. "I thought you'd miss her, too. Mr. McFly crank-started our flivver for me. I drove it here myself!"

In 1919 the country was now facing challenges transitioning from a wartime economy to a peacetime one. Many businesses struggled to adjust, leading to unemployment and economic uncertainty. Returning soldiers faced a difficult economic climate and struggled to find jobs. But, because of America's love of automobiles, the auto industry thrived, and so did Dave's livelihood. Molly was thrilled in August of 1919 when the 19th Amendment that granted women the right to vote was ratified. It was a cause that she believed in and campaigned for. She would say, "If you can send our men off to war, the least the country can do is give us the right to vote to determine our future."

By 1920 auto racing returned to Riverhead, but now it was on a dedicated oval on the Fair Grounds. On May 31st, 1920, more than 2,000 spectators attended the race. Molly and Dave were right there with them. Capt. Robert F. Wells of Stony Brook, an Essex automobile dealer and racecar owner, took first prize in all three races of the day with an Essex. His service manager Frank Gumbus drove the Essex in the races. The first race was a one-mile event on a half-mile track, which the Essex finished in 76.5 seconds. A time that broke all speed records of the day. The second event was a 25-mile race, with Gumbus and the Essex winning by two laps over the entire field. Wells was quoted in The Long Islander newspaper that he was "surprised to see the amount of reserve power and quick getaway." Gumbus, the paper reported, was said to have handled the Essex in the Riverhead races "with great coolness."

Molly and Dave continued attending the County Fair as they had done every year since their first meeting there. Dave took up Molly's idea to host an automotive display area at the fair. It fueled his business and gave him the opportunity to meet many men in the motor-trades.

Baseball was quickly becoming the national pastime. To the delight of many New Yorkers, the 1923 World Series took place between the New York Yankees and the New York Giants. Babe Ruth hit a home run in Game One, setting the tone for the all-New York City World Series. The Yankees came away victorious, by winning the series four games to two. Each of the winning players received $6,143, an enormous paycheck in 1923. Today's equivalent would be over $100,000.

Exhibition games and races were always a part of the Suffolk County Fair, and the organizers scheduled a special baseball game for November 9th, 1923. It featured none-other than the New York Yankee "Sultan of Swat," Babe Ruth. The town went crazy as thousands drove or came by train to Riverhead for the game. Yankee games weren't broadcast on radio until 1939 and television was even further into the future and most people had never attended a game live. The excitement to see Babe Ruth was intense. Local schools closed for the day to give students the chance to attend and see the Yankee hero play.

When he arrived at the fairgrounds, Babe Ruth received a great ovation from the huge crowd, who surrounded his big Twin Six Packard. The Twin Six 12-cylinder V-12 engine that was offered in higher-end 1923 Packards was a technological marvel and a symbol of luxury and automotive innovation at the time. Although, the 424 cubic-inch, 135 horsepower, water-cooled motor wasn't without occasional mechanical problems. Ruth's car sputtered to a stop.

The game was a delight to the fans. As reported in the Riverhead News and County Review in November 1923, "George Herman "Babe" Ruth, along with Jack Scott of World Series fame and a selection of All-Star players, defeated the Suffolk All-Stars 5 to 3 at a baseball game held at the Riverhead Fairgrounds on the afternoon of Friday, November 9, 1923. Babe Ruth lived up to his reputation as the "Sultan of Swat," slamming a home run in the first inning. The ball traveled over the grandstand and bounced back onto the racetrack. As Babe trotted around the bases with a long-distance stride, the crowd went wild with joy. Many of the fans in attendance had never seen Babe Ruth play in a baseball game."

It was late afternoon by the time Babe returned to the Packard. He had already devoured four hot dogs smothered in ketchup and a side order of pierogies and was now ready for dinner. He pressed the starter button. The otherwise smooth running V12 coughed and backfired to the surprise of the gaggle of fans that still surrounded him. It wouldn't start. He was embarrassed. Someone in the crowd hollered, "Find Dave!"

Two young men ran to the auto exhibition tent and grabbed Dave by the elbow. "Babe Ruth's car won't start. We need your help!" one exclaimed. They led Dave to the Packard. "This is a fancy car," Dave said as he rolled up his sleeves. Owning a Packard with the Twin Six engine was a mark of distinction. It signified wealth, status, and a taste for the finest things in life. "Let's see what we can see."

Dave lifted the hood and said, "I'm willing to bet the long drive over rough and dusty roads was the culprit. And I'd wager your magneto is knocked off kilter and there's dirt in your carburetor." Ruth was a gambling man. He shrugged his shoulders and said, "If you say so. I wouldn't bet against it. I'll stick to the horses and cards for gambling!"

"Unless," Dave countered, "the opposing pitcher sabotaged your motor." Babe Ruth often played practical jokes on teammates, managers and sometimes even members of the press. He wondered if he had been had.

"My word," Babe replied and started to sweat. "Not my beautiful car!"

"Oh, relax, Sir. I was only joshing you. Let me see if I can get it started and running good enough for you to limp over to my workshop. It's only a few blocks away. I can give it a proper fix there for your long ride back,"

"I'd be much obliged. By the way. It's nice out here. How's the fishing and duck hunting?" said the homerun king, who was also an avid hunter and fisherman.

"Both are excellent here," Dave answered. "Come back out here some time and I'll show you all of the best spots."

Dave tapped on the magneto and tried the starter. The v12 begrudgingly came to life and continued to misfire. "Let's go before It quits!" Dave called over the clatter. Dave was now the ride along mechanic for one of the best-known names in America. Once at the shop Dave set the magneto for a stronger spark, cleaned the carburetor, and checked the sparkplug gaps. He marveled at the technically advanced Twin Six engine design, which was way ahead of its time. It featured overhead valves, a pressurized lubrication system, and a crankcase with seven main bearings for added rigidity and durability.

"What do I owe you?" Babe Ruth asked.

"Not a dime, Sir. Just by coming out here you made a lot of people happy. Hitting that homer was a bonus. If you ever do come back to hunt or fish, you can buy me a coffee. That'll be fine."

"That's very generous of you, Dave. I'm extremely grateful. I must be back in the Bronx by tomorrow. I never would have made it without your help."

Molly couldn't believe that Dave had fixed Babe Ruth's Packard. "Wow, that's a story worth retelling," she said. At Thanksgiving dinner Dave and Molly truly felt thankful for all the good fortune in their lives. On the afternoon of Christmas Eve there was a knock at their door. It was the postman with a special delivery package. "Well, open it, Dave!" Molly said.

It was a box of cigars with a note that said, "Dear Dave. I don't know if you enjoy a good cigar the way I do. If so, please enjoy these. If not, please feel free to pass them along to your friends or customers. Thank you for fixing my Packard. Merry Christmas! – Babe" As Dave unfolded the letter something fell to the floor. Molly picked it up. "Oh my word," she said."

"What does it say, Molly?"

"Here, look." Molly handed Dave the sheet printed on a NY Yankees letterhead. Dave read it aloud. "Please accept the attached as a sincere token of my appreciation. Dave removed the paperclip that held a pair season guest passes to Yankee Stadium."

"That's dandy, Dave, but it could be a tough drive to the Bronx. It's a long way to go," Molly said.

"Well, maybe not. Let's take a walk over to the workshop and talk it over," he countered.

"Oh, Dave I have a lot to do to get ready for this evening and tomorrow. Can't we just wait until after Christmas?"

"C'mon, Molly. You won't be disappointed and it's a beautiful day."

"You never disappoint me, Dave."

The couple put on their coats and headed out the door. They walked the few blocks to Dave's shop. He slid open the barn door and flipped on the lights.

Glowing in the soft light was a Packard Twin Six 88 horsepower 12-cylinder 3-25 Series two-door luxury coupe.

"I wanted to wait until tomorrow morning to give you this. Now you can go anywhere in style. Merry Christmas, Molly."

Story Notes – The 1881 Vail-Leavitt Music Hall still stands on Peconic Avenue in Riverhead and is a registered historic landmark. The Music Hall played a role in the development of entertainment technology. In 1914, Thomas Edison used the venue to experiment with his kinetophone, an early attempt at synchronized sound and film. Auto racing is still going on in the Town of Riverhead at Riverhead Raceway, a quarter-mile asphalt oval track located two miles from the original County Fair Grounds and racetrack. I took part in motor racing in my early years, building and repairing sports cars and went on to manage a Buick powered prototype racecar team that competed at the 24 Hours of Daytona, Sebring 12 Hour, and many other endurance sports car races across America. I still attend the fair.

NINETEEN

Townsend, Tennessee

His father was sickly and therefore W.B. had to become a breadwinner for the family. By the age of ten he was working in the nickel mines of Pennsylvania. At 17 he apprenticed as a carpenter with a cabinet maker and builder in Lancaster, Pennsylvania. This was where his love of wood and lumber, and what could be done with it, began. W.B. built everything from cradles to coffins, and things that people needed in-between using either of them. As an apprentice he was initially paid four dollars per month for his first year. During his second year he earned eight dollars a month, and twelve dollars each month for his third and final year. It was a salary that was offset by housing provided by his master. He had to buy his own clothes, so, function rather than fashion was an issue. By age twenty he was a journeyman carpenter earning three dollars per day. That was a tremendous sum in those days. In 1879 he met Miss Margarett Johnson and married her in April of 1879.

W.B. was enterprising and self-motivated. He started a coal and lumber yard business on a couple of acres he bought. He sold the business at a hefty profit. Two years later he created the Clearfield Lumber Company to build sawmills and purchase timberlands. It was a large and impressive venture in its day.

In the late 19th century, the logging industry began to take hold in the Great Smoky Mountains. It didn't take long for the logging business to boom, and forests fell, mostly because of two new innovations, the bandsaw and logging railroads.

In 1900 Colonel W.B. Townsend bought approximately 85,000 acres of virgin forest stretching from Tuckaleechee Cove to Clingmans Dome, Tennessee. He had some military experience, but "colonel" was a title of respect given to him by those who knew him and appreciated his accomplishments. By 1901 he received his charter to create the Little River Railroad & Lumber Company in the town of Tuckaleechee, a tiny town along the Little River that gave loggers easy access. With the arrival of industry, Tuckaleechee went from a small agricultural community to a bustling mill town. The name Tuckaleechee was changed to Townsend in honor of W.B. for all the industry and jobs he brought to the area.

His business grew rapidly and within a year Colonel Townsend began to realize that he needed a better way to move his lumber around, so he started planning a railroad. The Little River Railroad used a narrow-gauge track and built a remarkable 150 miles of rail lines throughout Appalachia during its operational years. Narrow-gauge track, at only three feet wide, was cheaper to build and could make tighter turns than standard four feet eight-and-a-half-inch track. This helped the train negotiate the tight bends in the mountains.

The rail line interchanged with the Knoxville and Augusta, which later became the Knoxville and Charleston Railroad. In 1903 eight miles of track connected Walland to Townsend, along with three miles from Townsend to the forks of the Little River.

While W.B. was busy running the lumber company, his wife Miss Maggie was busy with cultural and charitable endeavors. Margarett Townsend was an angel to the poor people of Appalachia. While her husband set about building his lumber empire and railroad, Margaret worked with the mountain people. Her warmth and generosity aided many in need in Appalachia, especially children. She always tried to make Christmas special.

Although jobs were now plentiful, many of the men who worked the mill, ran the railway, or cut lumber lived in set-off houses along with their families. These houses, made of cheap materials such as wood and tin, were small, typically measuring 12 by 16 feet and only had one or two rooms, one door, two windows and a fireplace. Set-off houses were easy to move from one logging camp to the next. Although they didn't have much in the way of amenities, they offered the loggers and their families shelter. Also sometimes called 'skid houses' or 'string houses' they played a significant role in Tennessee logging because they provided housing for loggers working in remote areas. Set-off houses were sometimes built in rows called 'string towns.'

Set-off houses, string towns and their occupants were a kaleidoscope of rural living. In addition to the lumberjacks working the forests, the millworkers, and railroad men, they were home to farmers, blacksmiths, carpenters, and other skilled laborers who served the needs of the community, and hermits who shunned civilization.

They had to rely on resourcefulness and self-sufficiency and live off what nature could provide. Every day was a challenge. Although set-off houses were physically distant, people bonded through church gatherings and social events. String towns, on the other hand, were more cohesive because of their proximity to each other and shared experiences. This offered more opportunity to share or loan what was needed.

Access to services was limited in the rural hills. Healthcare and education were either unheard of or hard to come by and most had to travel to bigger towns for the services. It led to a lot of home doctoring and home learning. By the 1920s changes like the arrival of the automobile and radio led to an increased awareness of the wider world and solved some of the issues of isolation.

Aside from living in humble conditions and hardships in early 20th century rustic Appalachia, something else they typically had in common, whether living apart in set-off houses or grouped in string towns, was poverty. Regardless, Margaret Townsend looked after many of them.

The Little River Lumber Company cut 560 million board feet of lumber in the Great Smoky Mountains from 1901 to 1939. It was enough lumber if laid end to end it would cross the country twice. America was growing rapidly and the demand for lumber was high. There was a lumber company bigger than the Townsend's Little River Railroad & Lumber Company and several more that were smaller. It's believed that all the lumber companies combined cut ten billion board feet of wood from the landscape of the Great Smokies. It was enough to go round-trip to the moon three times.

Ironically, W.B. Townsend and others cutting lumber was the catalyst for the formation of the Great Smoky Mountain National Park.

Clear-cutting the trees of the Smoky Mountains was devastating. Logging was taking place on privately owned land. All the destruction raised the ire of many who then petitioned the government to do something to preserve the wilderness for future generations. This led to the creation of the Great Smoky Mountain National Park. It was the first time in history that private property was turned into a national park. Property owners in Tennessee and North Carolina were compensated at fair market value for their land under eminent domain laws of the United States Constitution. Congress passed legislation in 1934 to establish the Great Smoky Mountains National Park.

Colonel W. B. Townsend did sell 75,000 acres to the government to set up the Great Smoky Mountain National Park. Townsend, always shrewd and calculating, cut a deal with the government for the rights to continue logging sections of his formerly owned land for another 15 years. W.B. passed on in 1936 at the age of 81 and the last log was milled at the Little River Lumber Company in 1939. The glorious Smoky Mountain National Park lives on.

Margaret Townsend left a legacy as well. In 1903 she introduced Christmas Trees to Appalachia. Her generous spirit was shown by a Christmas gift list that included almost 1,000 people, most of which were children.

Story Notes - The Little River Railroad Museum in Townsend Tennessee commemorates logging and has exhibits of the narrow-gauge trains used in the Smoky Mountains during the lumber heydays. The Museum treasures the history of Margaret Townsend, her spirit of Christmas, and the impact Margaret had on the community. They celebrate Margaret's goodwill and Christmas at the Museum each Saturday night from Thanksgiving to Christmas.

TWENTY

Portsmouth, New Hampshire

Fueled by increasing rivalry between the Russian Empire and the Empire of Japan over control of Manchuria and Korea the Russo-Japanese War began on February 8, 1904. It started with a surprise attack by the Japanese navy on the Russian fleet at Port Arthur, a strategic naval base in Manchuria. This daring move caught Russia off guard and marked the start of the conflict. The loss Russia's fleet at Port Arthur was a devastating blow to the Russian Navy. Many of Russia's best ships were destroyed or captured. Japan's capture of Port Arthur allowed them to advance deeper into Manchuria and eventually defeat the Russian army at the Battle of Mukden. The battle didn't end the war. Meanwhile, half-way around the world the following year...

Henry Cliffens sat on the bank of the Piscataqua River and thought about the future of his career. Henry was an investigative reporter at the Portsmouth Herald. It was the era of muckraking, journalists seeking out and exposing real or alleged corruption, scandals, or other shenanigans in politics and business. Sometimes politics and business made strange bedfellows. It was becoming too stressful for Henry. He regularly met with threats, intimidation, and lawsuits for what he wrote. The newspaper faced the same. He had made enemies in the New Hampshire lumber industry after writing in great detail about the illegal land grabs of timberlands and the influence peddling and bribes that went along with them to skirt regulations and evade prosecution. Henry figured he was still young enough to change professions. And since he was already doing detective work, maybe applying for a job at the police department would be a good fit. It could also give him some protection from the thugs that ran interference for the corrupt politicians and crooked business owners. He got up and skipped a stone across the water then turned away and walked up Court Street through the Puddle Dock section of town to the William Pitt Tavern.

The three-story tavern had been around since 1766, 27 years before the newspaper Henry wrote for was founded. The William Pitt Tavern had a long, interesting history. Originally it was named the Earl of Halifax Tavern by its builder, Freemason John Stavers. The Earl of Halifax, a British statesman, was unpopular among American colonists who were quickly becoming disgusted with British rule. Rather than having his tavern trashed by angry colonists, Stavers decided to rename the pub after William Pitt, the Earl of Chatham, a British political figure who opposed the colony's taxation without representation. Pitt was seen as supporting the colonist's rights, which made him much more popular among them. Although the exact date of the name change from the Earl of Halifax Tavern to the William Pitt Tavern is not known, it was always clear to everyone in town that the place served as a foundational part of Portsmouth's heritage for decades. George Washington, Paul Revere, and Marquis de Lafayette were visitors and several of the Declaration of Independence's signers, including John Hancock, stayed at the tavern as did John Paul Jones while his flagship "The Ranger" was being built at a nearby shipyard. Before and during the American Revolution locals gathered in the tavern for heated discussions about Britain's taxation and policies that paved the way for revolt. Over the years the tavern played host to an array of sea captains and sailors who unfolded their wild tales of adventurous voyages and pirate raids over mugs of ale and rum. Within the tavern's walls The Grand Masonic Lodge of New Hampshire, one of the oldest in the United States, was formed on July 8, 1789. Since then, the William Pitt Tavern remained a noteworthy location for Freemasons in New Hampshire.

Henry was a frequent caller there. It was the perfect place to learn the latest scuttlebutt. He gathered a lot of gossip from Silas the bartender. What many thought were rumors Henry almost always found to be true, or part of a bigger story. Silas, a jovial Union Army Civil War veteran, liked Henry. Mostly because of the large tips Henry left on the bar when he left. Silas didn't know they weren't out of Henry's own pocket. Henry would go to his editor and explain that he needed information money. The editor would take the money out of the office petty cash box and straighten it out with the publisher later. It was easy to explain when Henry delivered a good story. Henry was never asked about his source, and as long as he kept writing groundbreaking newspaper articles for the Herald, everyone was fine with the arrangement. It was a win – win situation for Silas and Henry. At Christmas Henry gave him a much larger amount than usual as a Christmas present. Henry had to ensure the pipeline would keep flowing. Moreover, what Silas liked about Henry were the articles he wrote that revealed the dishonesty and corruption that was going on. Silas and Henry were members of The Grand Lodge that met upstairs in the tavern, which cemented a mutual trust between them. One rumor that Henry could not unravel was the one about the William Pitt Tavern being haunted. Late in the evenings after the usual crowd had left, as Henry and Silas sat at the bar exchanging stories, spooky squeaks and groans could be heard. Some said maybe it was the walls themselves muttering the secret tales told during days gone by there. Henry figured it was tavern's wooden beams creaking with age, but he had no way to prove it.

"Evening, Henry. What'll it be?" Silas asked as the writer, his only customer, perched on a barstool.

"The usual," Henry answered. As Silas reached for a bottled beer Henry stopped him and added, "How about a mint julep? It's been a tough day."

"Okay, coming up," the old timer said. "You want to talk about it?" Silas topped off the drink with another splash of bourbon.

"Maybe later," Henry replied as he shifted on the stool. "What's the news around town?"

"Well, let me think," Silas said as he wiped the top of the bar. "There were a couple of guys from the Navy shipyard over on Seavey's Island came in here yesterday. After a few drinks they started talking seems that something big is happening over there soon. A desk clerk from that fancy Wentworth Hotel was here at the same time and said the same thing. Said he's been checking in guests from all over the world the last few days including a few Asian blokes wearing expensive suits. Yep. Something big is coming up."

Henry stared into his drink and tried to connect the bits of information his tipster revealed. Henry knew the waters around Kittery Maine where Seavey's Island was located. He had gone duck hunting and fishing there many times. "Maybe I should snoop around the Wenworth," Henry said. "It's a long walk," Silas answered. "Better take a horse and get there before the story goes cold or you get scooped."

"I'm on it," Henry said as he downed his drink. He headed to the barn up the street where he stabled his horse. 20 minutes later he was at the Wentworth and sat in the lobby with a newspaper in front of him. Indeed, he overheard conversations in languages he didn't understand. When he did hear remarks in English, he decided to chance a chat using a covert approach.

"Good evening, Sir," he said to a dandy in a bowler hat. Oscar is the name. Real estate is my game. I'm here from Boston checking out property on the waterfront. What brings you to town?"

"Big meeting with important people," the visitor said.

"Oh, do tell," Henry countered. "Must be important if you're meeting here. What's it about?" Henry could see the man was now shifting in his seat. He looked perplexed. "What do you do?"

"I am a translator, I work for the government, and that is as much as I can tell you," he said.

"Interesting," Henry quipped. His curiosity was now piqued. "What do you translate?"

"I speak five languages. I interpret at international meetings." He was becoming frustrated.

"Rather spiffing, I'd say," the undercover reporter replied. Henry was getting frustrated, too. He wasn't getting anywhere. After looking in the dining room and checking the bar he did come across a couple of Asian men and others who clearly did not speak English. He decided to circle back to William Pitt for a nightcap and a closing chat with Silas.

"What did you find out?" Silas wanted to know.

"I did learn that, yes, there are more than several foreign nationals including some Orientals staying there. I still don't understand why they are here. One chap I met would tell me nothing except humbug. Maybe the world is about to go topsy-turvy."

"So, it's still a bad day, eh? What happened earlier?"

"Yeah. It is. I got an anonymous letter at the paper this morning. A death threat."

"Oh no, not again. Here, settle your nerves for the night." Silas poured him a bourbon neat.

"I'm going to go to the office early and see if anyone knows anything about the visitors."

The following morning Henry walked into the Hearld's office. It was quiet. In the journalism profession, the staff generally worked late into the night and came to work late in the morning. Perry, the newspaper's editor-in-chief, was at his desk.

"Good morning, Henry. You're in early," the boss said. Henry nodded. "I got this telegram just now. It's from Mayor William E. Marvin's office. Take a look. What do you make of this?" He shoved it across his desk to Henry.

PRESIDENT THEODORE ROOSEVELT TO ARRIVE PORTSMOUTH AUGUST 5 STOP

SET TO NEGOTIATE SETTLEMENT OF RUSSO-JAPANESE WAR STOP

PREPARE TO WELCOME THE PRESIDENT AND PROVIDE GENEROUS PRESS COVERAGE STOP

HOSPITALITY AT YOUR DISCRETION AS HOST CITY NEWSPAPER STOP

THANK YOU IN ADVANCE. THE OFFICE OF MAYOR WILLIAM E. MARVIN STOP

Henry let out a low whistle. ""Well, I declare!" he grunted. "This explains a lot." He told Perry what he learned about the activity at the Portsmouth Naval base, his evening ride to the Wentworth hotel, and encountering the foreign guests.

Perry cleared his throat. "Henry you are my best reporter with brilliant writing skills. Your articles are magic. I know you've been going through a tough time lately with covering the lumber scandals and all. I am giving you a break from the cloak and dagger activities and putting you on this story. You will be my lead man to cover President Roosevelt every minute he's in town. I'm here to help you with whatever you need. This is big. Really big. I'm holding out the front page for you for the next two weeks, and longer if there's more to report. Oh, and I will assign Lois to help you. Hmm. I'll send Jimmy the young photographer with that newfangled camera over when TR gets here. Maybe he can get something good."

"My word. Thank you, Chief," Henry stammered.

"Don't call me Chief! Just get back here with a story. I'll get together with the staff, and we'll do an editorial to go along with it."

Henry arrived at the train station with Lois and Jimmy and joined the press gaggle. A train with the presidential car on the end chugged into Portsmouth Station reached the platform. Theodore Roosevelt, the 26th President of the United States, stood in the railcar doorway and greeted the crowd. The high school band played Hail to the Chief. Roosevelt's body language exhibited the traits of a strong leader, backed up by the confidence in his voice. His fists pumped the air. His handshakes with the welcoming dignitaries were powerful.

Henry told Lois to get some quotes from the attending officials then headed to the front of the crowd. "Mr. President!" he shouted. "Henry Cliffens, Portsmouth Herald. How long do you think the negotiations will last?"

TR paused. "Steffens, Henry Cliffens? Yes, I know who you are." He slapped Henry on the back. "Quite the muckraker. Come see me at the hotel this evening. I would love to have an opportunity to chat with you privately. Let's say 8 PM. My secretary, Mr. William Loeb Jr, will give you the details. "William," the president called out. "Please take care of Mr. Cliffens. We will be meeting later for an interview."

Amidst all the hubbub William Loeb pulled Henry aside. "What time did the president tell you?" he asked Henry. "He said eight o'clock." William thought about it for a moment and said, "Fine meet me in the lobby of that Wentworth Hotel at 7:45. Do you know where it is? Henry replied. "I do. Very well." The clamor around the president subsided after a brief impromptu speech and he was put in a carriage and whisked away.

Lois got the quotes. Jimmy got some photos. Henry got an exclusive. Henry couldn't get back to the Herald office to file his story quickly enough. He burst into Perry's office then shut the door behind him and said, "Chief! You're never going to believe this!" he unraveled all the events that happened at the train station and the invitation for a one-on-one interview with the Hero of San Juan Hill.

"Great Caesar's ghost! That's incredible." Perry exclaimed. "You're just the man for the job. Go over there and hit a home run."

At quarter before eight Henry Cliffens strolled into the lobby. Once again there were men of different nationalities speaking several languages. He didn't see the translator around, not that he would need him for Mr. Loeb or President Roosevelt. The secretary approached Henry. "Good. You're on time. The President will see you now in a private dining room."

The President and his staff were finishing dinner. Roosevelt said, "Mr. Cliffens, pull a chair over here and sit next to me so I don't have to raise my voice." Then he dismissed the others. "Ask me anything you want. But if there's a question that might conflict with national security or if made public could harm foreign relations, I will answer it off the record. Are we together on this point?" Henry nodded that he understood. "Bully!" Teddy bellowed then polished his eyeglasses with a dinner napkin. "What are your interests and what do you like to do in your spare time?"

Henry wasn't sure why he was being asked. He wasn't aware how well Theodore Roosevelt understood the power of newspapers and cultivated relationships with journalists. "Honestly. Mr. President, I like to read about history, go fishing and hunting and enjoy the outdoors."

Teddy looked at his guest pensively. "We are very much the same. Those are my interests as well. I've been up to Maine on several occasions for big game hunting. I made a couple of hunting trips in the fall, with Bill Sewall and Wilmot Dow; and one winter I spent three or four weeks on snowshoes with them, visiting a couple of lumber camps. I was not a boy of any natural prowess and for that very reason the vigorous outdoor life was just what I needed. It's your turn to ask a question."

Henry thought about it for a moment. "Mr. President, do you favor Japan in these negotiations, and if so, can you tell me why?"

Roosevelt answered, "Please understand I must remain neutral as a mediator in the talks. However, yes, I do favor Japan to a certain extent for several reasons. There are a lot of global dynamics involved in balancing power. Favoring Russia for a better outcome could substantially increase their influence in the Pacific, which might potentially threaten American interests. I must say, as a military man, the Japanese victories over Russia in battles were stunning upsets. I respect the fortitude and skill of the Japanese navy and army. The United States has developing interests in Asia, and a powerful Russia there will pose a prospective threat to advancing American opportunities. Siding with Japan will help offset Russia's influence. Although, I understand both sides' perspectives and needs, so I must establish trust between Russia and Japan. In any event, my primary goal in mediation is to bring about peace, end the war, and prevent it from evolving into a larger conflict. Next question."

"Mr. President, why did you select me for this interview? There were much bigger papers from Boston represented at the train station today."

"Fair question. Simple answer. You uncovered that whole scandal about the logging industry and the corrupt deals with the railroads. The lumber companies deeply discounted the price of timbers for railroad ties in exchange for under the table kickbacks from the railroad owners. They had to make up the shortfall by charging consumers more for lumber. Meanwhile, America is growing and people are trying to build homes.

"As New York's Governor I ramped-up my anti-corruption efforts that I started as New York City's Police Commissioner. I went after issues like insurance fraud, railroad rebates, and political machine control. Furthermore, I also championed legislation to regulate public utilities.

"Conservation of our woodlands and fantastic forests are paramount to me. I've taken considerable steps to address land grabs, forest stripping, and logging corruption through the creation of national parks, forests, and monuments. This year in February I established the U.S. Forest Service. I put a good, honest man in charge, Gifford Pinchot, as its first Chief Forester. He knows the importance of scientific forest management. Pinchot studied forestry in Europe and brought those ideas back here. We traveled throughout the wildlands together and were often sparring partners at the Governor's Mansion in New York. I've known him for years, so I could trust him."

After I read your story about the antics going on with natural resources here in New England, I was keen to meet you. I like what you do and the way you write. As I have said before, far and away the best prize that life offers is the chance to work hard at work worth doing. That's why your newspaper got a telegram from the mayor."

Henry's jaw dropped. He never would have imagined that this colorful, bombastic president would reach out to him.

"I tell you what," Teddy continued. "It's been a long day, it's hot, and I don't enjoy stuffy hotels. I could use some fresh air and perhaps a sarsaparilla, or perhaps something more robust. Do you know of a place that's out of the way of the crowds?"

"I know just the place. Since you enjoy history, and I'm told you're a Freemason like myself, you will like it there. The barman is a trusted friend. Like you and I, he despises scallywags, crooks, and corruption. If I ask him to keep quiet, he will. It's a bit far from here, though. It's called Puddle Dock in a rundown section of town. It was originally named Strawberry Banke in 1623 by the British settlers because of all the wild strawberries that grew along the banks of the Piscataqua River. After many years of serving as a port for international trade the river silted in and the surrounding area fell into decline, and the name was changed to Puddle

Duck because of constant flooding. Puddle Dock was a tidal estuary but was filled in during the 19th century to create more land for expansion.

"I see. Do you ride?"

"It's a must up here, Sir."

"Can you get a pair of saddled horses?"

"Certainly, I can."

"Go fetch the horses and bring them around back to the service entrance. Find my bodyguards, tell them you're here for me, and give them the password... Bully Whitehouse pugilist."

By 10 o'clock they were at the Wiiliam Pitt Tavern. Aside from Silas, it was empty. Silas was astounded when Roosevelt stepped through the doorway. After overcoming the shock he blurted, "What'll it be, Mr. President?"

"Let's see. How about a sarsaparilla?" He slapped his hand down hard on the bar. "On further consideration let's have mint julep along with no talk of politics tonight."

"Coming right up. Mr. President. It's on the house." He poured three cocktails. Silas told Roosevelt the history of the William Pitt, and that he wasn't the only president to ever visit there. Silas listed the prominent guests who had been there during the tavern's history. He spoke about the Grand Masonic Lodge established there more than one hundred years ago. Roosevelt appreciated Silas' knowledge and told him how he had joined Matinecock Lodge No. 806 in Oyster Bay, New York, just five months before becoming President of the United States.

It was getting late and time to get back to the Wentworth. The next morning negotiations began with President Theodore Roosevelt presiding. The Treaty of Portsmouth, signed on September 5, 1905, formally ended the Russo-Japanese War of 1904-1905.

Roosevelt the gifted orator who could captivate audiences and deliver powerful messages didn't make public speeches immediately after the treaty was signed, his actions and subsequent comments reflected his satisfaction and pride in this diplomatic victory.

There was some criticism of the Treaty, particularly from the Japanese who felt they had not gained enough. Roosevelt believed it was a reasonable arrangement. He saw it as a crucial step in keeping the balance of power in the Pacific and avoiding further conflict.

Henry filed his final story about the international meeting. Excerpts from his first-hand accounts of Roosevelt's private interview session with him added to the depth of his articles. What was even more fascinating to the editor were the stories Henry told him that couldn't be printed. Demand for the Herald went up. Advertising revenues increased. He got a raise and Perry told him to take some time off, as much as he wanted, to go hunting and fishing.

Henry Cliffens returned to the office after the Thanksgiving holiday weekend with a clear head. Being alone in the woods had refreshed him and gave him newfound vigor. Still single he thought about finding the right woman and settling down. Preferably a woman who could enjoy outdoor lie. His paycheck was now enough to afford a bigger place. Perry greeted him warmly. Afterall, Henry was a lucrative asset to the newspaper.

"You've got mail," Perry said. Henry rolled his eyes. In the past the mail usually included threats, lawsuits, and hateful rhetoric. "One of them looks important. I'll let you open these in private."

Henry thumbed through the stack. Anything without a return name and address he put aside. He stopped when he got to an envelope with a return name and address that was obviously important. It said Theodore Roosevelt, President of the United States, The Whitehouse, 1600 Pennsylvania Avenue Washington DC. Henry slid his thumb under the envelope's flap, pulled the letter out and began to read.

Dear Mr. Cliffens, Thank you once again for the time we spent together and for your hospitality while in Portsmouth. I don't know if you have any Christmas plans, or if there is anything or anyone keeping you in Portsmouth for that time. If not, and you are interested and available, you are invited to my family's retreat residence at Sagamore Hill, Oyster Bay, Long Island New York for the holidays. Hunting opportunities abound. Kindly RSVP at your convenience. Either way, I appreciate the opportunity to invite you. Sincere Regards, Teddy Roosevelt.

"Perry!" he hollered. "I think I'm going to need some more of that as much time as I need off; off." Four days before Christmas Henry boarded a train for Long Island. Within an hour after arriving in Oyster Bay, he found himself standing on the wide veranda of the Roosevelt summer Whitehouse, which was used much more often than only in the summer months. He admired the Queen Anne style influences of the architecture; the non-symmetrical front, steeply pitched roofs with various angles and gables hosting a complex array of dormers and turrets. A housekeeper answered his knock on the door and invited him in as several of the Roosevelt children were taking turns sliding down the banister. "Mr. President is down at the stables looking after his horses. He's been expecting you. It's close by," She gave him directions to the stables.

Henry followed the short path to the barn. It wasn't hard to find. Like Roosevelt everything he did, it was oversized. Henry swung the barn door open and there stood the President with another man. Roosevelt spoke first. "Ah, Cliffens my good man! Glad to see you made it. Bully! Please meet Gifford Pinchot, our Chief of the Forest Service." Henry extended his hand to Pinchot and said, "pleased to meet you, Sir." Pinchot replied, "Likewise. Teddy has told me a lot about you."

Roosevelt stood beside three shotguns leaning against the wall and dozens of duck decoys scattered on the floor. "Cliffens, are you up to some duck hunting first thing in the morning? Pinchot and I are going to add tasty Teal ducks and wood ducks to the Christmas menu if we are successful. We hope you will join us. I'll have Noah Seaman or Robert Gillespie ask my staff to put these decoys out on Eel Creek near Cold Spring Harbor this evening. We have a good duck blind set up there. It's not too far of a hike from here. We'll walk rather than ride there to keep things quiet, but I'll have them pick us up by wagon afterwards."

"You can count me in," said Henry. "It would be an honor to be alongside you and Mr. Pinchot. The ducks won't stand a chance." "Bully!" roared President Roosevelt. "I'll have the house staff kit you out."

All the hunters were successful, Roosevelt, an excellent marksman, outscored the others. Teddy invited Henry and the Chief of the Forest Service to join him for coffee in the North Room of the Sagamore Hill mansion after breakfast. In the sprawling 20 by 40-foot room Henry marveled at an intriguing collection of items showing Theodore Roosevelt's active life. On display were a variety of gifts from foreign dignitaries and admirers, his cavalry saber and hat from the Spanish-American War, an extensive library of books, and numerous animal trophy heads that stared down at the mountain lion and bear rugs. Henry was also interested to see a huge, decorated Christmas tree in the corner tucked beneath the 20-foot ceiling.

"I must say, Mr. President," Henry began, "I'm not surprised to see so many magnificent hunting trophies, but I am flabbergasted to see a Christmas tree. My understanding is that you didn't have one."

Roosevelt laughed. "The newspapers love to speculate about whether the Roosevelts will have a tree each year, as if they didn't have something more to write about. Christmas trees are a recent development in the celebration of Christmas. I'm sure not as many people as some would think are put off by the White House not having one. Besides, we have visitors from around the world and not all countries celebrate the holiday. Not having a Christmas tree there is another reason to help with diplomatic relations. The fact of the matter is Mr. Cliffens, the White House is often crowded and in use for public events and gatherings. With six Roosevelt children it's difficult to find space for a Christmas tree. And I suppose what adds fuel to their Christmas tree stories is that I am undoubtably a conservationist, as you well know. However, I have never spoken out about Christmas trees. With more than 80 acres here at Sagamore Hill, the children and I take great joy in choosing and harvesting one of the cedars on the property. We sawed this one down a few days ago.

"I see," answered Henry. "Nonetheless, it's quite the impressive room you have here."

"Thank you, young man. Yes, Mrs. Roosevelt was getting tired of the constant flow of visitors waiting in her drawing room to see me. So, this year we added the North Room. The addition cost as much as I paid for the entire house. That mahogany you see there was imported from the Philippines.

"The Philippines are an interesting place. As you may or may not know, after we defeated Spain in the Spanish-American War, we acquired the Philippines as part of the Treaty of Paris deal in December of '98. I suppose going to Cuba and the Rough Riders victory at the battle of San Juan Hill had a benefit. Glad I could do my part."

Teddy leaned forward in his chair. "I have a thought, Henry. Back to that balderdash about me and Christmas trees. You can dispel the myth and set the record straight. I think it would be a great topic for an article. I would be very much obliged. It will help me with public relations. We can get a photographer up here to take a photograph of my family and me in front of this splendid tree. I'll have my secretary, Mr. Loeb, send clippings to the gadflies and put an end to the rumor. But, by all means, that's not the reason I invited you to Long Island. Pinchot and I will discuss that with you over cigars and good Port wine after we are done with Christmas dinner.

Christmas Day dinner was a lavish meal at Sagamore Hill. There were: oysters on the half shell from local waters, smoked salmon canapés, lobster salad, cream of celery soup, roast duck taken the day before on Eel Creek, roast turkey with chestnut stuffing, baked ham glazed with pineapple, mashed potatoes, cranberry sauce made from native cranberries harvested from Eastern Long Island bogs near Riverhead, roasted Brussels sprouts, green bean casserole, followed by pumpkin pie with whipped cream, fruitcake, and Christmas pudding with brandy butter.

"My word, that was quite a feast," Henry said to his hosts. "Thank you immensely for inviting me. As a newspaper man I don't get meals like this, even at special family occasions."

"Our pleasure, Henry," Teddy said. "Please thank your family. I am sure they have missed having you home for the holidays. Gentlemen, let's adjourn to more comfortable surroundings."

As they stood Henry said, "I am sure the family will understand, and they thank you. It's not very often a muckraker gets invited to the home of a president."

They returned to the North Room and the butler brought in cigars, the Port, and three small, tulip-shaped wine glasses. "Make yourself comfortable, Henry. There's something Gifford and I want to discuss with you."

Henry stammered, "Oh, Mr. President. Your Christmas tree article is almost finished, it will be ready tonight. I've titled it Presidential Holiday at Home. I think you will…" his voice trailed off as the tall, athletic Gifford Pinchot held up his hand.

"No, no, no. This is something entirely different. Let me explain the primary reason you were invited here while I would be visiting with the Roosevelts for the holidays. The President sent me clippings of your well researched and beautifully written articles that uncovered the corruption and dishonest land grabs in the logging industry up north. You made quite an impression. Plus, you're a good duck hunter to boot. In the U.S. Forest Service, I have a need for honest, dependable men. Men who can report back to me what they find in underhanded dealings in our great nation's wildlands. It must be someone who enjoys being outdoors a great deal of the time. It must be someone who can write clearly. I have discussed this with my long-time friend, President Roosevelt. We know about the death threats you have received, your long working hours, and the relatively low pay that goes along with them. We want to offer you a top position in the new U.S. Forest Service to help us conserve our nation's woodlands and natural resources with a substantial pay increase, job security and paid vacation leave to do as you please. The President has agreed."

Henry leapt off the couch and shook hands with each man. "I unconditionally accept!" he burst out. "Thank you, and Merry Christmas!"

"Merry Christmas, Henry," the President said as the butler stepped in. "Another round, gentlemen?" the servant asked. "Let's say yes. After all, we are celebrating more than Christmas tonight," Roosevelt answered as the butler poured the second round of Port. "After all… that was the easiest negotiation I have ever mediated. Bully!"

Story Notes - President Theodore Roosevelt was awarded the Nobel Peace Prize in 1906 for his positive results in overseeing the Russo-Japan Peace Talks. His effective mediation enhanced the United States' worldwide importance and positioned America as a substantial player in international affairs.

Roosevelt is known as the Conservation President. He created the U.S. Forest Service in 1905 with Gifford Pinchot as its first Chief Forester. Pinchot's acute eye for wildlife habitat helped add critical forests and wilderness areas to the preservation list.

During his presidential term from 1901 to 1909, Theodore Roosevelt preserved approximately 230 million acres of public land. He created the first eighteen national monuments, the initial 55 federal game preserves and bird reservations, 150 national forests, and five National Parks: Crater Lake National Park, Oregon, Wind Cave National Park, South Dakota, Sully's Hill National Park, North Dakota, which was later re-designated as a game preserve, Mesa Verde National Park, Colorado, and Platt National Park, Oklahoma.

Teddy Roosevelt, an avid ornithologist and naturalist, began a continuing experiment to shape habitats for his beloved wildlife by creating what would become the National Wildlife Refuge System on March 14, 1903. This early experiment included Pelican Island, Florida, to protect a critical rookery for endangered pelicans; Breton Island, Louisiana, the only refuge that it's believed Roosevelt visited after retirement; and the National Bison Range, Montana, which is considered America's first attempt at wildlife restoration. Roosevelt's first experiment with the four-acre Pelican Island Bird Reservation evolved to more than 560 wildlife refuges and monuments protecting 850 million acres of lands and waters.

I have made numerous visits to Sagamore Hill, Oyster Bay Long Island, New York. It is now run by the National Park Service. I highly recommend seeing the Theodore Roosevelts Summer White House.

TWENTY-ONE

Charleston, South Carolina

Church steeples reached for the morning sun in the Holy City. As the sun climbed higher Frank stepped from stone to stone along the battery sea wall making his way to Gadsden Creek. He held a large catch net in one hand and a bucket half-filled with saltwater in the other. He had finished his route early and decided to catch some crabs to use later in the day as bait. He had a bag slung over his shoulder that held a few chicken bones and string. Frank figured he'd hawk his last few copies of The News and Courier newspaper on a King Street corner before his final stop at Jim's Bakery. King Street was always productive for him. Merchants would buy a paper on the way to their shops that lined King Street. Frank Simmons was well known for his loud, colorful newspaper selling tactics. People sought him out and tipped well.

Frank got to the water's edge and crouched on a low ballast stone. He slid the net into the water and let it rest on the bottom. Next, he removed a chicken leg bone that held just enough meat from the shoulder bag and tied it to a length of string and tossed it in the center of the submerged net. He peered into the brackish water and waited patiently. Within moments a large blue crab crawled to the bait. "Gotcha!" he hollered as he snatched up the net. He flipped the net over on top of the pail capturing his prey. "That's one," he said confidently as he covered the pail with sheets of newsprint. "Three more and it'll be time to skedaddle." Sure enough. In rapid succession he caught three more. His cocker spaniel, Buff, sat in the shade at the top of the wall waiting for his master. The dog knew the drill well. Every morning it was the paper route followed by fishing or crabbing along the battery, then to town for a treat at Jim's. One of the shop girls always tossed him a snack. The girls in the bakery loved Buff and he always returned their affections with a wet nose and wagging tail.

Frank liked and appreciated the girls at Jim's. They were all a little older than him. Mandy, older by a year than the others, wanted to go to nursing school following high school at Roper Hospital on the corner of Barre Street and Calhoun Street that was newly reconstructed and opened in 1906. She had no idea how it might be possible. They all came from working class families that struggled. She was kind, caring and always had a pun or a riddle for Frank to figure out. Darcy had the most business sense, so Jim let her manage his books. Christin was Frank's information source on anything that swam, crawled, or flew around Charleston Harbor or the Wando, Ashley, and Cooper Rivers. Christin knew about them all and had a sketch book with drawings of the wildlife there. The three were students at the Memminger High School for Girls and worked before and after classes, summers, and holidays at Jim's. They didn't come from wealthy families, like the girls who lived in mansions on East Battery Street with a view of Charleston Harbor, but each household did what they had to do to send their daughters to the private school. They were finished by noon on Sundays. On Sunday mornings they took turns running the shop counter while one of them attended Mass down the street at the Sacred Heart Catholic Church at 888 King Street. The Sunday morning church rotation began at 7 AM. Jim encouraged it. Jim, a German immigrant, was allowed under the Blue Laws to open for a limited time on Sundays to accommodate the German custom of baking bread on that day. They worked part-time and it was all the help that Jim could afford. Business was tough for Jim, who was in the Catholic seminary in Germany to become a priest before a change of heart sent him to America. The theological school didn't offer business classes. Jim appreciated the young women being flexible about the schedule. It all worked out. The bakery closed before dinnertime, so they had time to do their schoolwork, have dinner with their families, and they could go fishing during the weekends and summers. Jim valued the three who were honest, polite, courteous and with a charming smile could double a customer's order. Jim's shop girls exemplified Southern hospitality in every sense of the words. They were sweet. And Jim knew they were good for his cash box.

What Frank valued more than anything about the three girls was that they all could fish. And he had to admit, they were better anglers than he was. More than that, they had a boat. It was Darcy's father's boat, but she had permission to take it out whenever she wanted to. Sometimes the trio would invite Frank to tag along and sail to John's Island and picnic beneath the giant branches of Angel Oak. Many believed that Angel Oak was at least 400 to 500 years-old, and some said it could be much older. None of them cared about the age of the tree, although it was a beautiful place to be. Darcy's boat also got them to some of the best remote fishing spots, or to the ocean beach to hunt for shark teeth, or for a sail past Fort Moultrie and wave to the men stationed there. Sometimes Darcy would beach the boat in a tidal marsh so Frank and Christin could jump over the gunnel to slog through the plough mud to look for critters in the nutrient rich mud. Darcy insisted they had to wash off the smelly mud before getting back on the boat. Mandy was always positioned in the bow on fishing outings ready to throw a cast net to haul in shrimp, finger mullet and mud minnows for bait. She claimed she could cast a net better than any man.

Frank loved history and could write well, or so he was told. He always got A grades in History and English at his school. Although, he often considered if either would get him a job in the future. His mother told him a teaching job or writing for a newspaper might suit him. Frank figured that he might be better off in the fishing trades since he didn't see a path to a college education. His father was a dock worker on the Charleston harbor front. It was hard work but paid well enough that the man could support his wife and three children but not enough to pay a college tuition. Frank was the oldest. Frank had a wealth of knowledge about local history. He would tell anyone who would listen stories about the history of Charleston. He always avoided talking about the unsavory past slave trade in the city. And he refused to write a word about it.

His grandfather was Harbor pilot in Charleston. During the Civil War on May 12th, 1862, he watched Robert Smalls, who was enslaved since birth, and was also a pilot, commandeer a steamer and sail out of the Harbor and past the blockade. He didn't stand in the way and watched as

Smalls craftily sailed to freedom and read the headlines in 1875 when Smalls was elected as the first black congressman from South Carolina. His grandfather told Frank he wasn't in the war in defense of slavery, he only wanted to protect coastal communities from being burned to the ground by the Union Army.

Frank liked to tell the story about how Fort Moultrie got its name. With dramatic flair he would deliver the tale, "Way back to the time of the American Revolution, during the beastly hot June of 1776, Colonel William Moultrie, with more than 400 men, consisting of members from his 2nd South Carolina Regiment of provincial troops along with Patriot volunteers, had started building a fort on Sullivan's Island to protect Charleston Harbor. They cut palmetto logs and stacked them ten feet high then the workers piled a 16-foot-thick bank of sand for reinforcement behind the palm logs. On June 28th the not quite finished Fort Sullivan came under attack by the British fleet with Admiral Sir Peter Parker in command. He had the Royal Navy open fire on the unfinished fort. Just before the battle Moultrie came up with a flag design using one of his soldier's blue coats and the crescent shape from his hat to make a signal to let the people of Charleston know if and when the British were coming. Before running it up the flagpole during the battle with cannon balls flying in both directions, good ol' Moultrie had somebody stich the word liberty on the navy-blue flag.

"Little did the Redcoats know, their cannon balls bounced off the tough palmetto trunks and all that sand absorbed the shock that followed. Moultrie and his men started laughing at the useless British fleet. Then the Patriots got serious and returned cannon fire, greatly damaging the British ships. It took 16 hours, but the British Navy was defeated for the first time in 100 years, and they wobbled off out to sea.

"Colonel Moultrie saved the Fort and Charleston for the time being. Everybody thought it would be a good idea to change the name of Fort Sullivan to Fort Moultrie. Moultrie made out okay. That September, they made him a General and after the Revolution the good folks of South Carolina elected him Governor." Frank would always take a long pause before his next point and put his hand over his heart. "And, I might add, that blue flag got shot down. A Sergeant named William Jasper scooted out in the open during the bombardment and grabbed the flag and rallied the troops until it could be put up again. Jasper's actions were seen as so heroic, saving Charleston from invasion for another four years, it made that flag the symbol of the Revolution, and liberty, in South Carolina.

They added a palmetto palm to the flag as a salute to the mighty tree trunks that built the fort and protected the men. Now we know it as our state flag."

Frank wrote stories about Edgar Alan Poe who was influenced by his time at Fort Moultrie and Sullivan's Island. Frank knew Poe wrote *The Gold-Bug* in 1843, a story that features a hidden treasure on an island, buried secrets and hidden messages. Frank imagined Sullivan's Island was creepy enough and the fort was eerie enough to inspire the novel. He penned stories about Fort Sumter in Charleston Harbor and the start of the Civil War. He wrote and told stories about how the Charleston Customs House, also known as the Old Exchange and Provost Dungeon, was used by Patriots during the American Revolution to hide gunpowder from the British Army that invaded Charleston in 1780. The Charleston colonists built a secret chamber below the Customs House that concealed about 100,000 pounds of gunpowder behind a false exterior wall. Although the gunpowder was literally under their feet, the British never found it, which was valuable to the American revolutionists later in the war after the British left Charleston. The Provost Dungeon below the Exchange became a prison during the British occupation of Charleston from 1780 to 1782. They held American prisoners of war there, including a few well-known Patriots including three signers of the Declaration of Independence: Edward Rutledge, Arthur Middleton, and Thomas Heyward Jr., and Colonel Isaac Hayne, who was in the Continental Army. Hayne was captured by the British after Charleston fell in 1780. The British offered prisoners of war freedom in return for signing an oath of allegiance to the Crown. Hayne signed the oath, probably to return to his family. Hayne, a true Patriot, couldn't stay away from the fight against the British and rejoined the Continental Army. The British saw his action as a violation of his oath, resulting in a treason charge. Hayne was tried and executed on August 4, 1781. It sparked the wrath of the colonists and reinforced American determination. Isaac Hayne became an icon of American patriotism and the harsh treatment that colonists had to endure from the British. Frank included that Christopher Gadsden was briefly held in the Provost Dungeon before the British shipped him to the prison at the Castillo de San Marcos fort in St. Augustine Florida.

Christopher Gadsden, a successful merchant in Charleston, was an outspoken rebel who played a key role for the cause. He was a forceful critic of British policies such as the Stamp Act, and a co-founder of the Sons of Liberty Charleston Chapter, a group known for taking a strong opposition against British rule. Gadsden also played a role in the effective defense of Fort Moultrie during the British naval attack in 1776. Gadsden was credited with designing the flag with the motto *Don't Tread on Me,* a statement of American defiance. Gadsden Creek, where Frank went crabbing, was named after Thomas Gadsden, the son of Christopher Gadsden.

Frank pushed his cart to his favorite spot on the corner of King Street and Meeting Street. He shouted to those passing by, "Extra! Extra! Read all about it! Forest fire burns Montana and Idaho! Almost 100 perish! If you don't believe me, read all about it in the News and Courier! A man in a derby hat bought a newspaper. "Ain't that something. Thanks, Kid. Can't wait to read all about it." Frank droned on, "Extra! Extra! Read all about it in the News and Courier!" Even in the early morning the August swelter didn't deter him, or Buff who greeted each customer with his stumpy tail wagging. Frank continued to his last stop before going home. He kept two newspapers. One for the bakery, the other for his mother and father.

Frank often came to the back door, although it was now eight o'clock and the bake shop was open. As a streetcar clanged past, he left his cart outside the front door in the shade of the bake shop, grabbed one of the two remaining newspapers, and entered. He left the crabs outside. "C'mon, Buff," he said to his dog. Bells on the door announced their arrival as they walked into the aroma filled shop. "There you are, extra, extra, Frankie!" Darcy called out from behind the counter. "What's the news of the day?" Frank didn't like to be called Frankie, and Francis even less. He flopped the News and Courier on the counter. "Here you go, Cupcake. Read the news for yourself before it gets stale," he said. Darcy fumed, "Cupcake?" Christin laughed. She put a springerle, an anise-flavored cookie with an intricate design that was pressed into the dough before baking, in front of Frank. "Here, eat this. You won't be so cross. Jim is in the back. I put fresh coffee on for him. Or, we have sweet tea if you want some," Christin said. Mandy knelt and gave Buff a brötchen. "Here's a bread roll, Buff. I put some butter on it for you," Mandy told the dog and patted him on the head. Buff gobbled the buttered roll and wagged his tail with excitement.

"Would y'all like to go fishing down on the dock by Murray Street this evening when it cools off? I already got some bait crabs this morning. I'm gonna use half a blue crab, just like Darcy taught me. I'm fixin' to try for redfish."

"Where is Murray Street?" Darcy wanted to know.

"It's that dirt road along the mud flats by the battery. The city is naming it Murray Street after Andrew Buist Murray, that local philanthropist and businessman. They are fixin' to pave it this year. There was a story all about it in the newspaper. I think they're going to make a big fuss with a ceremony and all at the dedication."

"How many crabs did you get?" Darcy asked. Frank proudly held up four fingers.

"Those will go fast, but I'm in," said Darcy. "Me too. I want to go," added Christin. Mandy chimed in, "I want to come, too. Don't worry. I'll bring a cast net if we run out of bait."

Frank rounded the counter and went into the back room that was full of heavy wooden tables covered with flour dust. Baking ovens lined the walls. Jim sat on a stool at one of the tables with his face planted in his hands.

"Good morning, Jim!" Frank called out from the doorway. "Are you alright?"

"Guten morgen, Frankie," Jim replied. Frank cringed and rolled his eyes. "Ja, I'm fine. Just tired. I started extra early this morning to get ahead of the heat. And I'm worried. I got a notice from the landlord yesterday that the rent will be going up a lot on the first of next year. I can barely pay the bills now. Wheat prices have been going up. Sugar has always been high and is going up now a bit, too." Jim sighed and continued. "I thought that once the Charleston Naval Yard opened business would be good with people from there stopping by. It's been a few years and not so much. Only a few from there. I think the sailors prefer saloons and not sweets on shore leave."

"Sorry to hear that, Mr. Jim. Is there anything I can do?"

"Nein, Frankie," Jim said as he got up to pour the boy a cup of coffee. "The holiday rush is still months away. I don't know if that will be enough. It's only Christmas once a year. Ja?"

Frank listened as he sipped his coffee and ate several quarkbällchen, cinnamon dusted deep-fried dough balls made with quark cheese, flour, eggs, and sugar. He didn't know what else to say to Jim other than, "I'll see you tomorrow." Frank worried about Jim losing his business and his friends losing their jobs.

Frank exited the back room and stopped to say goodbye and reconfirm the fishing plans for that evening. "Well. Ladies, shall I see you by White Point Gardens at seven this evening? If y'all are coming, could you bring some of that white bakery paper to wrap the catch in? I'll filet whatever we get," Frank said. Darcy stopped pushing a broom and answered, "You can count on it. We all will see you later at White Point. But hold on a minute. Before you run off, let me introduce you to Commander George Hopkins." She gestured towards a man at the counter in a Navy uniform. "He's a guest lecturer on history at the Citadel."

Darcy and Frank stepped to the counter. She made the introductions. "Commander, please allow me to introduce our friend, Frank Simmons. He's an avid American history student, quite a writer, and a darn good storyteller." Commander Hopkins shook hands with Frank. "Pleased to meet you, Sir," Frank said. "I certainly am a student of history. I read all I can about it. And I learn about who is making history by reading the newspaper every day."

"I see," the man said. "Yes, I recognize you and your dog from the street corner by Market Street. You're quite the showman as well, I must say. I have bought a newspaper from you a time or so on my way to the Citadel."

"Yes, I understand you teach history there? Isn't the Citadel about the Army?" Frank questioned.

"In a manner of speaking yes. As a guest lecturer on loan from the Navy I give talks to the students about the Navy's role in the Battle of San Juan Hill in Cuba during '98. I was selected to be on board the SS Yucatan, a civilian transport ship that carried Teddy Roosevelt and his volunteer force of Rough Riders to Cuba. After the USS Maine exploded in Havanna Harbor, the Navy was on high alert. We picked them up in Tampa in May and gave them a ride to the battle."

"Did you bring their horses, too?" Frank asked.

"No young man. Although the Rough Riders were a cavalry unit, the horses were left behind in Florida. The battle was mainly fought on foot. I talk about the methods used for getting the troops there, and other parts of the world, as part of my lectures on the Navy's role in warfare logistics. Seeing how as you're keen on history, perhaps one day you would like to attend a lecture as my personal guest."

Frank couldn't believe his ears. "Sir, I would be honored and delighted. Thank you for the opportunity!"

"Once I get my schedule for the semester, I will let one of the girls here know the date when I think I will be covering an area that will interest you. I often stop by here on my way to the school or on the way home. My wife's mother is a German descendant. She loves anything I bring home from Jim's."

For a moment Frank wished more people would come to the bakery to bring home Jim's cakes and cookies.

With the start of the new school year the summer of 1910 came to a close. As the days grew shorter Frank wondered when he would have the chance to attend one of Commander Hopkins' lectures. He continued delivering newspapers, selling what was left on the street and stopping at the bakery before school every day. One month led to the next and the girls juggled their work schedule around school, church, and fishing.

On a November morning Frank arrived as usual before the shop opened. Jim sat at a wooden table with papers spread out in front of him. Frank recognized the papers as the ledgers that Darcy recorded the sums on for the day and payouts for various vendors. Frank could see the look of frustration on the shop owner's face.

"Ich habe ein wirklich schlechtes Gefühl," Jim said.

"Good morning. I beg your pardon?" Frank countered.

"I have a really bad feeling, Frank," Jim replied.

Frank answered, "I can see that. What's wrong?"

"I have been going over the numbers. We have more going out than is coming in, and costs are rising faster than yeast on a hot day. Mir ist übel vor Ekel," Jim said.

"Disgusted, Eh?" Frank said.

"Ja, ekel. Christmas will be here soon, and I won't have enough money to cover the cost of baking supplies. Christmas cakes and so forth require much more expensive ingredients. It's more than just flour. I will need fruit and nuts, candied citrus peel and raisins to bake stollen. I have to have cinnamon, cloves, ginger, and some other spices to make lebkuchen. Pfeffernüsse are easy, they only need black pepper added to gingerbread cookies. Vanillekipferl vanilla crescent cookies are simple too, but I do have to have almonds for them. Dominosteine can be tricky to make, Ja? They are like tiny Advent calendars. Each layer represents a different day leading up to Christmas. For those I must have marzipan, jelly, and chocolate…"

Frank said, "Y'all are making me hungry, Jim." Jim went to a shelf and pulled out a Bremer Klaben, a sweet bread glazed with icing named after the northern German city of Bremen made with almonds, dried fruit, and spices. Jim cut a slice and pushed it towards Frank. "Here essen this. Es ist wunderbar. There's coffee over there." He nodded toward the stove.

Frank read the headline of the morning edition, 'Sugar Trust Facing Antitrust Lawsuit.' "That should help," he said. Often referred to as the Sugar Trust, The American Sugar Refining Company, founded in 1882 created a monopoly on a sizable portion of the sugar refining industry in the United States through a series of mergers and acquisitions. This gave the Sugar Trust ample power to control sugar prices. In 1910 Congress filed a lawsuit against the American Sugar Refining Company. They focused on the company's anti-competitive practices such as predatory pricing and exclusive railroad contracts.

Frank pushed the newspaper to Jim. "Here you go. Read all about it," Frank said as he stood up. "Mama says you're invited for Sunday dinner. She's putting up a seafood boil. Maybe that will cheer you up."

Frank went to the shop door to visit his friends. Christin greeted Frank "Good morning, Frank. Commander Hopkins stopped by yesterday and asked me to tell you that you should go with him to the Citadel next Wednesday for his lecture. Says he'll meet you here at 8 o'clock. You'll have to skip school or be tardy. I told the commander a little more about how knowledgeable you are on Charleston history. I must say, he was interested." Frank couldn't wait for Wednesday.

Frank was already at the shop when the Navy officer arrived. "Good morning, Sir! Should I call you Commander or Mr. Hopkins?"

"How about you call me George?"

Frank didn't feel comfortable about using the man's first name but went along with Commander Hopkins' suggestion. "Alright. George it is."

As they walked George told Frank stories about his world travels. And Frank told him about his life and family in Charleston, and about Jim, who had become his friend. Frank confided in George about Jim's financial struggles that might cost his friends their jobs. George took it all in. Other than nodding, he didn't respond. "Today I will begin a series of talks about foreign naval attacks on America. I'll start with the American Revolution," George said. Frank's ears perked up. They walked the 10 blocks to the Citadel and entered the lecture room. George showed Frank where to sit in the front row and took his place behind the podium as the cadets filed in. For the next 30 minutes Frank sat fascinated as he listened to accounts of coastal raids by British warships and privateers on coastal towns and villages including 1775 British raids on Virginia to destroy Revolutionist's military supplies and Falmouth, Massachusetts where the town was burned in retaliation for seizing British ships.

Commander Hopkins closed his notebook. "Cadets, I am going to stop there for today. For the remainder of our time together, I am turning the lecture over to a Charleston civilian resident who will speak on the 1776 Battle of Sullivan's Island at Fort Moultrie. Gentlemen, in closing, as I've mentioned here before; strategies are for amateurs, tactics are for experts, logistics are for professionals, which leads to a winning outcome." Frank was charged with excitement. He looked around the room of uniformed cadets and asked himself, *I wonder who the speaker could be?*

"Please allow me to introduce Frank Simmons who is an expert on the Fort Moultrie battle," Commander Hopkins told the class. Frank was shocked and walked to the podium. Hopkins leaned over and in a low voice said, "Your friends at the bakery told me all about your presentation on Fort Moultrie. The room is yours." Frank gulped, paused, then delivered a rousing talk on the Battle of Fort Moultrie. Frank had the rapt attention of all the students and Commander Hopkins.

The two walked back to the bakery dodging streetcars as they passed. "I was impressed," George Hopkins said. "What are your plans for the future? Job? College?" The Charleston paperboy explained what he would like to do, however in reality, what he would have to do… probably find a job on the waterfront or in the fishing trades. "I'm just an ordinary guy," Frank uttered. George asked more questions about Jim and Frank's three friends at the bakery. "Are Jim and the girls family?" George questioned. "No, but we could be. We all look after each other."

Frank gave George the details about Jim's business falling into decline due to the rise of wheat prices and the inflated cost of sugar. And that Jim wouldn't have enough money to cover the costs of the Christmas rush and was hoping there would be more business from the Navy yard and their families. He told George about the three young women, how smart they all were, and how they all needed their jobs to help out at home, and that Mandy wanted to go to nursing school at Roper Hospital, and Christin could go on to be a famous scientist like the botanist and educator Martha Jane Cory, an expert on algae and bryophytes. "We are all hoping to do something for people in Charleston this Christmas. Father Corrigan told us in church to do good works and help those less fortunate. We haven't come up with a plan yet. We're just young'uns, and we don't have much to offer."

George listened and nodded intermittently. After a long silence he said, "I have an idea. It involves a little strategy, tactics, and logistics."

As always, the bells on the door jingled as they entered the bakery. Buff greeted them both with a polite bark and a wagging tail. The girls wanted to know how Frank did with his speech. "Frank should be proud of himself. He did a fine job and left many of the cadets wide-eyed and astonished. I'll have to bring him back to lecture on the Patriot's sly shenanigans at the Customs House. Since I'm here, I would like to buy four Bremer Klaben cakes, four stollen, four dozen vanillekipferl cookies, and double that amount of springerle, and a same amount of Zimtsterne if you have enough of them. And Frank, I'm hiring you and your pushcart to get everything over to the officer's wardroom at the Navy Yard. A launch is waiting for me at the dock. They will ferry us up to the Navy Yard and bring you back later. Buff can come, too.

Jim panicked the next day when he learned about the size of the order that went out. "That's a lot of flour and sugar. I will not have enough left for my regular Charleston customers. I may have to close before Christmas," he said. Frank listened and shrugged. "Don't worry so much... I have a plan that will take a little strategy and logistics," Frank replied and added, "I got to scram. I have a stop to make on the way home. I'll see you first thing in the morning."

Frank went to the front of the shop at a rapid pace to say goodbye to the trio. "Ahh, Frankie," Darcy shouted. "Hold on a minute. We must chat with y'all."

"I'm in a hurry!" he exclaimed.

"This will only take a quick minute," she answered. Mandy and Christin stood behind her with their arms folded in front of their aprons.

"We came up with a plot for what we can all do for good works for others at Christmas. We need y'all's help." Her coworkers nodded in agreement. "It's something we can all do. But we must work together to pull it off. And... we will have to work hard and work fast."

"Are we robbing a bank?" Frank quipped.

"Hardly," Christin answered as she stepped forward. "We've seen how Jim sends bread and German baked treats on Christmas Eve to German families who have fallen on hard times. Right?" Frank nodded in agreement. She went on, "You know about the Italian families and how they have their Festa dei Sette Pesci, or the feast of the seven fishes, as we say. Right?" Again, Frank bobbed his head. "So, here's the plan. We got the names and addresses from Father Corrigan of a few of the Italian parishioners that have been having a tough time of things." Christin once again folded her arms and stepped back. Mandy smiled and came forward. "The four of us are going to get Darcy's boat out early on Christmas Eve morning. We will fish harder than we ever have before. We will bring all our catch nets, rods and reels, and fish traps. It's been warm so I'm sure we can hook, net, or trap at least seven different species between finfish, shrimp, clams, eels, and whatever else we can come up with. We will bring empty burlap flour sacks and split up the haul. Hopefully, we can spread the good cheer to everyone on the list. With the Good Lord watching over us, I believe we will do fine." Mandy closed with a question. "Are you with us, Frank Simmons?"

"You can count on me!" he replied forcefully.

"There's one more thing," Christin added. "This all has to take place under complete secrecy. We slip out before sunrise in the morning and drop the bags off at their front doors in the early evening darkness. We knock and run. The only other person who will know is Jim so he can cover the front counter in the morning. We can find a couple of kids to help him."

"What an idea," he told them. "I'll be back early tomorrow morning before you open. Christmas is still a ways off so we time to work out the logistics." Frank grinned as he realized George Hopkins' influence in his remark.

Frank arrived well before dawn as Jim pulled bread from the oven. Frank was the first to speak. "Guten morgen, Herr Jim. Are you well?"

"Ja, danke. Guten morgen."

Frank said, "I can't stay long. I wanted to get this to you early before the girls come in." Frank thrust a small bundle wrapped in newsprint towards the baker. "I want you to have this. I want you to keep baking for many years to come. I want Darcy, Mandy, and Christin to keep their jobs if they want them and for as long as you want them. Here, open it."

Jim reluctantly accepted the package and unwrapped it. It was full of crisp, new bills. Jim was red-faced. "Frankie! Where did you get this much money?" Jim was now stammering in German. Frank couldn't understand a word.

"Frankie, was ist das? What is this?"

"Over the years I've been putting all my tips in the bank. So, I did okay through the generosity of others. Now I'm giving it to you to save the bakery."

Jim put his face in his hands and wept. "Young Frank, I cannot accept your money. I might never be able to repay you."

"Like I've always told you. You worry too much. Get what you need to keep the bakery going and everything will be fine."

By the stroke of 8 AM there was a line of customers outside the front door of the bakery. Christin asked the others, "What in tarnation is going on today?" She unlocked the door. Mandy noticed they were all new customers, not the usual patrons. They all seemed to know each other. Each new visitor was greeted with a smile and warm welcome.

"What brings y'all to Jim's today?" Darcy asked. A burly man answered first. "We all work at the Navy Yard. Word has been going around about the delicious cakes and cookies y'all bake. Everybody is talking about y'all. Seems one of the officers, Commander Hopkins, brought some samples to the base and highly recommended this place. Told us to come early before y'all run out. Did y'all bake these goodies yourself?

The girls cackled with laughter. "Hardly," Christin replied. "Jim bakes everything."

The morning rush continued for a couple of days. On the Monday morning before Christmas they heard ding, ding, ding as a streetcar rolled to a stop in front of the bakeshop windows. "Why is he stopping here? Christin asked. "The streetcar never stops here," Darcy added. A gaggle of people hopped off the streetcar and went straight to the door of the bakery. Now Jim's Bakery was busier than it ever had been. The same thing happened the next day, And the next. With the sudden flurry of business Jim thought about opening Christmas morning for a few hours for customers who still needed his products for their Christmas Day dinner table. He would do it only if his three helpers were willing to come to work on the holiday. The three knew they might be exhausted from fishing on Christmas Eve and Midnight Mass then finally agreed and even Frank volunteered to help out.

Christmas morning arrived bright and glorious as Commander George Hopkins stepped off the trolley car and walked into the bakery. They were all excited to see him and gave sincere Christmas greetings. "It's Christmas morning and there are two miracles," Christin said. "A streetcar stopping out front and you being on it." George pulled Mandy aside. "May I have a word? In private," he said in a low voice. She was startled but went along with his request. They went out to the sidewalk and had a brief, quiet discussion. Her co-workers could see her nodding and then finally hug the officer before they came back inside.

Frank started an open discussion. "Jim has had as much business as we can handle since the streetcar started making this address a stop," Frank stated. Georged laughed. "Ha! Merry Christmas. Yes, I spoke with R. Goodwyn Rhett who, as you know, is both Mayor and president of People's National Bank. Actually, I paid him a visit with a Black Forrest cake from here. I told him that this place could eventually become a tourist attraction, and he could take credit for it. But... there would really need to be a trolley stop out front to shuttle visitors. He loved the cake so much, he said yes." The four teenagers laughed. "Don't tell Jim. Let's just let him think his baking brought the people." His audience agreed to keep the secret. The commander offered his farewells, jingled the bells on the shop door, and got on the next streetcar to go home for the holiday.

Frank asked Mandy, "What were you talking about out there?"

At 10 AM Mandy turned the key to lock the door from the inside. As Jim agreed they were done for the day and could go home for Christmas. After a long pause she answered. "We are all getting Christmas presents! It seems that Father Corrigan spilled the beans about our escapades last night. Mr. George wanted to come here and tell us directly, and since I'm the oldest among us, he's left it up to me to share his generous offer."

"Tell us! Tell us! The other three pleaded. Mandy could no longer suppress her wide smile. "Since Mr. George and his wife don't have any children of their own, here is what he's proposing. Darcy and Christin, after you graduate next year, if you wish to continue your education in your areas of interest, Darcy in finance and Christin in science, Commander Hopkins says he will find a way to get you into and through the school of your choice. As for myself, he's offered to help me through nursing school and has guaranteed me a job in the Navy Nurse Corps. I would get to travel and get a bonus for serving on a hospital ship or overseas service at an exotic place like the Naval Hospital Cañacao, located at the Cavite Navy Yard in the Philippines. Frank, as for you, when you finish school Commander George will get you into the Citadel, all expenses paid. He says Governor Coleman Livingston Blease owes him a favor for helping to get him elected. There will be a state sponsored scholarship waiting for you. He added that you would make an excellent history professor one day and doesn't want to see your talents go to waste. "Yes, I told Mr. George that," Christin added.

Mandy continued, "The Commander also told me to let y'all know to keep this under your hat. He said he gained a lot of respect for us and wouldn't do it for just anyone."

All of them were astonished. "Let's say goodbye and one last Frohe Weihnachten to Jim before we head home." Frank, Mandy, Christin, Darcy, and Buff quietly went to the back room. Jim was sound asleep on one of the large worktables. "Poor, Jim." Frank said. "He's worked himself to exhaustion the last few days. I think it's time for him to hire more help. Merry Christmas, Jim. Frohe Weihnachten," he whispered. "Merry Christmas to us all!"

Story Notes - Christin, Darcy, and Mandy, who are accomplished anglers that live in and around Charleston, suggested the location and year for the story as well as some of the places within the city and a cocker spaniel dog as a character. Frank is Mandy's grandfather's name. Simmons is Christin's mother's maiden name. Darcy's father's name is George. Mandy is a nurse in Charleston, Christin graduated from The College of Charleston, the oldest university in South Carolina, where she studied history and biology, and Darcy serves as an administrator at a real estate management company. Buff was the name of my grandmother's cocker spaniel.

The inspiration for the story came from true accounts. My father, Bill, was a newspaper delivery boy for the Brooklyn Eagle in the late 1920s. His last stop on his route was Jim's Bakery, owned by James Sterkel, a German immigrant who left the seminary and came to America. It became a morning ritual for Jim to give Bill coffee and a bakery item for breakfast. Although, despite their age difference they became good friends. When Jim's business began to faulter, Bill emptied his own bank account, which held every penny he had earned on his route and gave it to Jim. Bill told Jim not to worry about repaying him. The business survived and they remained close friends until Jim passed away in the early 1970s. Until then Jim was a frequent weekend dinner guest at the Gahan home, and always brought lavish gifts for the family. Stolen was one of Bill Gahan's favorite Christmas treats.

TWENTY-TWO

New Bedford, Massachusetts

Workers at Jethro and Zachariah Hillman's shipyard in New Bedford, Massachusetts watched the newly completed whaling ship Charles W. Morgan depart on July 21, 1841. Her masts stabbed the sky as sailors bellowed a sea shanty and began to heave-to at the anchor windlass. Their ladies waved their kerchiefs to them with tears in their eyes.

They could hear their men's voices fade as they made way out into the harbor...

"Well, a ship went to sailing over the bar
Away for Rio
She's pointing her bow towards the Southern star
And we're bound for the Rio Grand
(And it's) Away, boys, away,
Away for Rio
Sing fare-thee-well my Frisco girl
And we're bound for the Rio Grande

Well now, heave with a will boys heave with a song
Away for Rio
And we'll sing the chorus for it is a good song..."

It was at time in America when there were only 26 states and had a population of 17 million. There was a lot yet to happen in the United States, which had only declared its Independence 65 years earlier. Florida, Texas, and California were not states yet. Florida was a territory, Texas an independent republic, and California, a state of Mexico. Earlier in 1841 the Supreme Court pronounced the Africans free in the Amistad case. And people still depended on whale oil for lamps, soap and candle making, and as a lubricant for guns, watches, clocks, sewing machines and typewriters. Sperm whale oil could withstand high temperatures in manufacturing machinery, so it was necessary for the industrial age factories that churned out goods to expand America. Whaling fueled not only the United Sates, but the entire world. New Bedford, Massachusetts was the biggest whaling port in the world, exceeding Nantucket to lay claim to the title.

As America blossomed the Morgan eased forward powered by a light summer breeze.

At the turning point out of New Bedford, construction of the Old Stone Fort, Fort Rodman, then known as "Fort at Clark's Point, wouldn't begin for another 16 years. The light at Palmer's Island would not be erected for another eight years.

She raised all sheets for the first time and sliced through the waters of Buzzard's Bay. The Morgan rounded Martha's Vineyard and left Nantucket Island in her wake. Now running before the wind at full sail, Captain Thomas Norton set a due-east course for the Azores. The Morgan handled her maiden voyage by crossing the North Atlantic with ease. A stop was planned 2,200 miles east of New Bedford and 1,000 miles west of Lisbon Portugal at Porto Pim on Faial Island.

Although the ship had been outfitted at New Bedford's Rotch's Wharf, she lacked ample supplies for a whaling trip that would take many months. A whaling trip could mean three years away from a home port. Captain Norton's plan was to stop at Porto Pim to take on supplies before heading southwest toward Cape Horn at the southern tip of South America, the northern boundary of the Drake Passage. The waters of Cape Horn, where the Atlantic and Pacific Oceans meet, are treacherous. 19th Century mariners where aware of, and fearful of, the williwaw winds descending in sudden blasts from the mountainous coast to the sea. Williwaw wind gusts are unpredictable and are frequent off Cape Horn. The high winds that come without warning create bigger waves and extreme danger for sailors.

One hundred and fifty miles shy of her Faial Island, a Portuguese island in the Azores, destination a nasty squall arose. It would be the first of many sea storms the Morgan would encounter during her 80-year whaling career in the quest for leviathans in the South Atlantic, South Pacific, and Indian Ocean. Gale winds pushed the Morgan off course toward the tiny island of Corvo. Islanders had a custom of setting fires on the beaches to attract passing ships. It caught the captain's attention. Norton decided to make the best of the situation and dropped anchor off Corvo Island. He sent a party ashore in a whaleboat to judge if the island had enough provisions, which would eliminate the stop at the much larger port on Faial Island.

Half-way to the beach the whaleboat was met by a boy who swam out to meet them. It was easy for several of the crew who were from Portugal to converse with him. By the mid-19th century New Bedford bulged with immigrants from Portugal. Whaling ships carried crews from around the world. Along with Americans, the ship's crew, averaging 33 men per voyage, was manned by seamen from Cape Verde, New Zealand, the Seychelles, Guadeloupe, Norfolk Island and Portugal. Some never said where they were from, and they liked it that way.

"Ahoy," the first mate called out. "Throw him a line," he shouted to the crew.

As the rope sailed toward the boy he said in Portuguese, "I'm okay, really." He didn't mind the waters swirling around him and poked his head up between oars. In another moment he was hanging on to the gunnels. A lively conversation ensued with the oarsmen. The sailor asked, "What is your name?"

"Of course, my name is Braz Jacinto de Fraga," he told them.

"And your age in years?"

"I am fourteen years-old," Braz replied. Laughter broke out in the whaleboat.

"Fair enough," another sailor said. "You're old enough to go to sea. Come with us."

Braz became a seasoned sailor aboard the Morgan. He traveled the world and never concerned himself with its dangers. By the age of 15 he was in San Francisco.

In 1862 the Morgan headed for California to sell her cargo as the USS Monitor wins a Civil War battle against the Confederate ironclad Virginia. By September President Lincoln issues the Emancipation Proclamation.

The Morgan returns to Honolulu after whaling in the Sea of Okhotsk north of the Japanese island of Hokkaidō along a stretch of eastern Siberian coast. In Hawaii Braz joined the crew to weigh anchor and head for home. The ship and crew are in her home port of New Bedford in 1863.

Wampanoag Native Americans were the only people along the Acushnet River that ends in New Bedford. Before the arrival of Europeans, the Wampanoag had settlements throughout southeastern Massachusetts, Rhode Island, Martha's Vineyard, and Nantucket. It is believed that their population was approximately 12,000.

During his exploration of New England Bartholomew Gosnold landed on Cuttyhunk Island on May 15, 1602. He went on to explore Cape Cod and other nearby areas, including what became New Bedford. He did not settle the area. On the insistence of his crew they sailed back to England.

Europeans began to settle New Bedford in 1652. British Plymouth Colony settlers purchased the land from Wampanoag. History didn't record if the land transfer was legitimate. It's been the subject of intense scrutiny by scholars. Like native tribes across America, the Wampanoags may have believed they were granting land usage rights, and not giving up its ownership.

Braz Jacinto de Fraga arrived in New Bedford pretty much as Bartholomew Gosnold did. By boat, unaware, and unknown. Unlike so many generations before him, he found, and was welcomed by, the Portuguese community there. Now a young many with too many harrowing escapades under his belt, he thought maybe it was time to set down some roots on dry land. He had seen the world and he felt that maybe there wasn't much left he hadn't seen. A sailor's life was rough. There were events that he could not unsee. But the only thing he knew was sailing and the sea. America seemed like a good place to try a change.

Braz stood at the wharf and gazed at the Morgan. The Charles W. Morgan had been his home for the better part of his life. She would be sailing out in a few days after the crew finished loading provisions and a few live animals that could provide the crew with milk, cheese, and eggs. From the chandlery there were replacement sails, and repaired sails that couldn't be fixed on board, spare sail-cloth, rosin, tar, pitch, linseed oil, tallow, lard, varnish, twine, rope and cordage, hemp, and oakum, nails, spikes, barrel staves for whale oil, and mops for cleaning the decks and countless other items needed to keep the ship afloat and its crew fed. Mr. Santos the chandler scurried up and down the gangplank making sure every bit loaded on board the Morgan was entered in his invoice.

Duarte Santos was a curious man. He was likable despite his stern business demeanor. Santos shouted orders to his helpers who lined up wheelbarrows and carts that overflowed with the ships' needs. He also occasionally gave a cheerful shoutout to those passing by, whether they were a ship's captain that kept him in business, or a townsperson going about their daily business. He stayed friendly with everyone. It was part of what made him a successful businessman. He had no choice other than to be successful. He had a large family to feed. Santos had spent some of his early years on the maritime aboard a naval ship and although born in Massachusetts, was a Portuguese descendent. Braz appreciated him and respected him. New Bedford's population grew fast earlier in the 19th century with immigrants from Portugal. Santos' family was among them.

Braz learned from the men that to was customary while in New Bedford to visit the Seamen's Bethel before shipping out. Aboard the Morgan the captain had a Bible and Sunday worship services that where at the whim of the weather and the whales. Braz figured if he knew right from wrong and good from evil, it was enough to get him by for the time being. Nevertheless, he wasn't about to forego tradition and made his way up Johnny Cake Hill to the Bethel. Braz felt the Bethel was rather unassuming for a church. It had plain lines and there was nothing ornate about the exterior. He thought the steeple looked hacked-off with a weathervane where a cross should be and the windows looked like gun slits. *"Well, I suppose, if the Lord can be on board a stinking whaling ship, this is just fine,"* he thought.

Braz quickly stepped up the two short front steps, noting the corner stone marked 1830, and opened the door. Braz entered the darkened chapel and sat in one of the pews. As his eyes adjusted to the dim light, he noticed that the Bethel's interior was as plain as its overcoat. He lowered his head and asked for the Lord's blessing for either a safe whaling trip or the wisdom to know what to do for the rest of his life.

He shook himself awake. A young woman stood before and asked, "Sir, are you alright?"

"Yes, of course, yes," Braz said in a voice laced with a thick accent. Braz had mastered the English language learning it, and other languages, from the array of nationalities aboard the Morgan. But his tutors where most often the ship's captain, first mate, navigator and the ship's carpenter.

She gave him a questioning look and asked, "Have you been drinking?"

"Of course not! It was so dark, peaceful, and quiet in here it caused me to nod off."

"Well, good then. It would be a sin to be drunk in the Bethel."

"Me? Uh, no, of course. You are correct. I am heading out on the Charles Morgan soon or trying to decide if I should… and wanted to come here first."

"That's good. And I'm not judging you."

Braz's dark eyes where now accustomed to the soft light streaming through the narrow windows. He now realized the beauty of the young woman who stood beside him. He stood up. I am Braz. Braz Jacinto de Fraga originally from the tiny Island of Corvo and more recently from all over the world aboard the Charles W. Morgan. It is a pleasure to meet you."

"I know of Corvo Island. Portuguese?" she asked.

"Indeed." Braz beamed. This is my first time in the United States. Although, I was in San Francisco before California became a member of the United States."

"Another Vasco de Gama?" She laughed. "It's a pleasure to meet you as well, sailor. My name is Mariana. Welcome to America."

"You are Portuguese as well? Braz asked.

"I am American. A descendant of my Portuguese my ancestors." "Although, we do follow many of the Portuguese customs and traditions. There are many Portuguese families in New Bedford, who have settled here from the Azores, like yourself. Along with the Irish, Italians, and others, New Bedford grew into an important port. Yes, there are Portuguese people here who were brought by whaling, just like you."

Braz wiped his hand on his pants and extended it to her. She continued, "Well, let me wish you luck whether you decide to go back to whaling or whatever else you decide to do. I'm sure if you look within your heart, you will find your way." She felt he was rather forward in his gesture and ignored his hand. He withdrew quickly. In spite of his shabby sailor's clothes and a face that needed shaving and washing, she was enchanted.

"It's a hard choice," Braz said. "Whaling and sailing is all I've ever really known or done. I don't know what else I would, or could, do, or where."

"I see," she said. "Well, for the near future, do you have plans for this evening?" Braz said he didn't. "Perhaps if you got to know some of the people and places here it might help you with your decision. I am inviting you to our home for dinner this evening. You won't be disappointed. In any case, a good home-cooked meal would do you well. Mama is cooking something special." Mariana gave him the address and told him he would be expected at six o'clock, and her father would be home from work by then. "Get yourself cleaned up."

Braz wiped his hand and reached out to touch her hand. "Thank you so much! I am looking forward to seeing you again and meeting your family." He was beside himself with delight. "*Quite a place this America,*" he thought. He couldn't wait to spend time with her.

Braz returned to the ship and collected some of his belongings, including some scrimshaw that he had carved on his last voyage. He washed up at the horse trough near the wharf and found his way to the haberdashery. He traded a piece of scrimshaw with the shop owner for a new pair of pants and shirt. He put the other bits of whalebone scrimshaw in his pocket. He asked the shop owner for directions to the address Mariana gave him.

Braz arrived promptly at six. He was taken aback about what a fine home it was. He walked up the polished steps and rapped the door with its large brass knocker. Mariana opened the door. "Hello again, Braz, you found the place. Welcome to our home. Mama is expecting you. Father is not home yet so please join me in the parlor until he arrives. My sister will join us at the table. At the moment Sofia is helping Mama in the kitchen." Braz was impressed by the expensive furniture and artwork in the parlor. At least he assumed it was expensive. He didn't have much to compare it to, but it looked luxurious to him. Her father walked into the room ten minutes later.

Braz was astounded when her father entered. Her father was Duarte Santos. Braz stood up and greeted Santos. "Good evening Mr. Santos. I am Braz Jacinto de Fraga. I arrived here on the Morgan, the whaler you are outfitting." Santos gave Mariana a questioning glance.

"Ah, welcome young man," Santos said. "Yes, I thought I recognized you from the being at the docks." Braz reached into his pocket and pulled out one of his whalebone carvings and said, "This is for you and your family, Sir. It is for my appreciation of your hospitality." Santos was impressed. He placed the scrimshaw on the mantel. "Fine piece," he said. "You made this?"

"Yes, with my own hands. I had a lot of time to practice," Braz said as he sat on the sofa.

We're not in the habit of having a transient sailor as a dinner guest. But I must say, you have made a good impression with your generous gift."

Mariana's younger sister Sofia appeared in the doorway. "Dinner is served. Please join us in the dining room."

Mariana's mother, Antonia, served a sumptuous traditional Portuguese seafood dish originally from the Algarve coastal region, Cataplana de marisco. The stew is named after the pot that is used to cook and serve it in. A cataplana, a copper clam-shaped cooking pot, is a forerunner of the modern pressure cooker. Cataplana de marisco ingredients include chopped cilantro, diced tomatoes, onions, and bell peppers that are slowly steamed in their own juices and flavors along with white wine, herbs, and spices. Antonia combined local mussels, clams, and New England lobster as opposed to European lavagante lobster. Braz learned that although Antonia was also American and born in New Bedford, her parents were from the Azores.

The table was cleared after the Cataplana and Mariana brought out the desert course. A popular Portuguese dessert, Pastéis de Nata, which are petite, creamy, and sweet custard tarts. Santos brought a bottle of Port to the table and poured it for Braz and his family.

"Tell us your stories of the high seas," Santos said to Braz.

Braz had never before had such wonderful food. He raised his glass. "First, let me say thank you to Mrs. Santos for such a fine meal. Agradecido!" Antonia stopped him. "Our daughters Mariana and Sofia are both good cooks as well. They helped prepare tonight's dinner. Mariana made the desert. You should thank them, too."

"Well, here's to everyone who had a hand in preparing this meal!" Braz once again raised his glass in a toast and started to tell his stories. As he began, he stopped when he realized no one had ever asked him before to tell his tales.

Braz recounted being shanghaied in Corvo, about crossing the Tropic of Cancer several times, and the nerve wracking passings through Cape Horn. He told about the lush tropics of Hawaii, and the bitter cold of the arctic that caused the sails to freeze. His audience listened to every word. Mariana was spellbound. He left out the brutal business of whaling. He didn't want to upset the women. He figured he should quit while he was still welcome in the house. "Most days it was just hard work in tough conditions."

"How did you meet Mariana?" Santos questioned.

"In church," Braz answered. Santos gulped. Braz clarified. "We became acquainted while I was visiting the Bethel." Santos smiled and nodded at Braz's response.

"When does the Morgan sail?" Will you be on board?" asked Santos. Everyone, including his wife, called him Santos. Santos already knew the date because of his maritime supply business. He wanted to see how Braz would answer.

"A week from Tuesday and I'm not sure. That's why I was in the Bethel."

"How do you mean not sure?" asked Santos.

"I've been at sea since I was fourteen-years old. And, yes, as you have heard, I have traveled more, and seen more, than most young men would ever hope for. I was aboard a "lucky" ship. In spite of all of the hazards, it never sank, and I never was tossed overboard. I can't say the same for some others. Am I lucky? Maybe. Am I fortunate? Yes. I've come to a point in my life that I think it's time to settle down while my luck, or good fortune, holds out. And maybe it's time for me to not be away at sea for years at a stretch. I like America. The people are good and things seem prosperous here. The question is…what would I do here?"

Santos invited Braz to join him in his study. He motioned for the sailor to sit in one of the overstuffed leather chairs and stepped to the credenza. "Bourbon?" he asked and didn't wait for an answer. "Bourbon is an American made whiskey that comes from a mix of grains. This concoction is mostly corn, and the rest is a blend of rye, wheat, and malted barley. I have this shipped directly from Kentucky after it's been aged." He poured the bourbon in two cut-crystal whiskey glasses.

"You strike me as intelligent, certainly well-spoken, well-mannered, and personable. I know from your adventures that you're not a stranger to demanding work. How are you with numbers?"

"I'd say my math skills are better than average. I was schooled by the ship's carpenter and the navigator." Braz was growing nervous, but he tried not to let on."

"Understandable," said Santos. "And I see how Mariana looks at you. I don't know what your long-term intentions are, or whether you will return to whaling or not. I took to heart your concerns for your future wellbeing. That's a mature and understandable position." His voice trailed off as he looked for a response from Braz. Both men took a sip.

Santos continued, "The whaling industry is starting to change. And change not in a good way for those who rely on whaling to make a living. I've been very privileged over the years and have done well by outfitting whale ships that call on New Bedford or call it their home port. In Pennsylvania they are drilling in the ground for oil. If it can be produced in great quantities, which I believe it will. It will surpass whale oil. In addition, it will be a much safer process to obtain and more lucrative for those involved. I think the best days for America are ahead. And the best days for whaling are behind. Which brings me to my points. This region is growing in leaps and bounds. Building and homes are going up all over, factories are bustling. What I'm wanting to do is expand into more than just supplying ships. I believe building materials and hardware are a perfect opportunity right now. I've already got a lot of connections through the chandlery. I can make others. What I'm looking for is someone to help with the ship supply end of the business while I expand into other products. It must be someone who understands the wants of a captain and the needs of a ship well. Over time, even if whaling fails and whaleboats come to a halt, there will be a future for my business. As of yet…I haven't found the right person." Santos let his words sink in. He slouched back in his chair.

Once again, he leaned forward. "If you do decide to stay on dry land and are wondering what to do, this job could be a good fit for you if you have an interest. There's a spare room above the chandlery, so you'd have a place to stay. Don't give me your answer tonight. It's a big decision for you. Think it over. If you're interested; you know where to find me."

Braz was shocked. It was as if he had been struck by lightning. "*I guess praying about this decision paid off,*" he thought. The possibility of being near Mariana instantly made up his mind.

Braz stood up and shook Santos' hand, pumping it up and down. "I'm your man if you'll have me! I won't disappoint you. I can start as soon as you wish."

"Well then, it's decided. You can start a week from Wednesday. Take some time to enjoy yourself and look around town." Santos said this knowing the Morgan would already be out to sea by Tuesday and either Braz would be on it, or he wouldn't. He decided to give Braz a last chance if he changed his mind.

"May I say goodnight and thank you to Mariana for inviting me here?"

"I'll see if she's gone to bed," her father said. He left the room and returned a moment later. "She is in the parlor. You may see her and say goodnight."

Braz entered the parlor and found Mariana knitting. She looked up and said. "I hope you had an enjoyable time this evening. Will we see you again?"

"I had the most fantastic evening. In more ways than you know. Thank you so much for having me. I do intend to stay in New Bedford and I do

I hope I can see you again soon." He didn't mention the offer of a job at her father's company.

"You are very welcome. It seems you've made a good impression with our family. Will you see me again? Of course! Stop by the chandlery. I am the one you will find helping my father with the bookkeeping there. Goodnight." She smiled.

"Until next time we meet, I will say see you again. Goodbye is so final. Boa noite. Goodnight, Mariana."

The following Wednesday Mariana arrived early at her father's shop. She was surprised to see Braz already there. "What are you doing here so early?" she asked. "But wait a minute. The Morgan sailed yesterday and you're not on it. Have you decided to stay?"

"Please sit down there's something I want to tell you about," Braz said. Braz recounted the entire conversation he had with her father after dinner. "You made my decision easy. When I said yes to your father, I had no idea you worked with him here. It became even a better turn of events."

"Welcome to the family business," she remarked. Mariana gave him a wide smile.

As the weeks of summer unfolded into autumn, Braz went with Mariana to the outskirts beyond the edge of town on family picnics. When October arrived he accompanied her to church. On a mid-October Sunday carriage ride they marveled at the brilliant colors of the changed foliage and picked apples, which Mariana later used to bake pies. As they sat at the kitchen table she asked, "Isn't life grand?"

"Indeed it is...in so many ways," he answered. "Never in my wildest dreams did I ever think I could be so happy, and life could be so peaceful."

To Marian Braz was bigger than life itself. She admired him for his kindness and his hard work ethic. Even if he hadn't done something before, he was willing to try it and do his best. His handsome looks were a plus. Her admiration was apparent to Braz and his feeling toward her was mutual.

Braz worked hard at the chandlery making sure deliveries got to the docks on time and that every captain's and boat owner's needs were met. He saw to it that suppliers delivered on time, and they weren't being shorted on their orders. "Keep up the good work, Braz. You're keeping the business running without me," Santos told him. "I'm giving you an increase in your salary. You deserve it." Braz was delighted. Mariana overheard her father's remarks. They warmed her and deepened her feelings for Braz. Not only because of the extra money, which Braz could certainly use, but for the relationship that he and her father had forged. Her father treated Braz like the son he never had. Braz was often at the dinner table in the Santos household. Mariana was certain that her father was glad to have another man to converse with at mealtimes.

Late November delivered its usual chill to New England. It was a way of life, and no one minded the change. Snow was a frequent visitor. Braz trudged through the snow to the Santos home. He welcomed the Caldo Verde that Mariana made. She slid it before him. He let the steam fill his senses and let the warmth of the kale and potato soup warm him inside. At the end of the meal Mariana said, "Father is in the study if you care to join him. I'll finish up here. Braz acknowledged that he did and pushed his chair back from the table. Mariana was a bit disappointed that she wasn't getting to spend the time with him. But she heard laughter from both men coming from the study and accepted it that all was well, and, that she shouldn't complain.

Braz exited the study and was met by Mariana. She was concerned by his somber expression. "Are you alright, Braz?" she probed. "I couldn't be better, my dear Mariana," he said. "It will be Christmas soon. That will change everything." Mariana wrote off his odd expression and statement to him be tired. Afterall, he worked harder than anyone else in the company.

Christmas eve arrived and the Santos family wrapped it in their best traditional Portuguese Christmas fare. Braz helped himself to generous portions of the authentic Christmas meal, Ceia de Natal. Consoda, a dish of salted cod served with green vegetables, boiled potatoes and boiled eggs as served on Christmas Eve in Portugal. Following the Sofia brought the next course to the table. Santos applauded and raised his glass. "Boas Festas!" he said. Everyone clapped and Braz smiled. Although the family had blurred some of the lines of the Christmas traditions, they made up for it in spirit. Sofia placed the silver tray holding shellfish and roast wild turkey on the table.

Santos said, "It's time to go to Missa do Galo, Christmas Eve Service. We can visit the Christmas Madeiro, afterwards. We can do the creche and have our Bolo Rei when we get back. And perhaps we can see if Pai Natal will have arrived by then with Christmas gifts."

"What is Christmas Madeiro?" Braz wanted to know.

Santos explained, "It's a tradition in the Penamacor region of Portugal between Lisbon and Madrid that when young men or boys are about to enter the military, they are sent out to steal whole trees to make a huge bonfire in the churchyard. It is lit just before Midnight mass 'to warm baby Jesus's feet'! It creates a gathering place after the Service for people to meet, warm up, greet the pastor, sing a few Christmas songs, and exchange good wishes for Christmas."

They all scurried through the frosty night air to return home. "Come, let's fill the creche," Antonia said. They entered the parlor and filled the creche with figurines of Joseph and Mary, and small carvings of cows, sheep, horses, and shepherds. Braz placed an angel above the nativity. First thing in the morning Sofia, as the youngest child, would have the honor of placing Baby Jesus in the crib.

"Let's go to the table for Bolo Rei!" Antonia declared. "Braz helped me with the baking. We will give him the honor of serving the pieces. Let's see who gets the surprise!" Antonia brought the Bolo Rei to the table. Baked into the Bolo Rei, or King Cake, are a small gift and raw broad bean. Whoever gets the bean has to provide the Bolo Rei the following year. Sofia followed with fried cookies, and Mariana had apple pie. Santos brought out an array of liquors and an expensive bottle of Madeira wine for the occasion.

Braz sliced the cake and served the pieces one by one. "Let's see who will be the lucky one," he said. "Okay, then you go first," said Mariana. "Well, it should be ladies first, but if you insist," he said. Braz broke the slice apart with his fork. A large, flat bean popped onto his plate. The family laughed and clapped. "I guess it will be up to me to be here next year and bring the cake!" Braz supposed.

"Papa, you go next. "Afterall, you got the bean last Christmas." Santos mashed his slice of cake. "Nothing!" he exclaimed. "The prize is left for one of our lovely women. Antonio, you go now. Saúde…Cheers to you my Dear."

Antonia obliged and cut open her piece of cake. It revealed nothing. Her daughters giggled. "Sofia, you are the youngest," Antonia said and turned to cup Sofia's face. "In addition to placing the infant Jesus in the creche tomorrow morning, perhaps you will be blessed with the surprise gift. It is now down to you and Mariana. Good luck!"

Sofia eagerly tore into her dessert. "Nothing! she cried. "Mariana, I hope there is something good for you and Pai Natal hasn't played a trick on us!"

Mariana paused. "Okay, here we go…" She let her fork nibble at the edges and then took larger and larger pieces in search of a prize. Everyone heard a tinkling sound as something dropped on the porcelain china.

"Well, what did you get?" Sofia asked.

Mariana held up the surprise with two fingers. Covered in crumbs, but plainly visible was a ring.

"Oh, yes, a ring. That's a usual Bolo Rei prize," Sofia said.

"But wait," Mariana replied. She wiped the ring with her napkin. It began to sparkle, letting reflected candlelight dance around the dining room.

Braz knelt beside her. "Mariana, weeks ago I asked your father for your hand in marriage. I traded the jeweler some of the more exquisite pieces of my scrimshaw carvings… for this ring. What's more, I give it to you from my heart and with all my love. Your father said. Yes. Will you marry me?"

Mariana hugged him for a long time. "Of course I will!" she shrieked. "This is the best Christmas I could possibly ask for. I thank you with all of my heart. Muito obrigado. Eu te amo. I love you, too."

Over an 80-year whaling career, the Charles W. Morgan recorded 37 voyages. Most lasted more than three or more years. She was built for durability, not speed or comfort. The Morgan traversed the globe hunting whales. She was known as a "lucky ship." The captain and crew successfully survived a cannibal attack in the South Pacific and navigated through crushing Arctic ice and countless fierce snowstorms. They avoided being seized by the Confederate ship, Shenandoah, which did not know the Civil War had ended, and captured 11 whaling ships in the Bering Strait. They survived rounding Cape Horn and its deadly williwaw winds numerous times. As she rested at port, the Morgan even withstood the Hurricane of 1938 that devastated New England.

Charles W. Morgan's crew averaged approximately 33 men per voyage and had more than 1,000 whalemen of all races and nationalities in her lifetime. Braz Jacinto de Fraga was counted in their numbers and today his descendants live in New Bedford, Massachusetts.

The whaling ship Charles W. Morgan, now more than 180 years-old, rests at anchor at the Mystic Seaport Museum in Mystic, Connecticut. Tours of her historic decks are open to the public.

TWENTY-THREE

Savannah, Georgia

On Graduation Day in 1840 at the United States Military Academy in West Point, New York two cadets shook hands for the last time. One of them was two years behind the other cadet who was graduating. They were both named William. Class sizes were small at the times. There were 46 cadets who graduated that day. William and William completed their respective military obligations after school, fought in the Mexican American War, and then headed out into tumultuous times of the mid-19th century in America. Their paths would cross years later.

President Abraham Lincoln issued the Emancipation Proclamation on January 1, 1863. The Emancipation Proclamation freed slaves in Confederate-held territories. It became a key turning point in the Civil War that divided America. It established the Union cause as the abolition of slavery.

President Lincoln delivered his Gettysburg Address speech on November 19, 1863. It was a critical event in American history and marked a defining moment in the Civil War. Although, the end of the conflict was still on a distant horizon.

By 1864, the first successful transatlantic telegraph cable was laid, the First Geneva Convention was signed, in Virginia, the Battle of the Wilderness raged, and the Union Army's Siege of Petersburg isolated Confederate forces and weakened their capability, and will, to continue fighting. In August, the Atlanta Campaign was a substantial Union victory. The Northern Army had captured a major Confederate stronghold and destroyed much of Atlanta's infrastructure. It dealt a further blow to the morale of the Confederacy and their war effort. Nonetheless, conflict between the North and South continued.

Lincoln had another battle to fight, his 1864 re-election during the third year of the ongoing Civil War. The Democrat Party opposed Lincoln's new policies and the war effort, which included his emphasis on the importance of preserving the Union and ending slavery. They nominated George B. McClellan, a former Union general who Lincoln had relieved of his command. McClellan's campaign platform was less defined. He wanted a negotiated peace agreement with the Confederates. A fair share of voters thought this was a betrayal of the Union cause. In the end McClellan's position also alienated many war Democrats who supported Lincoln's policies. Lincoln won in a landslide victory getting over 212 electoral votes compared to only 21 for McClellan. The decisive win gave Lincoln the mandate he needed to persist in the battle for emancipation and to reunite the nation. As of Election Day in 1864, there was still much more to happen in the war between the North and the South.

It was General William Tecumseh Sherman who led the Union to victory in Atlanta. He was the cadet named William who graduated from West Point in 1840. Sherman, known for his aggressive tactics and brilliant strategies, was one of the most significant generals of the American Civil War. Although he was considered an excellent military strategist, he was also seen by some as a controversial figure because of his tactics, such as his "scorched earth" campaign that involved the methodical destruction of infrastructure and resources leaving a trail of destruction in his wake.

After Atlanta, Sherman's plan was to push east and devastate Confederate military strongholds and storehouses, railroads, bridges, factories, and farms to disrupt the Confederates supply lines, neutralize their will to fight, and bring about the South's surrender. With 60,000 men under his command Sherman had the opposition greatly outnumbered.

A week after Election Day and Lincoln's decisive win at the polls Sherman started their 250-mile march east, and the key shipping port city of Savannah, Georgia. Major General W.T. Sherman employed his scorched earth policy during their March to the Sea.

Ezekiel Jones from Bad Axe Michigan was in the 15th Michigan Infantry, the primary unit of Michigan soldiers that took part in Sherman's March to the Sea. Zeke hoped Savannah would be the last battle of the war and he could return home to the farm in the spring. He was just an average soldier and a dimwit who was smart enough to not get in the way of a Rebel Whitworth sniper rifle or any other Confederate's shot. He survived the Battle of Shiloh in Hardin County Tennessee, the Battle of Corinth Mississippi, Siege of Vicksburg in Mississippi, Battle of Resaca fought in Gordon County and Whitfield County, Georgia, the Battle of Kennesaw Mountain Cobb County Georgia, and the Siege of Atlanta Georgia. Seven conflicts in two short years. He was proud to be on the winning side in all of them and pondered if his luck was going to run out before the war was over. He trudged through the red clay dust and wondered if he would live to see Christmas and the ocean.

Day after day of marching made him as weary as the other men. Zeke, like his neighbors, volunteered to serve in the 15th Regiment. The only thing he appreciated about being in the south was being away from the icy winds off Lake Huron that whistled through Michigan. He was given an unusual field promotion to corporal. Not because of any heroic act, but rather, because of his harmonicas and knowing how to play them. His commanding officers noticed how his music calmed the men in the trenches and in the camps at night. Zeke could also draw and had a fantastic memory for events and their details. He would make charcoal sketches on tents depicting camp life.

After weeks of grueling marching over difficult terrain with limited supplies, and occasional encounters with Confederate troops and their sympathizers, General Sherman, Corporal Jones, and 60,000 Union troops arrived on the outskirts of Savannah on December 10th. Sherman's forces surrounded the city, effectively overwhelmed it with artillery fire, and cut off supply lines.

The Confederate garrison at Savannah numbered 15,000. They were commanded by Confederate General William J. Hardee. He was the other William who graduated from West Point two years before Willam T. Sherman graduated in 1840. Hardee ordered the garrison to burn defense installations, fortifications, including the naval yard, and anything else that might benefit the invading army. On December 20th the defenders surrendered and fled the city.

When Sherman advanced into Savannah the following day and he found it rather deserted. The civilian population of 23,000 free residents and enslaved people had evacuated following Sherman's siege, which cut off their supplies, and Hardee's scuttling actions, which finished off pretty much everything else of value. On December 21st, the Union Army completely controlled "The Gate City" at the mouth of the Savannah River. Sherman chose the recently vacated Green-Meldrim House at 14 West Macon Street for his headquarters. Located in Savannah's Madison Square, which was named after James Madison in 1837, the fourth president of the United States, the palatial home was designed by John S. Noris, a highly regarded architect in the city. The grand 7,300 square-foot main floor house was built in the Gothic Revival style with pointed arches, decorative woodwork and a unique entrance featuring a distinctive iron portico and columns, oriel and bay windows. Its interior features a wide center hall, double parlors, a dining room and sitting room appointed with American black walnut woodwork and silver-plated doorknobs. Its 15-foot-high ceiling rooms have elaborate hard stucco cornices and arches and fireplaces made with Italian Carrera marble.

On the eve of his arrival General Sherman sent President Lincoln a telegram. Sherman wrote, "I beg to present you, as a Christmas gift, the city of Savannah, with 150 heavy guns and plenty of ammunition, and also about 25,000 bales of cotton."

Lincoln was elated by the news. The Union Army had scored a significant victory and Savannah was the reward. It not only boosted morale, but also gave the North a much needed supply of cotton.

Zeke Jones was stationed on guard duty at Madison Square. He was completely unaware of the Square's historical significance. It was the site of a decisive battle during the American Revolutionary War. 14 years after Sherman's siege and conquest of Savannah a monument to Sergeant William Jasper, a hero of the American Revolution Siege of Savannah was placed there. A combined force of Continental Army troops, local militia and French troops laid siege to Savannah from September 16 to October 9, 1779. On October 9th they launched a last attempt to regain the city from the British, which in the end was unsuccessful. The British defenders repulsed the attack, inflicting heavy casualties on the Continentals. Sergeant Jasper was mortally wounded while saving his regiment's flag from the parapet. Zeke was more focused on the siege his army had just applied to Savannah. He was even more concerned about spending another Christmas so far from home. He took out a harmonica and started to play. The melody from his mouth organ wafted throughout Madison Square from his perch at Bull Street and Macon Street and flowed through the windows of the Green-Meldrim House. He knew Silent Night, The First Noel. And Jingle Bells, which was written in 1857 and had become popular.

Sherman's staff officers could plainly hear the Christmas music. A young Second Lieutenant who was assigned to guard the front door of headquarters heard the music and charged to the corner. "Corporal, what in tarnation are you doing?" the Lieutenant barked. "Standing watch," Zeke answered. "No, I am talking about what are you doing with that harmonica while you are on watch?" he fumed.

"I think I'm playing some songs," Zeke said flatly. The officer glared and Zeke continued. "Seeing how it's Christmas Eve and all, I thought I'd play some Christmas music for the men."

"On whose orders?" the Lieutenant snarled.

"Well, I suppose on my own orders…" Zeek's voice trailed off as a Major joined the conversation. Zeke saluted him. He didn't want any more trouble.

"Merry Christmas, Corporal. I am delivering you season's greetings from Major General Sherman. He could hear your tunes at headquarters. It's okay, Son. He appreciated the Christmas cheer. He wants to share it with his other officers and soldiers. I have orders for you. The General instructs you to pack up your gear and head to the cotton warehouse on the riverfront that we commandeered on the 21st. There's a bunch of sergeants, lieutenants, and a captain or two billeted there, along with some enlisted men. Some of the soldiers are nursing wounds. Play for them. Help them sleep peacefully. God bless you, Corporal." The Major saluted Corporal Jones and added, "You'll have plenty of soft cotton to sleep on tonight. With my compliments."

Along the Savannah River is the Historic River Street and the location of the original Port of Savannah where the colony of Georgia was founded in 1733 by James Edward Oglethorpe and 114 British settlers. In the 18th century it was the primary port for goods coming into Georgia. By the mid-1800s Savannah was the world's leading exporter of cotton. By Christmas 1864 the Union Army was in control.

In 1859, John S. Norris, who designed the Green-Meldrim House where Sherman was headquartered, designed a building on the Savannah riverfront that was originally divided into a cotton warehouse and a shipping company. Little did Norris realize what the cotton warehouse with a commanding view of the Savannah River and River Street would eventually be used for.

Zeke hefted his pack on his back and slung his Springfield rifle over his shoulder. He put his harmonicas in his coat pocket and started the 15-minute walk to the cotton warehouse. He went to the Bay Street entrance on the top floor loft. Corporal Jones, the harmonica playing soldier from Bad Axe Michigan snaped a salute to the sentry who directed Zeke to the officer in charge. Zeke tried to explain to the captain as best he could how General William Tecumseh Sherman sent him out of 60,00 troops to spend the night in a comfortable cotton loft. Zeke said, "Hold on a moment. Let me show you." He pulled a harmonica out of his pocket and played a tune for the captain."

Zeke spent the rest of Christmas Eve entertaining the men. He woke up on Christmas morning and went down to the River Street level. He waited his turn in the mess line. The soldiers were glad to have a break from battle for the holiday. Everyone knew their Christmas peace would end with the next skirmish or engagement with the rebel forces. After biscuits and coffee, Zeke ambled over to the camp cookfire and pushed pieces of charcoal out of it with his boot. Once they were cool, he wrapped the charcoal in a bandana and climbed back up to the loft.

He used the charcoal bits to start a sketch on a whitewashed wall. A window with an arched top facing the river gave him more than enough natural light. Officers and enlisted men gathered around him. When they realized what he was doing they cheered him on. A map was beginning to take shape on a cotton warehouse wall. They helped him spell the names of the towns and cities they marched through on the way to Savannah. The men shouted out the spellings of Chattanooga, Kennesaw Mountain, Milledgeville and Griswoldville. Zeke knew how to spell Atlanta. He added the locations to his map. His drawing was accurate in every detail, or at least to the degree that the officers in attendance could say. It traced the Union Army's campaign from Chattanooga, through Atlanta, and into Savannah. The campaign started on May 7th and ended at one of the crown jewels of the south and the Confederacy's strategic seaport four days before Ezekial Jones drew his map.

Sherman's forces stayed in Savannah for a relatively brief time. The Union Army used Savannah as a base of operations for further military operations in the south. They restored the infrastructure in the city, created supply lines, and planned for future campaigns to hopefully put an end to the war. Sherman's army continued their march north and up through South Carolina.

At Appomattox Court House in Virginia on April 9, 1865, the surrender of the Army of Northern Virginia brought about the end of major fighting in the Civil War. The conflict wasn't officially over between the North and South until August 20, 1866, when President Andrew Johnson issued a proclamation declaring the end of the insurrection and the restoration of peace in America.

Story Notes - Although haphazard Zeke Jones from Bad Axe Michigan is a historical fiction character, and didn't draw the map, the other persons, places, and events in the story are true.

In 1901 the actual aged cotton warehouse on the Savannah riverfront mentioned in the story underwent renovations. Workmen removed old wallpaper and paint from a wall and discovered a map drawn on its plaster. In great detail it depicted General William Tecumseh Sherman's "March to the Sea" from Tennessee through Georgia. Historians verified the authenticity of the map, which was likely drawn by Sherman's officers billeted there. It is believed it was wallpapered over to hide any military secrets from the enemy.

Only a portion of the wall showing the route of Sherman's Chattanooga campaign could be saved. It was preserved under tempered glass and protected from humidity and UV light and remains to this day. Visitors to the Hostess City of the South can relive history and see the map in its original location on the wall of what eventually became Vic's on the Riverfront Restaurant at 26 East Bay Street, Savannah.

TWENTY-FOUR

Bethlehem, West Bank

She swept the bits of hay and debris into the fire and stoked the coals. Yellow flames danced in reaction to her thrusts. She gathered her apron and stepped back. It had grown exceptionally cold, and the warmth came to her like a welcomed friend. The master of the house who kept the inn was a quarrelsome man. Rebecca, (in Hebrew, a name meaning servant of God) accepted his harshness not out of choice, but design. She had worked there almost her entire life.

The innkeeper inherited the roadhouse from his father, who had inherited it from his grandfather. Nothing much had changed over the generations. It was meager and even the most tired traveler was quick to point out the lumps in the straw mattress and the cracks that let the wind whistle through. He ignored their complaints knowing they would be on their way in the morning.

Travelers from afar were on the move heading to their father's home town to be counted as directed by Caesar Augustus. The proprietor was ecstatic during the last few days. He raised portions and offered smaller portions and watered down the wine. His place was filled to capacity. It was something that didn't happen during this time of year, if at all.

Rebecca continued to make the rounds sweeping, filling water buckets and tending to the patron's needs. Many of the travelers arrived on mules, some on horses and a few in ox drawn carts. Most of them walked on their journey. The setting sun cast deep chilling shadows over the expansive courtyard and Rebecca began to think about the comfort of the animals. Some, but not all, could take shelter in the manger, a simple stable, which was a good distance from the inn. She noticed that as the evening wore on the animals in the outbuilding became extremely quiet. Neither a nay nor a bah came from within. The girl approached and saw the animals with their heads hung low. Steam billowed from their nostrils and from their thick breaths into the gathering chill.

Rebecca was startled as two sheep, followed by an ox, made their way to the door and out into the makeshift corral. Another sheep and three mules followed in procession. All of the animals remained silent and one by one quietly made their way outdoors. In a noble act the horses waited to be last. The crude barn stood empty. Never before had the servant girl seen anything like this. She ran across the courtyard to a shepherd boy who was warming himself by the fire. "Have you ever seen such a thing?" she asked and sat beside him then stirred the coals with a stout branch.

"Can't say that I have. I wonder what's wrong. Word has come down from the hills that the sheep have either laid down or are headed this way." He stretched his hands out to the fire. "The other strange thing is they all always point their noses downwind. Tonight, they are all facing east, into where the wind is coming from. And...they are all gazing toward the heavens. It's like they're waiting for something to happen." he said and shrugged his shoulders. "I don't expect a storm. It's not only the sheep. Same thing with any other four leggers that are out and about." He pulled his blanket tightly around his wiry body and felt its coarseness against his skin. "If I hear any news. I will be sure to let you know," he said.

Rebecca frowned. "Are you going to be alright out here tonight?" she said.

"Sure, I will," he said, holding his hands out to the flames. "I came down from the hills to find a lost sheep."

"What about your flock?" she asked and poked the fire once again. They watched sparks spiral up with wisps of smoke.

His eyes watered as the wind changed direction and pushed the smoke towards him. "Each and every life in my herd is as important as the other. I left them to search for the lost one. The life of that sheep is every bit as important and needs to come back to the flock."

Rebecca was amazed that this young boy would see the value in looking after one lost sheep while leaving the others behind. "Won't you be upset with that sheep for running off?" she said.

"We all stray at times. I'll be very happy to find it…not upset. I'll bring it back like nothing ever happened." Rebecca weighed the wisdom of his words and looked back toward the animals.

"Perhaps the animals left the stable because it's too dirty from being overcrowded," she said. "Yes, that's it. I must clean it out. It will be bitter tonight. They can't be outside," she said to the boy.

Rebecca hurried across the expanse to the manger. Pungent odors met her that wrinkled her nose as she mucked the stalls and swept out the entire place. Noise and boisterous laughter erupted from time to time at the inn and drifted to the outbuildings as Rebecca cleaned the animal's quarters. "The travelers must be quite comfortable and having a merry time this evening," she remarked to a dove who had stayed behind. She only paused long enough to catch her breath then added fresh water to the troughs and placed clean straw everywhere she could. The animals stayed outside.

Rebecca's busyness, the loud banter from the inn, and the distance prevented her from hearing a young couple's knock on the inn's door and the husband's desperate pleas for a room. "There is nothing I can do," the innkeeper said in an aggravated voice. "I have no room for you."

Rebecca had finished her work. It was the cleanest she had ever seen the manger. *Any animal would be happy in here,* she thought. She looked up in time to see the proprietor talking to the couple and gesturing toward the stables.

"Oh no! I've neglected the true guests and have disappointed my master," Rebecca said in a loud whisper to the dove. She tossed her hair back and watched as the couple approached. The wife dressed in worn peasant clothes road on a donkey. It was obvious to Rebecca that she was with child and her time was near at hand. She was young, even younger than herself. Her husband was older, quite a bit older. Rebecca stepped aside and smiled politely. The wife placed her hand on Rebecca's shoulder and thanked her for the wonderful preparations she had made for them. Rebecca bowed her head in shame knowing that this would be the place where the young mother's baby would be born. Rebecca ran to the inn and collected the few spare blankets that she could find and brought them to the manger. When Rebecca returned, she found the woman visitor curled in the fresh straw.

While Rebecca was away the oxen, mules, horses, donkey and sheep had returned to the stables and now surrounded the girl lying on the ground. They tread softly to not disturb the expecting mother and nudged each other into position. Their great bulk and shaggy bodies blocked the drafts. Their warm bodies and breaths filled the air of the manger chasing away all traces of cold. The servant girl folded a blanket and placed it beneath the woman's head for a pillow.

The animals stood watch through the night and were there the next morning to see the greatest birth the world has ever known. Before sunrise, shepherds, and the one who sought his lost sheep, were directed to the manger by a powerful chorus of voices far greater than themselves. They gathered around to welcome the newborn child. It was a birth of a child, a Servant and Master, who would tend to the needs of all people… forever.

Story Notes – This was the first of the 24 short historical fiction stories I wrote. For the way it really happened, please read the Bible Luke 2:8-20.